Literary Odysseys

Photograph courtesy of Rafael Kapelinski

To the people and places I have known and loved

Literary Odysseys

An Interactive Introduction to the Short Story

Mary Ziemer

Ann Arbor
THE UNIVERSITY OF MICHIGAN PRESS

Copyright © by the University of Michigan 2000
All rights reserved
ISBN 0-472-08603-0
Published in the United States of America by
The University of Michigan Press
Manufactured in the United States of America

2003 2002 2001 2000   4 3 2 1

No part of this publication may be reproduced,
stored in a retrieval system, or transmitted in
any form or by any means, electronic,
mechanical, or otherwise, without the written
permission of the publisher.

Acknowledgments

The writing of this textbook represents an odyssey in my own life, from my years as a student of literature to those I have spent teaching language and literature to students from various cultural and linguistic backgrounds. I would like to thank those who have helped me along the way.

To my literature professors who have given so much to their students, in particular, Rosemary Boston, John Brugaletta, Elizabeth Ching, Jean Hall, Thomas Sawicki, and Elaine Tumas, I offer my continual thanks. Special thanks are due to Jane Hippolitto, who made the study of literature a creative experience, and to Dee Kilker, whose influence is evident throughout this work. To Zoe Gibbs, I would like to say thank you for sharing the life that is your namesake.

I'd like to express my heartfelt thanks to Sandy Silberstein of the University of Washington, who first encouraged me to write this literature textbook and who then gave me her valuable guidance as I prepared much of the manuscript. And, to Jim Tollefson, let me say thank you for making me more sensitive to the relationship between language and power.

I would also like to acknowledge the University of Michigan Press for having published this work, and I appreciate the help of Kelly Sippell, ESL manager—Kelly, thank you for your suggestions and input. Thanks also to Liz Suhay, assistant editor, for her help in preparing the manuscript.

Here I'd also like to thank Joan Borsvold for having introduced me to the essay "From Outside, In" by Barbara Mellix. Thanks go to the United States Peace Corps volunteer in Poland who introduced me to the lesson based on the "The Little Red Hen" and to a former student of mine, Jolanta Lewandowska, for sharing Richard Wright's *The Ethics of Living Jim Crow* with me. And, special thanks to my friends Cheryl Coatney and Penny Ziemer for their insights into literature and life. The chapter on feminist criticism was written with them in mind. Finally, I will always be grateful to the students who have continually challenged me to make the study of literature meaningful and worthwhile. The lessons they have taught me about literature and life are found in this textbook.

The author has endeavored to credit all known persons holding copyright or reproduction rights for text quoted and for photographs reproduced in this book, especially:

Frankl, Viktor. Excerpt from *Man's Search for Meaning* by Viktor E. Frankl. © 1959, 1962, 1984, 1992 by Viktor E. Frankl. Reprinted by permission of Beacon Press, Boston, and by Hodder and Stoughton Limited, London.

Hemingway, Ernest. "A Clean, Well-Lighted Place." Reprinted with permission of Scribner, a Division of Simon & Schuster, from *Winner Take Nothing* by Ernest Hemingway. Copyright 1933 by Charles Scribner's Sons. Copyright renewed © 1961 by Mary Hemingway. Copyright © Hemingway Foreign Rights Trust.

Hughes, Langston. "On the Road" from *Something in Common* by Langston Hughes. Copyright © 1963 by Langston Hughes. Copyright renewed © 1991 by Arnold Rampersad and Ramona Bass. Reprinted by permission of Hill and Wang, a division of Farrar, Straus, & Giroux, Inc., and by Harold Ober Associates Incorporated.

Jacobs, Harriet. From *Incidents in the Life of a Slave Girl* by Harriet Jacobs. Copyright © 1987 by the President and Fellows of Harvard College. Reprinted by permission of Harvard University Press.

Maugham, Somerset. "Appointment in Samarra," from *Sheppey* by W. Somerset Maugham. Copyright 1933 by W. Somerset Maugham. Used by permission of Doubleday, a division of Bantam Doubleday Dell Publishing Group, Inc., and the Random House Group Ltd., and William Heinemann, Publisher.

Mellix, Barbara. From "Outside, In" originally appeared in *The Georgia Review,* Volume XLI, No. 2 (Summer 1987), © 1987 by The University of Georgia, © 1987 by Barbara Mellix. Reprinted by permission of Barbara Mellix and *The Georgia Review*.

Olsen, Tillie. "I Stand Here Ironing," copyright © 1956, 1957, 1960, 1961 by Tillie Olsen. From *Tell Me a Riddle* by Tillie Olsen. Used by permission of Delacorte Press/Seymour Lawrence, a division of Bantam Doubleday Dell Publishing Group, Inc., and Elaine Markson.

Olsen, Tillie. Excerpt from *Silences* by Tillie Olsen. © 1965, 1972, 1978 by Tillie Olsen. Used by permission of Delacorte Press/Seymour Lawrence, a division of Bantam Doubleday Dell Publishing Group, Inc., and Elaine Markson.

Plato. "The Allegory of the Cave" from Plato's *The Republic.* Translated by Benjamin Jowett. 4th ed., 1953. Reprinted by permission of Oxford University Press.

Singer, Isaac Bashevis. "Gimpel the Fool" by Isaac Bashevis Singer, translated by Saul Bellow, copyright 1953, 1954 by The Viking Press, Inc., renewed © 1981, 1982 by Viking Penguin, Inc., from *A Treasury of Yiddish*

Stories by Irving Howe and Eliezer Greenberg. Used by permission of Viking Penguin, a division of Penguin Putnam, Inc.

Woolf, Virginia. Excerpt from *A Room of One's Own* by Virginia Woolf, copyright 1929 by Harcourt Brace & Company and renewed 1957 by Leonard Woolf, reprinted by permission of the publisher and The Society of Authors as the Literary Representative of the Estate of Virginia Woolf.

Wright, Richard. Excerpt from "The Ethics of Living Jim Crow" from *Uncle Tom's Children* by Richard Wright. Copyright 1937 by Richard Wright. Copyright renewed 1965 by Ellen Wright. Reprinted by permission of HarperCollins Publishers, Inc.

Photographs

I would like to thank Marco Fenaroli for his photographs, which bring so many of the readings to life. Marco, thanks for spending so much time going through your photographs, slides, and negatives in search of just the right image for a text.

Thanks to Lucile Leister of Bethel, Virginia, for sharing a photograph of one of her award-winning quilts. Lucile has pointed out that the circle effect is an optical illusion as "there is not one curved seam" in the entire work.

And, thanks to my husband, Rafael Kapelinski, for all the shared love and memories in his photographs and our life.

Photograph courtesy of Rafael Kapelinski

"I long for home, long for the sight of home. If any god has marked me out again for shipwreck, my tough heart can undergo it. . . . Let the trial come." —Homer, *Odyssey*

Contents

Chapter headings indicate the main topic or reading of a chapter. Unless otherwise stated, an activity applies to the main reading. Critical approaches to the literature are underlined.

Introduction: To the Instructor   1
To the Student   13

Chapter 1. The Fable   16
   Activities
     1.1.   Introduction to the Fable   17
     1.2.   Origins of the Fable and <u>Intertextuality</u>   17
     1.3.   Morals: "The Tree and the Reed"   19
     1.4a.   Vocabulary Preview: "The Little Red Hen"   20
     1.4b,c. Cloze Exercise: "The Little Red Hen"   20
     1.4d.   Morals: "The Little Red Hen"   23
     1.4e.   Plot Terminology   23
     1.4f.   Cultural Values   24
     1.4g.   Personalization   24
     1.5a.   Sequencing: "The Wind and the Sun"   24
     1.5b.   Morals: "The Wind and the Sun"   25
     1.6a.   Biographical Information: The Buddha   25
     1.6b.   From the Buddhist Scriptures: "The Restraint of the Senses"   25
     1.6c.   "The Dog and the Reflection"   27
     1.7a.   Biographical Information: Plato   27
     1.7b.   Prereading Activity: "The Allegory of the Cave"   28
     1.7c.   From "The Allegory of the Cave"   29
     1.8a.   Biographical Information: Marcus Aurelius   33
     1.8b.   From *Meditations,* by Marcus Aurelius   33
     1.9a.   "The Lion King"   34
     1.9b.   Plot Terminology: "The Lion King"   34
     1.10.   Writing a Fable   35

1.11. Word Association 35
1.12. Review of the Fable 35

Chapter 2. "The Tell-Tale Heart," by Edgar Allan Poe 36
Activities
2.1a. From "The Tale and Its Effect," by Edgar Allan Poe 37
2.1b. Narration: "Appointment in Samarra,"
by Somerset Maugham 37
2.1c. <u>Formalism</u>: "Appointment in Samarra" 38
2.2a. Narrative Terminology 38
2.2b. Point of View 39
2.3. <u>New Criticism</u>: "Appointment in Samarra" 40
2.4. Narration 41
2.5. Vocabulary Preview: "The Tell-Tale Heart" 41
2.6. "The Tell-Tale Heart" 41
2.7. Narrating a Story 46
2.8. Plot Terminology 46
2.9. Oral Reading 46
2.10a. Irony 47
2.10b. Irony: "Appointment in Samarra" 47
2.11. Narration: "The Tell-Tale Heart" 47
2.12. Theme 47
2.13a. Psychological Theories: Case History 48
2.13b. Vocabulary Preview: The <u>Freudian Approach</u> 49
2.13c. Summary of the <u>Freudian Approach</u> 49
2.13d. <u>Freudian Approach</u>: Case History 53
2.14. Title Analysis 54
2.15. Point of View: The Narrator 54
2.16. Point of View: Filming a Story 54

Chapter 3. "Young Goodman Brown," by Nathaniel Hawthorne 55
Activities
3.1. <u>Historical Approach</u>: The Puritans 56
3.2. Puritan Values: From "A Young Puritan's Code,"
by Jonathan Edwards 57
3.3. Allegory 58
3.4. Cross-Cultural Values 59
3.5a. <u>Mythic Approach</u>: Archetypal Symbols 59
3.5b. <u>Structuralism</u>: Binary Opposites 60
3.5c. <u>Structuralism</u> and Cultural Values 61

3.5d.	<u>Poststructuralism and Deconstructionism:</u> Introduction 62	
3.6.	Writing a Story 62	
3.7.	Puritan English 63	
3.8.	"Young Goodman Brown" 64	
3.9.	Narration 76	
3.10.	Irony 76	
3.11.	Dream Analysis 77	
3.12.	Point of View 77	
3.13.	Symbols and the <u>Freudian Approach</u> 77	
3.14.	Interview: Brown and a Freudian Psychologist 78	
3.15.	Review of Cross-Cultural Values 78	
3.16.	Theme 78	
3.17.	A Cross-Cultural View of "Young Goodman Brown" 79	
3.18.	Archetypal Symbols: Visual Focus 79	

Chapter 4. "On the Road," by Langston Hughes   80
Activities

4.1.	<u>Sociological Approach</u>: Constitutional Amendments 81
4.2.	From *Incidents in the Life of a Slave Girl,* by Harriet Jacobs 82
4.3.	Constitutional Amendments 83
4.4.	From "A Paradox and a Dream," by John Steinbeck 84
4.5.	From *The Ethics of Living Jim Crow,* by Richard Wright 86
4.6.	"From Outside, In," by Barbara Mellix 90
4.7.	"On the Road" 92
4.8.	Dr. Martin Luther King Jr. and the Civil Rights Movement 98
4.9.	Nonviolent Civil Disobedience 99
4.10.	From "Civil Disobedience," by Henry David Thoreau 100
4.11.	From *The Fire Next Time,* by James Baldwin 100
4.12.	Freedom March on Washington, DC 101
4.13.	Time Line: Civil Rights Movement 102
4.14.	"On the Road": Review 104
4.15.	Homelessness 104
4.16.	Point of View: Harriet Jacobs 104

Chapter 5. "I Stand Here Ironing," by Tillie Olsen   105
Activities

5.1a.	<u>Feminist Criticism</u>: Analysis of a Quilt 106
5.1b.	Question from *In Search of Our Mothers' Gardens,* by Alice Walker 107

5.1c. Questions on *In Search of Our Mothers' Gardens*   107
5.1d. Discussion of *In Search of Our Mothers' Gardens*   108
5.1e. Discussion of "Everyday Use," by Alice Walker   108
5.1f. Writing a Story   109
5.1g. Review of 5.1a–f   110
5.2.   Survey   110
5.3a. Shakespeare's Sister   110
5.3b. From *A Room of One's Own,* by Virginia Woolf   111
5.4.   Alice Walker and Virginia Woolf   114
5.5a. Survey   114
5.5b. From *Silences,* by Tillie Olsen   115
5.5c. Harriet Jacobs and Feminist Criticism   119
5.6a. Prereading Questions for "I Stand Here Ironing"   119
5.6b. Vocabulary Preview for "I Stand Here Ironing"   119
5.6c. "I Stand Here Ironing"   120
5.6d. Feminism and Psychology   128
5.7.   Chapter Review   129
5.8.   AIDS: Analysis of a Quilt   129

Chapter 6. "A Clean, Well-Lighted Place," by Ernest Hemingway   131
Activities
6.1.   Preview Questions for Existentialism   132
6.2.   The Mahabharata and Existentialism   132
6.3.   From *The Myth of Sisyphus,* by Albert Camus   133
6.4.   "A Clean, Well-Lighted Place"   135
6.5a. Biblical Allusions   141
6.5b. Worldviews   142
6.6a. Universalizing Techniques: Setting   143
6.6b. Universalizing Techniques: Characterization   144
6.7a. Characterization Techniques Continued   144
6.7b. Characterization and Hemingway's Writing Style   145
6.7c. Characterization and Hemingway's Writing Style   145
6.8.   Reader Response Criticism: Summary   145
6.9.   Debate on Existentialism   147
6.10a. Deconstructionism: Summary   152
6.10b. Deconstructionism: Advertisements   155
6.10c. Deconstructionism: The Bhagavad Gita   155
6.10d. Deconstructionism: Language   156
6.10e. Deconstructionism: *The Myth of Sisyphus*   156
6.11. Review of Existentialism   156

Chapter 7. "Gimpel the Fool," by Isaac Bashevis Singer   157
  Activities
  7.1.   Historical Background   158
  7.2.   Vocabulary: Historical Background   159
  7.3a.   From *Man's Search for Meaning*, by Viktor Frankl   159
  7.3b.   Existentialism and the Freudian Approach:
            The Doctor and the Soul and *Man's Search for
            Meaning*   165
  7.4.   Deconstructionism   166
  7.5.   From *Farewell to Reason*, by Paul Feyerabend   166
  7.6.   From *The Story of English*, by William Cram,
            Robert MacNeil, and Robert McCrum: Yinglish   167
  7.7a.   Preview of Idioms in "Gimpel the Fool"   168
  7.7b.   Preview of Proverbs in "Gimpel the Fool"   169
  7.7c.   Prereading Activity for "Gimpel the Fool"   170
  7.8.   "Gimpel the Fool"   170
  7.9.   Characterization   183
  7.10a.   Setting   183
  7.10b.   The World of the Story   183
  7.10c.   Feminist Approach to Setting and Characterization   184
  7.11.   Freudian Approach: Characterization   184
  7.12.   Deconstructionism: Language   184
  7.13.   Existentialism: Characterization   184
  7.14.   From *Inside the Third World*, by Paul Harrison   184
  7.15.   Review of 7.1   185
  7.16a.   "Gimpel the Fool" and the Fable   186
  7.16b.   Thoughts on Literature   186
  7.16c.   Thoughts on Literary Criticism   186

Chapter 8. Using Source Materials and Critical Approaches
          to Write about Literature   187

Chapter 9. Biographies   197

Answer Key   219

I would stay up until the sacred Dawn
as long as you might wish to tell
your story.
—Homer, *Odyssey*

Introduction: To the Instructor

What Kinds of Students Would Enjoy Using This Textbook?

Literary Odysseys is intended for students who want to read literature for their intellectual enrichment and language study as well as for those who plan to major in literature. The textbook would work well in introductory literature courses at the junior college and university levels. Additionally, this textbook could work as part of an advanced placement literature course in high schools.

In an English as a second or foreign language (ESL/EFL) context, students who use this text should be at a high-intermediate or advanced level. This text could be used in intensive English programs that have elective courses for more advanced students as well as in English programs abroad wherein students are required to study a year or more of literature along with their language studies.

As the name *Literary Odysseys* suggests, this study of literature is meant to provide students with an adventurous journey through literature and literary theory. Although *Literary Odysseys* focuses on the short story form, many of the analytical skills that students gain from working through the materials in this textbook can also be applied to the analysis of poetry, drama, and the novel. The readings and the activities found in the textbook will involve your students in literature, language, and life. In either teaching context, teachers should find that there is more than enough material to fill a nine-week quarter or a fifteen-week semester.

What Kinds of Teachers Would Enjoy Using This Text and Why?

Literary Odysseys is designed for instructors who have been trained in literature and for those who enjoy literature but who have had little or no formal training in literary analysis. Often, instructors who are trained in teaching ESL/EFL, but not literature, are asked to teach literature courses, and even those who have degrees in the subject can find it daunting to think of teaching literature—a job that is altogether different from the research done at the university. In fact, most degree programs in literature do not provide students with courses in teaching methodology. Such courses are usually picked up if a teacher decides to get a secondary teaching credential or in conjunction with teaching composition or ESL/EFL courses, as happened in my case. Similarly, many ESL/EFL programs do not include classes on teaching literature in an ESL/EFL context. In the section "How Can Teachers Use *Literary Odysseys* in an ESL/EFL Context?" I describe in more detail how ESL/EFL teaching techniques are used to approach the texts in *Literary Odysseys*. I discuss the text's layout in the section "How Is *Literary Odysseys* Organized"? Whether you will be teaching in an ESL/EFL context or in a class with students whose first language is English, it would be helpful to read both sections, but, for now, please read on.

A background in teaching methodology, particularly as it relates to ESL/EFL, is helpful when teaching literature, yet, even for teachers who do have such a background, the actual task of putting theory into practice can be overwhelming. Anthologies can be over two thousand pages long, and it is generally up to the instructor to decide how to break down the materials into manageable chunks for the students. Ironically, literature textbooks rarely introduce students to the range of critical theories that is used to analyze literary texts. Thus, teachers find themselves in a paradoxical situation: they must teach literature without teaching the theory that is used to analyze it. In turn, students find themselves in a situation where they are expected to talk and to write about literature without having been introduced to the concepts and vocabulary terms they need to do an effective analysis.

As a student of literature myself, I remember many moments in introductory literature classes when an instructor asked a question hoping for an answer but received only blank looks and an awkward silence in response. Other times, a response was offered, but it often seemed to fall short of what the instructor desired because we lacked the analytical tools necessary to explain why we felt a certain way about a work of fiction. Consequently, the resultant classroom discussion was often very subjective and based on the students' emotional reaction to a text. I can remember the relief when the instructor finally began his or her lecture. We students would open our notebooks, pens poised to take down the words of wisdom that we would receive.

While I was fortunate to have instructors who gave interesting lectures, sometimes, no matter how riveting the instructor was, I found my attention drifting away. My job as a literature student often seemed to be to take notes, to pass exams, to write research papers, and to occasionally offer my opinion in class. In general, I was not required to be actively involved in each lesson. I can even recall one dear instructor who lectured to the upper far-right corner of the room, as if the students weren't there.

Fortunately, I also had instructors who recognized that students could never make the literature their own until they had the chance to really work with it. Just as a student learning a foreign language needs to use a language and not just learn about it, so we needed to work with the literature and not just listen to lectures about it. In such classes, the teachers gave us creative tasks. For example, we developed role plays and debates based on characters in a text; we were asked to apply what we had learned in class to everyday, human situations so that the literature seemed a part of life rather than abstracted from it. We were asked to consider a text from many angles—from the view of a psychologist, a feminist, a social critic—so that we could appreciate ways of viewing the world that may have differed from our own. Such activities demanded our active involvement. As a result, the literature became more personal and more alive—more connected to daily life.

As an undergraduate and graduate student in English literature, I picked up teaching techniques from watching teachers who modeled how it could be done. I also learned much from the courses in rhetoric and teaching methodology that I was required to take while teaching writing to both native and non-native speakers of English. I discovered that the techniques used in teaching English as a second or foreign language—the communicative activities, the emphasis on learning styles, and the interaction of students and their teacher—could also be used to make literary texts more accessible to students—whether those students spoke English as a first, second, or foreign language. Over the years, I have used such techniques to help make literature a vehicle for language study and the study of literary theory.

Literary Odysseys came out of my own experiences as a student and as a teacher of the English language and of literature. When I found myself teaching an introduction to literature course, I did not want my students to be passive learners who simply took notes as I lectured. As a teacher, I hoped to draw out my students and draw them into the literature. For this reason, *Literary Odysseys* is not set up like many literature anthologies in which students read a text in isolation, answer a few questions, and then write an essay about the text. Instead, each of the short stories presented in this textbook is related to a critical approach to literature so that the students have the concepts and vocabulary they need to answer the question, "What did you think about the story?"

Ideally, both teachers and students will find that the textbook activities are organized in a way that makes the stories and concepts nonthreatening and accessible. Instructors will find the textbook particularly helpful because classroom activities accompany each of the readings included in the text: the text layout provides much of the groundwork that teachers would have to do in order to present both literature and literary theory to their students.

Many of the activities in *Literary Odysseys* have been shaped by much trial and error, and by much success, in classroom settings with students ranging from their late teens to middle age. My intent has been not only to provide a selection of literature and supplementary readings but also to make the materials ready for classroom use. *Literary Odysseys* aims to provide you and your students with paradigms—intellectual maps—so that, together, you can explore and discuss a short story with pleasure. To this end, I would ask that you read both of the sections that follow whether you are teaching students who are majoring in English literature or those who are studying English as a second or foreign language.

How Can Teachers Use *Literary Odysseys* in an ESL/EFL Context?

As an undergraduate and graduate student of literature, I took courses in rhetoric and ESL/EFL methodology as part of my training. Additionally, as a United States Peace Corps volunteer in Poland (1990–93), I received further training in teaching English as a foreign language and in teaching English for special purposes. My interest in ESL/EFL methodology prompted me to obtain a master's degree in teaching English to speakers of other languages, eight years after having received my master's in English literature.

As a literature student, I had begun to feel that my studies were too esoteric, too disconnected from everyday life—an ironic situation considering that literature comes from life. So, after receiving my master's in literature, I felt the need to apply what I had learned. As a Peace Corps volunteer working at a teacher training college, I was given the opportunity to combine my studies in literature with the training I had received in ESL/EFL. In Poland, I was also fortunate to have students who welcomed the more interactive teaching style, even though they were used to the lecture format. Since then, I have used the materials in *Literary Odysseys* in a number of ESL/EFL contexts.

Those who have used ESL/EFL teaching materials will recognize the ESL/EFL techniques at work in *Literary Odysseys*—techniques that require both teachers and students to interact collaboratively. In ESL/EFL classes, the teacher sets up a lesson framework wherein students can learn, practice, and apply new structures. As a result, the teacher is not the focal point of the lesson but rather is more of a facilitator. This is not to imply, however, that such an instructor is not involved in the lesson. On the contrary, the instructor has done much behind-the-scenes work to set up a lesson. He or she has set clear objectives and meaningful tasks that reinforce the learning process, encourage interaction, and appeal to a variety of different learning styles. In class, the teacher elicits information from the students and presents the concepts and vocabulary terms that the students need to accomplish an activity. The instructor also sets the pace, adjusts the lesson to the students' needs, gives them feedback, and coordinates the classwork that may be done individually, in pairs, or in small groups (Kinsella 1996).

In *Literary Odysseys,* I have sought to provide activities that help teachers to achieve these goals. Let's look at parts of chapter 1 to see how the chapter has been set up to do this. In chapter 1, the deceptively simple form of the fable is used as a vehicle for introducing students to concepts related to plot structure and intertextuality—the way in which texts "dialogue" with one another and the way our knowledge of a text influences our reading of other texts. The activities in the chapter also familiarize students with a more interactive learning experience.

Activity 1.1 serves as a lead-in that elicits what students already know about fables and introduces terms related to fables. Students are asked to discuss the following terms associated with the word *fable*.

      Folk wisdom
  mor**A**l
      Brief
anima**L**s
    A**E**sop

Then, activity 1.2 gives the students more detailed background information in outline form about the development of the fable. The students work with the information in the outline by transferring the information from it to the blanks found in a written text (a cloze passage) and by trying to summarize the text verbally. In this way, the students read, write, and talk about the content area, thus integrating three of the four skill areas focused on in ESL/EFL contexts: listening, speaking, reading, and writing.

Activity 1.4b develops the students' listening and reading skills. Students are asked to predict the words that go in the blanks based on the parallel structure of the text. They are given a sequencing exercise that familiarizes them with the information found in the text. They are then asked to fill in the missing words of "The Little Red Hen" as the teacher reads the fable aloud. After the fable has been completed, the students are asked to do a role play in which each student assumes the identity of a character in the fable.

Only after the students are thoroughly familiar with the fable, having read it, listened to it, and done a role play, are they then asked to write a moral for "The Little Red Hen." They personalize the moral by applying it to their own lives and/or to situations in everyday life. Since the structure of "The Little Red Hen" is rather simple, it also is used as a means of introducing students to the more complex vocabulary associated with plot structure.

The fables in the chapter are also used to introduce the students to the notion of intertextuality. As an illustration, the fable "The Dog and the Reflection," thought to be of Indian origin, is shown to echo teachings found in extracts taken from the Buddhist Scriptures. Before reading the extracts, the students read a short passage about the Buddha's life and write questions based on answers taken from the biographical text. They also discuss their associations with some of the key words found in the excerpted passage. These prereading activities allow teachers to preteach some of the concepts found in the text and to elicit what their students may already know about Buddhism. Since the passage is full of similes, the students are asked to identify the similes and, if possible, to sketch them out. They can then use the similes and/or their sketches to summarize the passage. The students are also invited to think of additional similes that reflect the themes found in the excerpt. Once the students are familiar with the ideas from Buddhist thought that are presented in the text, they read "The Dog and the Reflection" and are asked what the Buddha might have thought of the dog's behavior.

The next portion of the chapter focuses on an excerpt from "The Allegory of the Cave," by Plato. Although Plato's allegory is not a fable, it uses a technique that is employed in fables—characters and situations are made to represent people and situations in life. The lead-in to this reading is based on a photograph of shadows. The students are asked to consider what is casting the shadows and how the shadows were made. They are then asked whether they would say that the shadows are real or that they are reflections of reality. Such questions prepare the students for Plato's allegory in which prisoners in a cave believe that shadows *are* the real world rather than reflections of it. This reading has been divided into four parts with comprehension questions following each section. An instructor could ask the students to work in groups that are responsible for providing the answers that accompany a given section of the text. Each group could then share its responses with the class. Once the students understand the passage, they are then asked to think of the allegory as a fable and to write a moral for it. They are also asked to find similarities between Plato's writing and the excerpt taken from the Buddhist Scriptures.

To wrap up the chapter, students are again asked to associate a word with each letter of the word *fable*. However, this time around, their associations should be based on the new knowledge they have gained from the chapter. For example, a student may come up with the following.

   Eight-**F**old Path
    Indi**A**
      Buddha
    P**L**ot
      Enlightenment

Thus, the chapter comes full circle with a review of what the students have learned. As demonstrated by the activities found in chapter 1, much of the behind-the-scenes work has already been done in *Literary Odysseys*. Not only does the text provide the readings, it also provides activities based on those readings. A quick review of the activities noted in chapter 1 reveals the following ESL/EFL teaching techniques.

A. Word associations
B. Outlines
C. Cloze passages
D. Summarizing
E. Transferring information
F. Sequencing
G. Predicting
H. Role plays
I. Personalization
J. Question formation
K. Preteaching of vocabulary
L. Using a visual focus
M. Second identity (putting yourself in someone else's shoes)
N. Comprehension questions
O. Recycling/reusing information

Such techniques enable the students to integrate the skills of listening, speaking, reading, and writing as well as to work individually and in pairs or groups.

The activities encourage interaction and involve the students in the materials. They are also varied to appeal to different learning styles. More analytical thinkers will like working with the outline and sequencing tasks whereas those who are visual learners will appreciate the photograph and drawing activities. Learners who like taking a hands-on approach to learning will enjoy the role plays. More reflective students should enjoy the predictions and taking on a second identity. The point is that ESL/EFL teaching techniques allow for a wide variety of creative approaches to teaching literature. As a result, the lessons do not become predictable or static, and students become involved in the materials.

Repeatedly, I have found that, just as I have had to learn how to teach more interactively, so my students have had to learn what it means to be an active participant in class. They have had to learn how to take responsibility for what happens during a lesson and how to be prepared to participate individually as well as in pairs or groups. You may find that your students are not used to an interactive classroom environment. If this is the case, you will need to give them time to become familiar and comfortable with interactive teaching techniques. Many of my students have had to learn how to do activities that are common to communicative ESL/EFL classrooms. At first, some of the students were hesitant to take part in such activities, but, in my experience, I have found that even the students who seemed the most skeptical about the approach soon came to realize that they were learning and enjoying the process. When students realize that each activity has a purpose, they are more willing to be flexible and interactive learners.

When using *Literary Odysseys,* ESL/EFL teachers who are not trained in the teaching of literature should feel confident in the knowledge that they are able to apply the teaching techniques they use in ESL/EFL classes when teaching literature. The same holds true when ESL/EFL teachers find themselves teaching courses in specialized English classes such as English for computers or English for finance. In such situations, the teacher may not have expertise in the content area but does know how to teach language, how to encourage interaction, and how to elicit information from the students that can be used in class. In the same way, ESL/EFL instructors should feel comfortable when using this text in a literature class for high-intermediate or advanced level students. You may have to take some time to familiarize yourself with the content area, but the approach to the materials will be familiar to you. If you are not familiar with teaching in an ESL/EFL context or with using interactive teaching techniques, you will find that such an approach is a natural outgrowth of using *Literary Odysseys.*

How Is *Literary Odysseys* Organized?

The stories and the supplementary readings in *Literary Odysseys* reflect the diverse cultural movements that have shaped literature and literary analysis. For instance, in chapter 2, on Edgar Allan Poe's "The Tell-Tale Heart," the students learn to describe the short story form and to analyze the narrator's psychological state. "On the Road," by Langston Hughes (chap. 4), becomes a vehicle for a study of the Civil Rights movement in the United States. In chapter 5, the students read Tillie Olsen's "I Stand Here Ironing" in order to consider the world from a feminist viewpoint. Hemingway's "A Clean, Well-Lighted Place" (chap. 6) is used to illustrate the mindset of the twentieth century. Students may or may not agree with the ideas presented in the literature and in the literary theories, but they can become aware of other worldviews and how these shape our perception of reality as well as literature. Additionally, the students will become aware of how our use of language shapes our perception of reality. In the process, you will need to clarify that the language used in a given text reflects the cultural mores of a given time and may contain expressions that are no longer considered appropriate, particularly as such expressions refer to racial or cultural groups.

In my note to the students, I emphasize that the summary of a given theory or philosophy simply outlines the basic concepts and vocabulary terms associated with it. To round out the summaries, I invite the students to share any additional knowledge they may have about a given topic in class. I realize that the very nature of a summary limits its scope—my hope is that the overviews will serve as a springboard for students, drawing out what they may already know about a topic and inspiring them to take a deeper look into a subject area. Generally, the readings toward the end of a chapter explore a topic in more depth. In chapter 9, both you and your students can find more detailed information about many of the writers, philosophers, and political figures that are featured in the textbook.

In *Literary Odysseys,* classroom activities have been built into each unit. The activities prior to a reading prepare the students to deal with the concepts and the vocabulary terms that are found in the text. Tasks accompanying each reading serve to guide the students through each piece and to check the students' comprehension. Generally, the exercises that follow each reading enable the students to apply a critical theory to the analysis of a literary work and to the larger world.

The material in this textbook is presented in stages so that the students are not distracted by unfamiliar concepts or vocabulary terms when they try to analyze a story or to complete an activity. Also, much of the information presented in each chapter is "recycled" or reused so that the students' knowledge is continually being reinforced. Because of this, activities and/or questions in a given chapter may relate to materials introduced previously. To maintain continuity, I recommend that you follow the sequence laid out in the text. If you decide to skip activities to save time or because you think that they do not fit the level of your students, then, in subsequent chapters, you will need to select activities that are not based on materials that you have passed over. Activities labeled with a number and a letter, such as *1.1a* and *1.1b,* contain materials that are closely interrelated, so the students will need to have completed the first activity in order to have the tools they need to complete the one that follows.

For the purposes of analysis, many of the readings have been broken into sections. When this is the case, my personal preference would be to have the students read the work in its entirety before they analyze its various parts, though they may prefer to do so after the analysis. In either case, it's good for students to get a feeling for the reading as a whole as well as for its parts. To aid the students in their comprehension of a text, words, idioms, and historical information that may be unfamiliar to them have been glossed. Such definitions are related to the context in which each term is used.

The answers to most of the activities found in the textbook are listed in the answer key. When this is the case, the activity will be identified by the "answer key" icon ➭. Generally, the key lists the answers to matching exercises, fill-in-the-blank activities, and sequencing exercises. I have also included sample answers to questions that relate to literary theory and to concepts presented in the textbook. However, these answers are not meant to be definitive, and your students may come up with equally convincing answers. I have not provided the answers for questions that require creative and open-ended responses from the students. The answer key is meant to be a resource for teachers, but you may choose to have your students refer to it to check their answers.

When using *Literary Odysseys,* you may want to vary your approach to the activities found in the textbook. For example, you may choose to assign an activity as pair or small group work. Or, if you think a story is particularly long, such as "Young Goodman Brown" in chapter 3 or "Gimpel the Fool" in chapter 7, you could have small groups of students summarize a part of the story for the class. To vary the approach to the activities, you might decide to have the students present their work orally rather than in written form or the opposite. To save class time, you could assign certain activities as homework rather than as classwork. The point is to take a flexible approach to the materials: feel free to adjust the activities to the needs, the level, and/or the personality of your particular class—and to your personality as well. In conjunction with some of the activities, you may want to have students listen to songs or refer to texts that are copyrighted. When this is the case, you will need to obtain permission from the copyright holder if you wish to make copies for classroom use. Additionally, when completing activity 2.15, you may want to make a film of your students. Should you do so, be sure to obtain written permission from your students as a release to show the film.

Since students generally end up writing essays or research papers about the literature they have read, chapter 8 provides basic guidelines for using source materials and critical approaches when writing about a short story. The guidelines follow the *MLA Handbook for Writers of Research Papers* (5th edition) and include sample citations that have been taken from the readings found in chapter 1. The chapter also includes two sample essays based on the formalistic and psychological approaches that are introduced in relation to "The Tell-Tale Heart." Because of this, I recommend that the students review the materials found in chapter 8 only after they have completed chapters 1 and 2.

The sample essays in chapter 8 focus on a content-based approach to the materials presented in the textbook—the content itself serves to shape the form of the essays. Each chapter in the textbook is organized in such a way that by working through the materials the students will have done much of the prewriting and prethinking necessary to write a thoughtful and well-organized essay. Throughout *Literary Odysseys* you will find a number of writing tasks. The phrasing of such tasks and/or the organization of the materials provide a framework for a response. In a similar manner, you should find that the organization of *Literary Odysseys* provides a framework for interactive and thought-provoking lessons.

What Else Should I Know?

A former student of mine who went on to take a literature class at a university told me about an experience she had during the first week of class. In the middle of a lecture, when the instructor asked, "Now, why do you think that the author has used such a symbol?" this student raised her hand to share her ideas. However, from the instructor's surprised look, it became clear that the question had been asked rhetorically—the teacher hadn't really expected or wanted an answer from her students. My hope is that a textbook such as *Literary Odysseys* can help to create a classroom environment wherein students and their teachers can speak with assurance and familiarity about literature, as though they were talking about a friend. I would like both students and their teachers to find using *Literary Odysseys* a positive experience.

I welcome feedback and constructive criticism about the experiences instructors and students have had using *Literary Odysseys*. I would also welcome suggestions for activities related to the analysis of poetry and drama. If you have ideas for interactive lessons, please send your comments to me care of the University of Michigan Press. The Press can be reached via e-mail at the Web site: http://www.press.umich.edu/esl/. Should I use your idea(s) in a future publication, the reference will be fully cited. Thank you in advance for your contributions. I invite you to read my note to the students, and I hope that your literary odyssey proves to be enjoyable.

Reference

Kinsella, K. 1996. Designing group work that supports and enhances diverse classroom styles. *TESOL Journal* 6: 24–30.

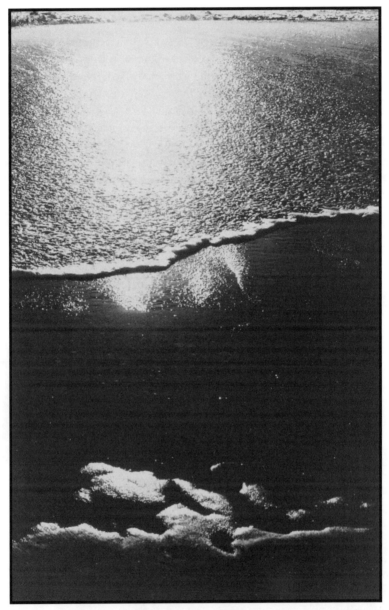

Photograph courtesy of Marco Fenaroli

"In the dawn tomorrow, you shall put out to sea."—Homer, *Odyssey*

To the Student

You are about to embark on a literary odyssey—an adventurous journey through literature and literary theory. Perhaps you are already familiar with Odysseus, the hero of the Greek epic the *Odyssey,* which tells of Odysseus's adventures as he makes his way back home to his family after the **Trojan War.*** Odysseus is willing to undergo whatever he must to return home to his wife and son. He says, "I long for home, long for the sight of home. / If any god has **marked me out** again / for shipwreck, my tough heart can undergo it. / . . . / Let the trial come" (4.220–24). On his return trip, Odysseus undergoes many trials and adventures; among these, he outwits the Cyclops, a one-eyed giant who had taken him and his men captive; he overcomes the temptations of the sensual witch Circe; and he returns alive from a visit to the **underworld.**

In much the same way as Odysseus, you are going to use your intelligence and your life experiences to deal with the many different **worldviews** and social contexts found in this textbook. Like a person on an odyssey, you will become involved in the "world" of each text and how it relates not only to you personally but also to the larger world. Your journey should lead you to feeling "at home" and comfortable when you talk and write about literature, particularly as it relates to the short story form.

Literary Odysseys is meant to be an introduction to literature and to the strategies that can enable you to successfully analyze literary works. It is not a **survey** of English literature from the Middle Ages to the present. Rather, the idea is to become familiar with some of the major trends that have influenced and shaped literary theory—as well as humanity. You will find that *Literary Odysseys* is not set up like many anthologies in which you read a text in isolation, answer a few questions, listen to lectures, and then write an essay. Instead, each of the seven short stories presented in this textbook is related to a critical approach to literature and/or to a social, historical, or philosophical context. Each chapter includes excerpts from **supplementary** readings and a variety of activities to help you better understand and analyze a given story. Also, the information in each chapter "dialogues" with the information found in other chapters so that you are continually reusing what you have learned and applying your knowledge to different contexts.

---

*To aid in your understanding of a given text, words written in boldface type are footnoted. The definitions are related to the context in which each term is used.

Trojan War: a ten-year war between the Greeks and the Trojans that ended in the destruction of Troy

to be marked out: to be called for a special purpose

underworld: a place where the spirits of the dead live

worldviews: the ways people understand and interpret life; from the German *Weltanschauung*

survey: an overview of the major literary works from a specific period of time

supplementary: adds information to what is already known

The intent of *Literary Odysseys* is to provide you with paradigms—intellectual maps—so that you can explore and discuss a literary text effectively. Although this textbook is organized around the short story form, many of the analytical techniques dealt with in the materials can also be applied to an analysis of poetry, drama, and the novel. In the process of using this textbook, you will learn not only about language and literature but also about the world of ideas. For example, as you analyze the short stories in this textbook, you will use ideas developed in Freudian and Jungian psychology; a **host** of "isms"—the philosophies of stoicism, existentialism, and deconstructionism, to name a few; and historical events that continue to impact society such as the Civil Rights movement in the United States and the Holocaust in Europe. The critical approaches used to analyze literature will also help to make you more aware of how our use of language shapes reality. When reading the materials found in this textbook, please keep in mind that the language used in a given text reflects the cultural perceptions of a given time and may contain expressions that are no longer commonly used or are no longer considered appropriate, particularly as such expressions refer to racial or cultural groups. Finally, the critical approaches used to analyze literature will help you to read more carefully the book of life that you open every day.

In this text, the critical approaches to literature are often presented in a summary form that outlines the main concepts and vocabulary terms associated with them. By nature, summaries are **reductive,** so if you are already familiar with a concept or theory introduced in this textbook, you are invited to share your knowledge in class—any information you can bring to the learning process will help to flesh out the materials. Of course, some theories may appeal to you more than others, and you may or may not agree with a stated point of view. In any case, all of the ideas should challenge you to think critically and creatively. The summaries are there to familiarize you with concepts and to encourage you to pursue a more thorough understanding of those areas that interest you. Also, in chapter 9, you can find more detailed information about many of the writers, philosophers, and political figures mentioned in this textbook.

In chapter 8, you can find tips for writing about literature using the approaches introduced in *Literary Odysseys*. The answers to questions that are not open-ended are listed in the answer key. When this is the case, the "answer key" icon (↪) can be found next to the activity. However, keep in mind that you may come up with slightly different and equally convincing answers.

Your instructor may take different approaches to the activities found in each chapter: he or she may ask you to focus on particular exercises to the exclusion of others; you could be asked to divide up the activities into pair or small group work; or you may be asked to do some activities orally and others in written form. In either case, the activities in *Literary*

---

host: a large number of something

reductive: too simplified

Odysseys will get you involved in your literature class. When using *Literary Odysseys,* be prepared to take an active part in each lesson; to share your ideas in class; to work individually, in pairs, and in groups. The point is that the approach to the materials is flexible and varied. There is more than one way to reach your intended destination. Sometimes you may need to take a more direct route, while at other times you may want to take a side trip or even linger in one place for a few days.

For the purposes of analysis, some of the stories and supplementary readings have been broken up into sections followed by activities and/or questions. My personal preference would be to read through each work in its entirety and then to focus on a given section in more detail. But you could also complete each section in turn and then go back and read through the entire work in one sitting. Whichever approach you take, it's good to get a feeling for each work as a whole as well as for its parts. After you have finished reading this "To the Student" section, I invite you to read the preceding section, "To the Istructor," so that you will have a better idea of the approaches your instructor may take when using *Literary Odysseys.*

The readings and the activities in this textbook ought to involve you in literature, language, and life. Should you ever take a survey course of literature or one that focuses on a particular period or **genre** of literature, you can readily adapt much of the knowledge you will have gained from this textbook. More importantly, what you learn from this study of literature can serve as **guideposts** as you make your own odyssey through life.

genre: a specific type of literature; i.e., poetry, drama, the novel

guideposts: signs or signals used to direct a person on a path or road

Chapter 1
The Fable

Kamakura, Japan. Photograph courtesy of Marco Fenaroli

"Hidden and unknown, like the new moon, I will live my life."—Shantideva, a Buddhist text

Activity 1.1

In this chapter, you will learn what a Greek philosopher, a Roman emperor, and the Buddha, a religious teacher, might have thought about the behavior of a little red hen, a cat, a duck, and a pig. To do so, you will analyze the fable, a **precursor** of the short story form. The following words are often associated with the fable. Do you know why this is so? Discuss your ideas with a classmate.

>   **F**olk wisdom
> mor**A**l
>   **B**rief
> anima**L**s
>   A**E**sop

precursor: something that comes before and contributes to what follows

Activity 1.2 ⇨

Although a fable may seem **deceptively** simple, fables come from around the world and have a rich history. To truly understand the importance of the fable, it is helpful to be aware of the cultural and philosophical influences that have shaped the form. Literary critics use the term *intertextuality* to refer to the interrelationships between a literary text and texts that have influenced it. The term also refers to how our knowledge of one text influences our reading of other texts.

Read the outline below to gain a better understanding of the intertextuality that has shaped the development of fables.

deceptively: seemingly having one sort of characteristics; really having a different type

Fables from around the World

Greece and Rome	Asia/India	Arabia and Europe
550 B.C. Aesop—thought to have been a Greek slave—uses fables to refer **covertly** to his master's behavior and the behavior of politicians. Fables used as a **rhetorical** device to criticize political leaders and for entertainment at dinner parties.	563–483? B.C. Influence of Buddha. Buddha uses fables to teach moral lessons. Animals represent **incarnations** of the Buddha.	164 A.D. Over 60 fables brought to England by the **crusaders** and translated into Latin.
	50 A.D. 100 Indian fables brought to Alexandria.	1200 A.D. Alfred the Great, king of England, has fables translated into French and English. Fables are popular themes for tapestries.
300 B.C. Demetrius Phalerus, founder of the **Library at Alexandria,** collects over 200 fables.	30 A.D. Many fables from India and Tibet are translated into Latin by Phaedrus, a Roman writer.	1480 A.D. German collection of fables published as *Aesop's Fables.*

(continued)

covertly: secretly

rhetorical: having to do with the forms of speech and writing—rhetoric

crusaders: those who took part in military actions of the eleventh–thirteenth centuries to take Jerusalem from the Muslims

Library at Alexandria: A collection of over five hundred thousand ancient texts started by the Egyptian king Ptolemy I in 200–300 B.C. The library, the largest in the Roman Empire, was destroyed by fire.

incarnations: lives lived in different forms, e.g., human or animal; the forms a god or spirit can take on earth

Fables from around the World—*continued*

Greece and Rome	Asia/India	Arabia and Europe
161–80 A.D. Marcus Aurelius, a Roman emperor, has **rhetoricians** collect over 300 fables. He believed fables taught moral lessons.	1609/10 A.D. Shakespeare, an English playwright, refers to the fable "The Tree and the **Reed**" in his play *Cymbeline*, 4.2.267: "To thee the reed is as the oak." The fable is of Indian origin and is found in the **Mahabharata**.	1483–96 A.D. *Aesop's Fables* is translated into Italian, Dutch, French, English, and Spanish.

reed: a tall, slender grass that grows in wet areas by waterways

rhetoricians: those who study rhetoric

Mahabharata: A Hindu holy book that contains what is considered to be the longest poem in the world—over one hundred thousand verses. The book was written in Sanskrit, the oldest language known. *Maha* means *great* or *complete. Bharata* means *India* in particular or *man* in general. The title can be translated as *The Great History of India* or *The Complete History of Humankind.* The book contains the Bhagavad Gita, seven hundred verses about the nature of the divine.

Use the preceding outline to fill in the following blanks. After you have filled in the blanks, compare your answers with a classmate's. Then use your outline to tell your partner about the origins of fables. Try not to refer to the text when giving your summary.

What is commonly known as *Aesop's Fables* is a collection of fables from around the world that were brought together in a German collection of fables in the year (1) _____. Aesop was thought to have been a Greek slave who told nearly seven hundred fables. He is said to have lived before 550 B.C.

Fables were not simply considered stories. In Greece and Rome, when it was dangerous to speak openly about one's political opinions, fables were used to criticize (2) _____. Even during periods when free speech was encouraged, the use of fables was continued as a rhetorical device to illustrate a point or for (3) _____ at dinners. In the Roman world, (4) _____ collected fables for Marcus Aurelius, the emperor of Rome (161–80 A.D.). Aurelius was interested in the question of how to live a (5) _____ life, and he thought that fables helped to provide an answer.

Fables from Asia and India are thought to have come from stories about the (6) _____ . In these fables, the Buddha is incarnated as an (7) _____ . Some of these fables came to Alexandria in (8) _____ and were eventually translated into Latin. Shakespeare refers to an Indian fable called "The Tree and the (9) _____" in his play *Cymbeline* (1609–10 A.D.).

Another sixty fables in the Aesop collection come from Arabia. These fables were brought to England by the crusaders, and they were (10) _____ into Latin. In 1200 A.D., King Alfred the Great had them translated into (11) _____ and French. With the publication of *Aesop's Fables,* fables became widely popular and were often **alluded to** in literary works.

alluded to: referred to indirectly or by association

© 2000 University of Michigan.

Activity 1.3 ⇨

A fable is a brief story that teaches a lesson called a *moral*. Morals are generally quite short and stated in one sentence. You will be reading the fable "The Tree and the Reed," referred to by the English playwright and poet William Shakespeare in his play *Cymbeline*. Before you read the fable, look at the pictures of a tree and a reed. Which do you think is the stronger? Why? Discuss your views with a partner. Then, read the fable and answer the questions.

Photograph courtesy of Marco Fenaroli

Photograph courtesy of Marco Fenaroli

The Tree and the Reed

"Well, little one," said a tree to a reed that was growing at its feet. "Why do you not plant your feet deeply into the ground, and raise your head boldly in the air as I do?"

"I am happy the way I am," said the reed. "I may not be so grand, but I think I am safer."

"Safe!" laughed the tree. "Who will **pluck me up** by the roots or bow my head to the ground?" But soon the tree had time to regret its boasting, for a hurricane arose that tore it up from its roots and threw it as a useless log on the ground, while the little reed, bending with the force of the wind, soon stood upright again after the storm had passed over.

to be plucked up: to be pulled up from the ground

This fable is in the public domain. Exercise © 2000 University of Michigan.

dirge: a sad song sung at a funeral

1. Shakespeare referred to this fable in a funeral **dirge** sung for King Cymbeline, a medieval king of Britain. What do you think Shakespeare meant when he wrote of Cymbeline that "To thee the reed is as the oak" (4.2.267)?
2. Write a moral for "The Tree and the Reed." Discuss your morals in small groups and choose a moral to share with the class.

Activity 1.4a ⇨

"The Little Red Hen" is a well-known American fable. Before you read the fable, study the following list of phrases. Use your dictionary if necessary. Once you know the definition of each phrase, put the phrases in a logical sequence by numbering them 1–6. Then compare your sequence with a partner's.

___ to thresh the wheat

___ to bake bread with flour

___ to grind the wheat

___ to take the wheat to the mill

___ to cut a stalk of wheat

___ to plant a grain of wheat

Activity 1.4b ⇨

Many fables come from an oral tradition. Often key words and phrases are repeated to make it easier to remember the story. As you read through "The Little Red Hen," try to fill in the blanks with words or phrases using the word order in the first paragraph to help you. Compare your predictions with a classmate's. Your instructor will read the completed version of the fable aloud. Check your answers. Make any necessary changes.

The Little Red Hen

One day, when the little red hen was scratching around for food, she found a grain of wheat. Instead of eating it right then and there, she turned to the other animals in the barnyard and said, "Who will help me plant this wheat?"

"Not I," said the duck.

"Not I," said the cat.

"Not I," said the pig.

"Then I shall plant it myself," said the little red hen.

And she did.

The wheat grew into a tall stalk. "Who will help me cut the wheat?" she asked.

"Not I," said the duck.

"Not I," _____ the cat.

"_____," said the pig.

"Then I _____ cut it myself," said the little _____ hen.

And she did.

At the top of the wheat grew a large cluster of grain. "Who will _____ me thresh the wheat?" she asked.

"Not _____," said the duck.

"Not I," said the cat.

"_____ I," said the _____.

"Then I shall _____ it myself," said the _____ hen. And she _____.

Soon she had a sack of grain. "_____ will help me take the wheat to the mill?"

"_____ I," said the _____.

"_____ I," said the _____.

"_____ I," said the_____.

"Then I shall _____ myself," said the _____.

And _____.

The mill ground the wheat into flour for baking bread. "_____ bake the bread?" said the little red hen.

"_____," _____.

"_____," _____.

"_____," _____.

"_____," said _____. _____.

And she baked a big round loaf of bread. "Now, _____ _____ the bread?" she asked.

"I will!" _____.

"_____!" _____.

"_____!" _____.

"Oh no," said _____. "You did not help me plant the wheat. You _____ cut the wheat. You _____ to grind into flour for baking bread, and you _____ it. So you will not help me _____ the bread. I will eat it myself." And _____.

This fable is in the public domain. Exercise © 2000 University of Michigan.

Activity 1.4c

In groups, read the fable aloud with one person taking the role of the **narrator** and others the roles of the hen, the duck, the cat, and the pig.

narrator: the one who tells a story

Activity 1.4d ⇨

Write a moral for "The Little Red Hen." Discuss your morals in small groups and choose a moral to share with the class.

Activity 1.4e ⇨

A fable is similar to a very short story. Even though it is not long, it follows a sequence that is common to the form of a longer story. This sequence is called the story's *plot*. We can talk about the story's plot using the terms found below. Identify the parts of "The Little Red Hen" that correspond to the plot terminology by answering the questions that follow each definition.

A. *The introduction or exposition*
   The part of the story that sets the scene for the action or the dramatic situation in the story.
   1. Where does the action take place?
   2. How does the action in the story get started?
   3. Who is involved in the action?

B. *The dramatic conflict*
   The dramatic conflict is between the protagonist, the character with a problem or a task to complete, and the antagonist, the character(s) or situation that causes the protagonist's conflict.
   4. What is the little red hen's problem in this fable?
   5. If the hen is the protagonist, who is/are her antagonist(s)?

C. *The rising action*
   The sequence of events in the story that increases the feeling of tension.
   6. Give the sequence of events in the rising action of "The Little Red Hen." Refer to activity 1.4a for help.

      Example
      1. The hen is scratching for food and finds a grain of wheat.

D. *The climax or crisis*
   The moment of highest tension in the story. The turning point that determines how the story ends.
   7. What happens when the hen asks, "Who will help me eat the bread?"

E. *The resolution*
   How the dramatic conflict is **resolved**. How the story ends.
   8. At the end of the fable, what does the hen do by herself?
   9. How do you think the other animals feel at the end of the fable?

resolved: solved; concluded

metaphorical: One idea or object is used in place of another to communicate a similarity between two things. For example, if we say a computer has a mind, we are likening the way it is organized to processes in the brain.
A work of literature can be metaphorical in that it suggests a similarity between a work of fiction and real life.

symbolic: When an object stands for itself and more than itself. For example, a rose is a flower yet it can also symbolize love.

universal: something that is true for the majority of people

to personalize: to relate something to one's personal experience

Activity 1.4f ⇨

In "The Little Red Hen," the characters and their actions have a **metaphorical** and **symbolic** significance; that is, they represent themselves and yet stand for something that is experienced in everyday life. When you state the moral and describe how it relates in general terms to the values of a culture, then you are speaking of the work's symbolic significance in general or **universal** terms. What cultural values are illustrated in "The Little Red Hen"?

Activity 1.4g

You can **personalize** this fable by applying the moral illustrated in "The Little Red Hen" to a specific incident in your life or in another person's life. Or, you can write about a specific instance in history that illustrates a similar moral. Write a short paragraph in which you relate "The Little Red Hen" to life.

Activity 1.5a ⇨

The fable "The Wind and the Sun" is an example of a fable that was used in ancient Greece to talk about a sensitive topic covertly. Sophocles, a Greek dramatist, is quoted as saying that the fable describes the relationship between the well-known Roman historian Plutarch and his wife.

The sentences that appear in the fable are in the wrong order. Order the sentences by writing the numbers 1–6 in the blanks. Compare your version with a classmate's.

___ But the harder he blew, the more closely did the man hold his coat until the wind gave up trying to make him take off his coat.

___ The sun said, "Whichever of us can make that man take off his coat is the stronger."

___ The wind and the sun were arguing about who was the stronger.

___ The wind began to blow cold air on the man.

___ Then the sun came out and shone upon the man, who soon became very hot and took off his coat.

___ Suddenly they saw a man walking on the road, and the sun said, "I see a way to end our argument."

This fable is in the public domain. Exercise © 2000 University of Michigan.

Activity 1.5b

1. Why do you think people told this fable rather than speaking directly about the relationship between Plutarch and his wife?
2. Write your own moral for "The Wind and the Sun." Discuss your morals in small groups and choose a moral to share with the class.

Activity 1.6a

In order to become more aware of the intertextual influences that have shaped fables, you will be reading excerpts from the Buddha's teachings, Plato's *Republic,* and Marcus Aurelius's *Meditations.* In preparation for the readings from the Buddhist Scriptures refer to the biographical information about the Buddha found in chapter 9. (Note that the Buddha is listed under *Gautama, Siddhārtha,* his family name.)

Use the information about the Buddha to write questions for the following answers. The first one has been done for you.

1. <u>What does the name Buddha mean?</u>

    Enlightened one.

2. _____

    A way of life that leads to enlightenment.

3. _____

    At the age of twenty-nine.

4. _____

    When he gazed at the morning star.

Activity 1.6b

In writings such as the Buddhist Scriptures, images and situations from life are used to teach a moral lesson much as they are in the fable. Before you read the adapted passage from the Buddhist Scriptures, think about what is meant by the following words.

A. the senses
B. mindfulness

In this passage, the Buddha compares the senses to objects and situations in everyday life. He often uses the word *like* to make these comparisons. For example, he says that the five senses are like five arrows. A direct comparison that uses *like* or *as* to compare things is called a *simile.* As you read the passage, underline the similes that the Buddha has used to describe the senses. Your instructor may ask you to sketch out these similes and to use your drawings to summarize the passage.

From the Buddhist Scriptures: "The Restraint of the Senses"

By taking your stand on mindfulness you must control your five senses which are **unsteady** by nature. Fire, snakes, and lightning are less dangerous to us than our own senses which are so much more dangerous. For they **assail** us all the time. Even the most **vicious** enemies can attack only some people at some times, and not at others, but everybody is always and everywhere **weighed down** by his senses. . . . Those attacked by external enemies may, or may not, suffer injury to their souls, but those who are weighed down by the senses suffer in body and soul alike. For the five senses are rather like arrows which have been smeared with the poison of **fancies**, have cares for their feathers and happiness for their points, and fly about in the space provided by the range of the sense-objects; shot off by Kama, the God of Love, they hit people in their very hearts as a hunter hits a deer, and if men do not know how **to ward off** these arrows, they will be their undoing; when they come near us we should stand firm in self-control, be **agile** and **steadfast**, and ward them off with the armor of mindfulness. As a man who has **subdued** his enemies can everywhere live and sleep at ease and free from care, so can he who has **pacified** his senses. For the senses constantly ask for more by way of worldly objects, and normally behave like **voracious** dogs who can never have enough.

Buddhist Scriptures, edited and translated by Edward Conze. Penguin, 1959.

restraint: control of the senses and their desires

unsteady: not stable; easily confused or influenced

to assail: to attack

vicious: extremely cruel

to be weighed down by something: to feel that one is carrying a heavy load

fancies: desires; dreams

to ward off: to keep something from hitting or finding its target

agile: moving quickly and easily

steadfast: dependable; true

subdued: brought under control

pacified: satisfied; calmed

voracious: having a great appetite

1. Compare the sections of the excerpt that you have underlined with those of a classmate. Discuss any differences you may have.
2. If you have drawn pictures based on the similes found in the excerpt, use these to help you summarize the passage.
3. Write similes about the five senses that are not in the passage.

   Example

   The five senses are like a lava flow.
4. Now, what do you think the Buddha means by *mindfulness*?

Activity 1.6c ⇨

Read "The Dog and the Reflection," a fable believed to be of Indian origin. But, first, look at the picture. What do you think the dog is looking for?

Photograph courtesy of Marco Fenaroli

The Dog and the Reflection

It happened that a dog had got a piece of meat and was carrying it home in his mouth to eat it. Now, on his way home he had to cross a log lying across a running stream. As he crossed, he looked down and saw his own image reflected in the water. Thinking it was another dog with another piece of meat, he made up his mind to have that also. So he tried to snap at the reflection in the water, but as he opened his mouth, the piece of meat fell out, dropped into the water, and was never seen again.

This fable is in the public domain.

1. What is the dog actually looking for?
2. What might the Buddha think about the dog's behavior?

Activity 1.7a ⇨

The reading from Plato's "The Allegory of the Cave" is taken from his book the *Republic*. The word *allegory* comes from the Greek word *allegorein*, meaning to speak figuratively—to use symbolic images to communicate a message. In an allegory, the characters themselves symbolize general truths about life. Although Plato's "The Allegory of the Cave" is not, strictly speaking, a fable, Plato employs a technique that is used in the fable—characters and situations are made to represent people and situations in life. In this excerpt, Plato has Socrates, a Greek philosopher, and his student, named Glaucon, discuss the cave and the people who live there.

Before you read the excerpt from "The Allegory of the Cave," take a moment to read the biography of Plato found in chapter 9. Then write questions for the following answers. The first one has been done for you.

1. <u>What did Plato think about objects in the physical world?</u>

   that they were imperfect and reflections or shadows of the ideal forms

2. _____

   because he thought that mathematical solutions reflected the ideal forms

3. _____

   through study and analytical thinking

4. _____

   a series of dialogues in which a question is asked and then answered

Activity 1.7b ⇨

Look at the picture. In pairs, describe what you see. How would you answer the questions that follow?

Photograph courtesy of Rafael Kapelinski

1. What is casting the shadows that are shown here?
2. How are shadows made?
3. Would you say that shadows are real or reflections of reality? How do you think Plato would answer this question?

Activity 1.7c ⇨

Plato's "The Allegory of the Cave" describes an imaginary situation in which prisoners have been chained to a wall deep in a cave since their births. They are unable to move their heads to see what is behind them. The prisoners can only see the wall in front of them. On this wall, they can see the shadows of people and objects that are cast by a great fire that burns on a raised **ledge** behind them. However, because the prisoners can not turn their heads, they can not see the people as they walk across a passageway between the fire and the prisoners. Since the prisoners cannot see the people and objects that are casting the shadows, they believe that the shadows are "real."

ledge: a raised edge

This excerpt begins after Socrates has described the cave and its prisoners to Glaucon. The reading has been divided into four parts followed by questions. As you read this adapted text, think about the symbolic significance of the cave, the shadows, and the light. Although the situation described in the allegory is imaginary, answer the questions as if the situation were real.

Your instructor may have you read the dialogue aloud in pairs.

Part 1

> ### From "The Allegory of the Cave"
>
> *Socrates:* They [the prisoners] are like ourselves. They see only their own shadows, or the shadows of one another which the fire throws on the opposite wall of the cave.
>
> *Glaucon:* True, how could they see anything but the shadows if they were never allowed to move their heads?
>
> *Socrates:* And they also see only the shadows of the objects which are being carried, isn't that so?
>
> *Glaucon:* Yes.
>
> *Socrates:* And if the prisoners were able to talk with one another, wouldn't they try to explain the shadows that they were seeing before them?
>
> *Glaucon:* Very true.
>
> *Socrates:* And suppose a sound echoed off the walls in the cave when one of the passers-by spoke, wouldn't the prisoners think that the sound came from the shadows?

Glaucon: Without a doubt.

Socrates: To the prisoners, the truth would be **literally** nothing but the shadows of the images.

literally: in reality; in actuality

Glaucon: That is certain.

1. Try to draw a sketch of the scene in "The Allegory of the Cave."
2. How do the prisoners explain the shadows?
3. How are the prisoners like us?

Part 2

Socrates: And now look again, and see what will naturally happen if one of the prisoners is released and shown the truth about the shadows. At first, when he is freed, he will stand up and turn around and walk and look towards the light, and the **glare** of the light will hurt his eyes and upset him. He will be unable to see the realities which in his former state he had seen as shadows. And then imagine what would happen if someone tried to explain to him what the objects are as they pass and asked about them, will he not be **perplexed**? Will he not think that the shadows which he formerly saw are **truer** than the objects which are now shown to him?

glare: a light so bright that it causes pain

perplexed: confused
truer: more real

Glaucon: Far truer.

Socrates: And if he is **compelled** to look straight at the light, will he not have a pain in his eyes which will make him turn away **to take refuge** in the shadows which he can see and which he will **conceive** to be in reality clearer than the things which are now being shown to him?

compelled: forced to do something
to take refuge: to look for safety and protection
to conceive: to think of something in a certain way; to come up with an idea

Glaucon: True.

Socrates: And suppose that, once more, he is reluctantly dragged up the **ascent** to the entrance of the cave and is forced into the presence of the sun. Is he not likely to be pained and irritated? When he approaches the light his eyes will be **dazzled**, and he will not be able to see any of the objects which are now called realities.

ascent: an upward slope

dazzled: blinded by a bright light

Glaucon: Not all in a moment.

Socrates: He will require time to grow **accustomed** to the sight of the upper world. And first he will see the shadows best, next the reflections of people and other objects in the water, and then the objects themselves; then he will gaze upon the light of the moon and the stars; and he will see the sky and the stars by night better than the sun or the light of the sun by day, won't he?

accustomed: having become used to something

Glaucon: Certainly.

Socrates: Last of all he will be able to see the sun, and not mere reflections of the sun in the water, but he will see the sun in its own proper place in the sky, and he will see the sun as it is.

Glaucon: Certainly.

Socrates: He will then proceed to argue that the sun is what causes the seasons and the years and that the sun is the keeper of all that is in the visible world, and in a certain way the cause of all the shadows which he and his fellow prisoners have been accustomed to seeing.

Glaucon: Clearly, he would first see the sun and then reason about the sun and its purpose.

4. When the prisoner is first brought out of the cave, how does he react when someone tries to explain the shadows to him?
5. How does the prisoner react to the light the first time he is brought out of the cave? Why?
6. Once the prisoner has grown accustomed to the light, what does he realize about the shadows?

Part 3

Socrates: And when he remembered the cave and the way that he and his fellow prisoners had thought about life, do you not think that he would be happy that he now knew the truth about the shadows and that he **pitied** the other prisoners?

Glaucon: Certainly he would.

Socrates: And if the prisoners had been in the habit of giving honors to the prisoner who was the quickest to observe the passing shadows and to remember which had passed before and which followed after, and which were together and who were, therefore, the best able to draw conclusions about the future, do you think that the former prisoner would care for such honors and glories, or envy the possessors of them? Would he not say with **Homer**, "Better to be the poor servant of a poor master," and to endure anything, rather than think as the other prisoners do and to live like them?"

Glaucon: Yes. I think that he would rather suffer anything than live with a false belief in the shadows and in such a miserable manner.

Socrates: Imagine once more that the same man went suddenly back into the cave to be put back into his old situation. Would he not be certain to have his eyes full of darkness?

Glaucon: To be sure.

Socrates: And if there were a contest and he had to compete with the other prisoners to identify the shadows while his eyes were getting used to the darkness, would he not appear ridiculous to the other prisoners? Wouldn't the others say that he had returned to the cave without his eyes and that it was better not to think of leaving the cave, and if anyone ever came to unchain one of the prisoners and

pitied: felt sorry for someone; to be the object of pity

Homer: A Greek poet believed to have lived in the ninth century B.C., though nothing is known of his life. The epic poems the *Iliad* and the *Odyssey* are thought to be his works. Socrates uses Homer's saying to show that it is better to live with a knowledge of the truth and to be poor than to be rich and not know what is true.

> lead him or her up into the light, let them catch and put that person to death?
>
> *Glaucon:* No question.

7. The prisoners play a memory game in which they try to remember the kinds of shadows that had passed by on the wall. What does the released prisoner think about this contest after he has seen the sun?
8. Why does the prisoner have trouble playing the memory game when he returns to the cave?
9. How do the people in the cave react to the prisoner who tries to tell the truth about the shadows?

Part 4

> *Socrates:* I will now explain this entire allegory to you. The prison cave is the world of sight [the physical world], the light of the fire is the sun, and you will not misunderstand me if you interpret the journey upwards out of the cave to be the ascent of the soul into the intellectual world which, according to my poor belief and your request, I have explained to you, whether rightly or wrongly, God knows. But, whether true or false, my opinion is that in the world of knowledge the idea of good appears last of all, and is seen only with an effort: and, when seen it is also **inferred** to be the universal author of all things beautiful and right, parent of light and lord of light in this visible world, and the immediate source of reason and truth; and that this idea of good is the power upon which a person who would act rationally, either in public or private life, must **have his eye fixed**.

inferred: concluded from the evidence given

to have one's eye fixed: to focus on something and to keep it in sight or in mind

"The Allegory of the Cave" from Plato's *Republic* is taken from *The Dialogues of Plato,* translated by Benjamin Jowett. 4th ed. Copyright 1953 by Oxford University Press. Reprinted and adapted by permission of Oxford University Press.

10. What does the cave represent in real life?
11. What does the light of the fire represent?
12. What does the journey out of the cave represent?
13. What do you think is meant by the "idea of the good"? What is required to understand this idea?
14. What ideas from "The Allegory of the Cave" are similar to those found in the excerpt from the Buddhist Scriptures?
15. If you thought of "The Allegory of the Cave" as a fable, what would the moral be?

Activity 1.8a

The Roman emperor Marcus Aurelius (121–80 A.D.) was fond of collecting fables for the morals they contain. Read the biographical information about Aurelius found in chapter 9 to write questions for the following answers. The first one has been done for you.

1. <u>What did Aurelius believe about the power of reason?</u>

    He believed that it could be used to live a moral life.

2. _____

    a short, insightful statement

3. _____

    to live a morally upright life

Activity 1.8b

The lessons Aurelius learned from fables can be seen in his own philosophical writings called the *Meditations*. Before reading the following excerpt, which deals with issues presented in fables, answer the following questions.

A. What do you think makes people truly happy?
B. Why do you think human beings exist? Why are they on earth?
C. Have you ever been in a great deal of pain, either physical or mental? How did you deal with the pain? Or how has someone you know dealt with a terrible pain?

Read this adapted excerpt from Aurelius's *Meditations*. Compare your answers to questions A–C with the answers given in the excerpt. Then complete the questions that follow.

From Meditations

A man's true delight is to do the things he was made for. He was made to show goodwill to his kind, to rise above his senses, **to distinguish** false appearances from realities, and to study Nature and her works.

We have three relationships: one to this bodily shell which **envelops** us, one to the divine Cause which is the source of everything in all things, and one to our fellow human beings.

Pain must be an evil either to the body or to the soul. But the soul can always refuse to consider pain an evil, and so keep the soul's skies calm and unclouded. For there is no decision, no impulse, no move-

to distinguish: to tell the difference between things

envelops: surrounds

ment or reaction, but must come from within the self; and into this self no evil can force its way.

Erasing all desires, keep on saying to yourself, "It lies in my own hands to ensure that no viciousness, greed or chaos of any kind finds a home in this soul of mine; it is up to me to perceive all things in their true light, and to deal with everything as it deserves." Remember this power of reason which is Nature's gift to you.

Meditations, by Marcus Aurelius, translated by Maxwell Staniforth. Viking, 1964.

1. Why do you think Aurelius would have liked the fable "The Dog and the Reflection"?
2. Although Aurelius probably did not know of the Buddha's teachings, what beliefs does he have that are similar to the Buddha's?
3. What ideas about light do Aurelius and Plato share?

Activity 1.9a

Phaedrus refers to the fable "The Lion King" in one of his writings. The fable comes from India, where it is known as "The Elephant and the Mouse." Read the fable and think about what Aurelius might have learned from it. Be prepared to discuss your ideas in class.

The Lion King

Once when a lion was asleep, a little mouse began running up and down upon him. This soon wakened the lion, who placed his huge paw upon the mouse and opened his big jaws to eat him. "Pardon, O King," cried the little mouse. "Forgive me this time; I shall never forget it. Who knows, someday I may be able to do something good for you." The lion thought the idea that the mouse might help him was so funny that he lifted his paw and let the mouse go. Days later, the lion was caught in a trap, and the hunters, who wanted to carry him alive to the king, tied him to a tree while they went in search of a wagon to carry him on. Just then the little mouse passed by and, seeing the sad plight of the lion, went up to him and soon gnawed away the ropes that bound the king of beasts. "Was I not right?" said the little mouse. "I was able to help you even though I am little."

This fable is in the public domain. Exercise © 2000 University of Michigan.

Activity 1.9b

Identify which parts of "The Lion King" correspond to the plot terminology listed in activity 1.4e.

Activity 1.10

Now that you have read a few fables, write a fable from your own culture or simply a fable you know of that has not been discussed in this chapter.

Activity 1.11

As in activity 1.1, write a word that you associate with each letter in the word *fable* but use words that differ from those used in activity 1.1. You may have more than one possible association for each letter.

Activity 1.12 ⇨

Answer the following questions about "The Little Red Hen" using terminology from the readings in this chapter.

1. How would the Buddha have described the behavior of the cat, the duck, and the pig in "The Little Red Hen"?
2. What might Plato have said about the behavior of the animals in "The Little Red Hen"?
3. Why would "The Little Red Hen" have **appealed** to Marcus Aurelius? What would he say about the behavior of the animals in this fable?
4. Why is it helpful to be aware of the intertextual relationships that have shaped fables?

appealed: attracted the attention of someone in a positive way

Chapter 2
"The Tell-Tale Heart," by Edgar Allan Poe

Photograph courtesy of Rafael Kapelinski

"It is the beating of his hideous heart!"—Edgar Allan Poe, "The Tell-Tale Heart"

Activity 2.1a

The American writer Edgar Allan Poe (1809–49) is well known for his short stories. In addition to stories, Poe also wrote critical essays about the act of writing. One such essay is entitled "The Tale and Its Effect." Traditionally, a tale is similar to a fable in that the characters are not described in detail. Like a fable, a tale comes from an oral tradition and has a moral—whether stated or **implied.** Unlike a fable, however, a tale presents strange events and has a strong emotional effect on the reader. Sometimes writers, like Edgar Allan Poe, call their short stories *tales* when they contain particularly strange events. To Poe, it was important that the author create a story in which every event contributed to the story's intended effect on the reader. In "The Tale and Its Effect," he writes:

> A skillful literary artist has constructed a tale. If wise . . . he conceived, with **deliberate** care, a certain unique or single effect to be **wrought out.** He then invents such incidents—he then combines such events as may best aid him in establishing this **preconceived** effect. If his very **initial** sentence tends not to the **outbringing** of this effect, then he has failed in his first step.

In other words, every part of the story should contribute to the creation of an emotional effect within the reader.

implied: suggested

deliberate: with extreme care; with conscious action

wrought out: made; completed

preconceived: thought of before something was done

initial: the first

outbringing: The bringing out of or causing of an effect. The term *outbring* is no longer used.

Activity 2.1b ⇨

Read the tale "Appointment in **Samarra**," by the English writer Somerset Maugham (1874–1965), and, as you read, think about the effect Maugham wanted to achieve. (This work is based on an Arabic story Maugham retold in English.)

Samarra: a city about sixty miles outside of Baghdad, Iraq

Appointment in Samarra

> Death speaks: There was a merchant in Baghdad who sent his servant to market to buy **provisions** and in a little while the servant came back, white and trembling, and said, Master, just now when I was in the marketplace I was **jostled** by a woman in the crowd and when I turned I saw it was Death that jostled me. She looked at me and made a **threatening gesture;** now, lend me your horse, and I will ride away from this city and avoid my fate. I will go to Samarra and there Death will not find me. The merchant lent him his horse, and the servant **mounted** it, and he dug his **spurs** in its **flanks** and as fast as the horse could gallop he went. Then the merchant went down to the marketplace and he saw me standing in the crowd, and he came to me and said, Why did you make a threatening gesture to my servant when you saw him this morning? That was not a threatening gesture, I said, it

provisions: supplies

jostled: moved or shaken slightly

threatening gesture: a movement that suggests something bad will happen

mounted: got up on something above the level of the ground; e.g., mounted the horse

spurs: metal spikes attached to the heel of a shoe that are used to urge a horse to go faster

flanks: the sides of the horse

was only a start of surprise. I was astonished to see him in Baghdad, for I had an appointment with him tonight in Samarra.

"Appointment in Samarra," from *Sheppey* by W. Somerset Maugham. Copyright 1933 by W. Somerset Maugham. Used by permission of Doubleday, a division of Bantam Doubleday Dell Publishing Group, Inc., The Random House Group Ltd., and William Heinemann, Publisher.

1. Is the very first sentence of the story effective? Why or why not?
2. How would you react if you were to meet Death in person?

Activity 2.1c ⇨

When you study how an author has formed a work such as "Appointment in Samarra" to create a particular effect, then you are analyzing the work in the same way a formalist critic would. A formalistic criticism of a work attempts to answer questions such as, "How are the effects of a literary work achieved?" and "How does the form of a work contribute to this effect?" For example, a critic who is interested in the form of "Appointment in Samarra" would analyze how the author has shaped the plot to create a literary work and its effect. A formalist critic would also analyze the narrative techniques an author has used to create an effect, that is, the way the story is told. In Maugham's "Appointment in Samarra," the narrator is Death. Answer the following questions about the narrative techniques Maugham has used.

1. Why do you think Somerset Maugham has chosen to have the tale narrated by Death?
2. To whom is Death speaking?
3. In this tale, Death is personified—she has the characteristics of a human being. What do you learn about Death's character from reading her **narrative**?
4. What moral is implied by Death's narrative?

narrative: A story told by someone or something. *Narrative* can be used as an adjective.

Activity 2.2a ⇨

To describe the narrative techniques used by writers to tell a story, you will need to be familiar with the following adjectives that are often used to describe the type of narrator who is telling a story. If necessary, use your dictionary to help you define these words.

a. Omniscient
b. Objective
c. Selective
d. Participatory
e. Editorial (omniscience)

Match up the type of narrator with the definition you think best fits the adjectives you have defined. Write the letter of the appropriate adjective in each blank.

___ 1. This type of narrator simply reports the events in a story but does not know what anyone in the story is thinking. Like a journalist, the narrator tries to report the events without revealing his or her opinion about the events and the characters in the story. Generally, the pronouns *she, he,* and *they* are used when telling the story.

___ 2. This type of narrator reports the events in a story but only knows what one or two characters are thinking. These characters generally have major or minor roles in the story.

___ 3. This type of narrator is actually a character in the story. Because of this, the story is told from the first-person point of view using the pronoun *I*.

___ 4. This type of narrator knows what all the characters in the story are thinking. Such a narrator does not participate in the story; instead, the narrator reports what happens, what people say, how they feel, and what they are thinking. However, the narrator does not judge the characters' actions.

___ 5. This type of narrator knows what all the characters in the story are thinking. Such a narrator does not participate in the action that takes place in the story; instead, the narrator reports what happens, what people say, how they feel, and what they are thinking. The narrator also judges or comments upon the characters' actions.

A. Which type of narrator does Maugham use to tell "Appointment in Samarra"? How do you know this?

Activity 2.2b ⇨

The author also chooses the point of view from which the story will be told. Generally, formalists speak of the first-person or third-person point of view. In "Appointment in Samarra," you can tell that the first-person point of view is being used because the narrator uses *I* to tell the story. In chapter 1, look for a fable that is told from the third-person point of view using *he, she,* or *they*. Which type of narrator has the author of the fable used?

Activity 2.3

coined: made into a new word or expression

paraphrased: retold something in one's own words

Edgar Allan Poe was, in fact, a formalist critic, although the term was not **coined** until the 1930s when a group of students at Vanderbilt University took a new approach to discussing literature. Their approach to literature became known as "New Criticism," because, unlike the "old criticism," their approach demanded a more careful analysis of a given text. Previously, students of literature had simply **paraphrased** what a text might be about and described their personal reactions to a text. In contrast, the New Critics focused on the structure of a literary work and analyzed how the form related to the content of a work. For example, when analyzing a literary text they might look at its plot structure and the narrative techniques and explain how such formal characteristics of the work shaped its main ideas.

organic: belonging to a living structure of interdependent parts whose roles are determined by how they function in an organism

affective: having to do with emotional effects

fallacy: a false idea

New Critics conceived of a literary text as an **organic** whole that could best be understood by an analysis of its parts; that is, each image and word had a special function in the creation of a text's overall effect. When a reader simply paraphrased a text rather than explaining how the parts of the text worked together or when a reader simply described how a text affected him or her, New Critics called this the *affective fallacy*. Also, unlike previous critics, formalist critics did not take into account the life of the author when analyzing a given work.

One of the main spokespersons for formalistic criticisms was Cleanth Brooks (1906–94). In an essay entitled "The Formalist Critic," he outlined some of the principles of this approach. Three of those principles are as follows.

a. "That the primary concern of criticism is with the problem of unity ... the relation of the various parts to each other in building up the whole."
b. "That in a successful work, form and content cannot be separated."
c. "That literature is ultimately metaphorical and symbolic."

Take a moment to think about Brooks's ideas as they relate to the following questions about "Appointment in Samarra."

1. In "Appointment in Samarra," do all the parts of the story build up to one effect? Which part of the story, if any, could be excluded or removed without changing the story's effect?
2. Can the form and the content of "Appointment in Samarra" be separated?
3. Is the tale "ultimately metaphorical and symbolic"? In what way?

Activity 2.4 ⇨

Read the initial sentence of Poe's "The Tell-Tale Heart" and answer the questions that follow.

> True!—nervous—very, very, dreadfully nervous I had been and am; but why *will* you say that I am mad?"

1. Based on this sentence would you say that this narrator seems to be **reliable** or unreliable? Why?
2. Which point of view has Poe chosen for the narrator?
3. What does the narrator want you to think about him?
4. What is the effect of this first sentence? Would you say that it succeeds in creating a powerful effect? Why or why not?
5. Based on this first line, what do you think Poe's story will be about?

reliable: dependable; trustworthy

Activity 2.5

In "The Tell-Tale Heart," the narrator uses the words and expressions listed below. Discuss the meaning of each item with a partner. If necessary, use your dictionary. Then use these words to write a tale. Choose a specific type of narration to tell your tale. Keep in mind Poe's advice—your story should have a single effect upon the reader.

lantern	to be black as pitch
planks (of wood)	a villain
the beating of a heart	midnight
terror	a ray (of light)
a vulture	cunningly
hideous	

Activity 2.6

Although Poe calls his short story *a tale,* he has changed the usual form of the tale by using it to present the character of the narrator who is telling the story. After you read each section of "The Tell-Tale Heart," draw a sketch to help you to recall the actions in each section. Don't worry about the artistic quality of your drawing; you can use simple stick figures and symbols. Try to avoid referring to the written text as you are drawing your sketch. You can draw your sketches on a piece of paper. There are nine pictures all together. The first drawing has been done for you. (You may be asked to draw your sketch as each section of the text is read aloud by a classmate or by the instructor.)

The Tell-Tale Heart

1. True!—nervous—very, very, dreadfully nervous I had been and am; but why *will* you say that I am mad? The disease had sharpened my senses—not destroyed—not dulled them. Above all was the sense of hearing **acute.** I heard all things in the heaven and in the earth. I heard many things in hell. How, then, am I mad? **Hearken!** And observe how healthily—how calmly I can tell you the whole story.

It is impossible to say how first the idea entered my brain; but once conceived, it haunted me day and night. Object there was none. Passion there was none. I loved the old man. He had never wronged me. He had never given me insult. For his gold I had no desire. I think it was his eye! yes, it was this! One of his eyes **resembled** that of a vulture—a pale blue eye, with a film over it. Whenever it fell upon me, my blood ran cold. And so, **by degrees,** very gradually, I made up my mind to take the life of the old man, and thus rid myself of the eye forever.

Sample drawing for "The Tell-Tale Heart," activity 2.6, part 1

2. Now, this is the point. You **fancy** me mad. Madmen know nothing. But you should have seen me. You should have seen how wisely I proceeded—with what caution—with what foresight—with what **dissimulation** I went to work! I was never kinder to the old man than during the whole week before I killed him. And every night, about midnight, I turned the **latch** of his door and opened it—oh so gently! And then, when I had made an opening **sufficient** for my head, I put in a dark lantern, all closed, so that no light shone out, and then I thrust in my head. Oh, you would have laughed to see how cunningly I thrust it in. I moved it slowly—very, very slowly—so that I might not **disturb** the old man's sleep. It took me an hour to place my whole head within the opening so far that I could see him as he lay upon his bed. Ha!—would a madman have been so wise as this? And then, when my head was well in the room, I **undid** the lantern cautiously—oh, so cautiously—cautiously (for the **hinges** creaked)—I undid it just so much that a single ray fell upon the vulture eye. And this I did for seven long nights—every night at midnight—but I found the eye always closed, and so it was impossible for me to do the work; for it was not the old man who **vexed** me, but his **Evil Eye.** And every morning, when the day broke, I went boldly into the **chamber,** and spoke courageously to him, calling him by name in a **hearty** tone,

---

acute: strong

to hearken: to listen

resembled: looked the same as or similar to something else

by degrees: little by little

to fancy: to imagine

dissimulation: the hiding of the truth about something

latch: the handle

sufficient: large enough

to disturb: to bother

undid: opened

hinges: metal clasps holding the door of the lantern

vexed: angered

Evil Eye: The *Evil Eye* refers to a curse put on someone by looking them in the eye.

chamber: room

hearty: lively; energetic

and inquiring how he had passed the night. So you see he would have been a very **profound** old man, indeed, to suspect that every night, just at twelve, I looked in upon him while he slept.

3. Upon the eighth night I was more than usually cautious in opening the door. A watch's minute hand moves more quickly than did mine. Never before that night had I *felt* the **extent** of my own power—of my sagacity. I could scarcely contain my feelings of **triumph**. To think that there I was, opening the door, little by little, and he not even to dream of my secret **deeds** or thoughts. I fairly **chuckled** at the idea; and perhaps he heard me; for he moved on the bed suddenly, as if startled. Now you may think that I drew back—but no. His room was as black as pitch with the thick darkness (for the shutters were close fastened, through fear of robbers), and so I knew that he could not see the opening of the door, and I kept pushing it on steadily, steadily.

I had my head in, and was about to open the lantern, when my thumb slipped upon the **tin fastening,** and the old man sprang up in the bed, crying out—"Who's there?"

I kept quite still and said nothing. For a whole hour I did not move a muscle, and in the meantime I did not hear him lie down. He was still sitting up in the bed listening—just as I have done, night after night, hearkening to the **death watches in the wall.**

4. Presently I heard a slight groan, and I knew it was the groan of **mortal** terror. It was not the groan of pain or grief—oh, no!—it was the low **stifled** sound that arises from the bottom of the soul when **overcharged** with **awe**. I knew the sound very well. Many a night, just at midnight, when all the world slept, it has **welled up** from my own bosom, deepening, with its dreadful echo, the terrors that distracted me. I say I knew it well. I knew what the old man felt, and I pitied him, although I chuckled at heart. I knew that he had been lying awake ever since the first slight noise, when he had turned in the bed. His fears had been ever since growing upon him. He had been trying to fancy them causeless, but could not. He had been saying to himself—"It is nothing but the wind in the chimney—it is only a mouse crossing the floor," or "It is merely a cricket which has made a single chirp." Yes, he had been trying to comfort himself with these **suppositions;** but he had found all in vain. *All in vain;* because Death, in approaching him, had **stalked** with his black shadow before him and enveloped the victim. And it was the **mournful** influence of the unperceived shadow that caused him to feel—although he neither saw nor heard—*to feel* the presence of my head within the room.

5. When I had waited a long time, very patiently, without hearing him lie down, I **resolved** to open a little—a very, very little **crevice** in

profound: extremely sensitive and thoughtful

extent: the limits to which something reaches

triumph: success; victory

deeds: actions

chuckled: laughed softly

tin fastening: The small door over the lantern was made of tin. The fastening is the hook that opens the door.

death watches in the wall: the sound of beetles crawling in the wooden walls, considered a sign of approaching death

mortal: extreme; showing an awareness that one will die

stifled: cut off or held back

overcharged: filled with too much emotion

awe: fear

welled up: rose up

suppositions: guesses

stalked: followed someone secretly for a harmful purpose

mournful: extremely sad

resolved: decided

crevice: a long, thin opening

the lantern. So I opened it—you can not imagine how **stealthily**, stealthily—until, at length, a single dim ray, like the thread of a spider, shot out from the crevice and full upon the vulture eye.

It was open—wide, wide open—and I **grew furious** as I gazed upon it. I saw it with perfect **distinctness**—all a dull blue, with a **hideous** veil over it that chilled the very **marrow** in my bones; but I could see nothing else of the old man's face or person: for I had directed the ray as if by instinct, precisely upon the **damned** spot.

6. And now, have not I told you that what you mistake for madness is but over-acuteness of the senses?—now, I say, there came to my ears a low, dull, quick sound, such as a watch makes when it is enveloped in cotton. I knew *that* sound well too. It was the beating of the old man's heart. It increased my **fury**, as the beating of a drum **stimulates** the soldier to courage.

But even yet I **refrained** and kept still. I scarcely breathed. I held the lantern motionless. I tried how steadily I could maintain the ray upon the eye. Meantime the hellish **tattoo** of the heart increased. It grew quicker and quicker, and louder and louder every **instant**. The old man's terror must have been extreme! It grew louder, I say, louder every moment!—do you mark me well? I have told you that I am nervous, so I am. And now at the dead hour of the night, amid the dreadful silence of that old house, so strange a noise as this excited me to uncontrollable terror. Yet, for some minutes longer I refrained and stood still. But the beating **seized** me—the sound would be heard by a neighbor! The old man's hour had come! With a loud yell, I threw open the lantern and leaped into the room. He **shrieked** once—once only. In an instant I dragged him to the floor, and pulled the heavy bed over him. I then smiled gaily, to see the deed so far done. But, for many minutes, the heart beat on with a **muffled** sound. This, however, did not vex me; it would not be heard through the wall. At length it ceased. The old man was dead. I removed the bed and examined the **corpse**. Yes, he was stone, stone dead. I placed my hand upon the heart and held it there many minutes. There was no **pulsation**. He was stone dead. His eye would trouble me no more.

7. If you still think me mad, you will think so no longer when I describe the wise precautions I took for the **concealment** of the body. The night **waned**, and I worked **hastily**, but in silence. First of all I **dismembered** the corpse. I cut off the head and the arms and the legs.

I then took up three planks from the flooring of the chamber, and **deposited** all between the **scantlings**. I then replaced the boards so cleverly, so cunningly, that no human eye—not even *his*—could have **detected** anything wrong. There was nothing to wash out—no **stain** of any kind—no bloodspot whatever. I had been too **wary** for that. A tub had caught it all—ha! ha!

---

stealthily: carefully and slowly like a cat on the hunt

grew furious: became very angry

distinctness: clarity

hideous: terrible

marrow: a tissue in the bones

damned: cursed

fury: extreme anger; wild anger

to stimulate: to excite

refrained: kept from doing something; in this case, from murdering the old man

tattoo: a rapid, rhythmic sound

instant: moment

seized: grabbed; took control of

shrieked: yelled

muffled: wrapped or covered with something to dull or weaken a sound

corpse: a dead body

pulsation: the beating of the heart that can be felt in a person's veins; the pulse

concealment: the hiding of something

waned: passed

hastily: quickly

dismembered: cut off parts of the body

deposited: put into something

scantlings: the spaces between the boards under the wooden floor

detected: noticed

stain: an unwanted mark on something; e.g., a spot of wine on a tablecloth

wary: careful about things

8. When I had made an end of these labors, it was four o'clock—still dark as midnight. As the bell sounded the hour, there came a knocking at the street door. I went to open it with a light heart—for what had I *now* to fear? There entered three men who introduced themselves, with perfect **suavity**, as officers of the police. A shriek had been heard by a neighbor during the night; suspicion of **foul play** had been **aroused**; information had been lodged at the police office, and they (the officers) had been **deputed** to search the **premises**.

I smiled,—for *what* had I to fear? I **bade** the gentlemen welcome. The shriek, I said, was my own in a dream. The old man, I mentioned, was absent in the country. I took my visitors all over the house. I bade them search—search *well*. I led them, at length, to *his* chamber. I showed them his treasures, secure, undisturbed. In the enthusiasm of my confidence, I brought chairs into the room, and desired them *here* to rest from their **fatigues**, while I myself, in the wild **audacity** of my perfect triumph, placed my own seat upon the very spot beneath which **reposed** the corpse of the victim.

9. The officers were satisfied. My **manner** had convinced them. I was singularly **at ease**. They sat, and while I answered cheerily, they **chatted familiar things**. But, **ere long**, I felt myself getting pale and wished them gone. My head ached, and I fancied a ringing in my ears: but still they sat and still chatted. The ringing became more distinct:—it continued and became more distinct: I talked more freely to get rid of the feeling: but it continued and gained **definitiveness**—until, at length, I found that the noise was *not* within my ears.

No doubt I now grew *very* pale:—but I talked more fluently and with a **heightened** voice. Yet the sound increased—and what could I do? It was a *low, dull, quick sound—much such a sound as a watch makes when enveloped in cotton.* I gasped for breath—and yet the officers heard it not. I talked more quickly—more **vehemently**; but the noise steadily increased. I arose and argued about **trifles,** in a high key and with violent **gesticulations,** but the noise steadily increased. Why *would* they not **be gone**? I paced the floor **to and fro** with heavy **strides,** as if excited to fury by the observation of the men—but the noise steadily increased. Oh God! what *could* I do? I foamed—I **raved**—I swore! I swung the chair upon which I had been sitting, and **grated** it on the floorboards, but the noise arose over all and continually increased. It grew louder —louder—*louder!* And still the men chatted pleasantly, and smiled. Was it possible they heard not? Almighty God!—no, no! They heard!—they suspected!—they *knew!* —they were **making a mockery** of my terror!—this I thought, and this I think. But anything was better than this agony! Anything was more **tolerable** than this **derision**! I could bear those **hypocritical**

suavity: smooth, polite behavior
foul play: trickery; something that is done illegally
aroused: caused
deputed: sent
premises: the property; the area
bade: asked
fatigues: labors
audacity: boldness; daring
reposed: rested
manner: behavior; way of being
at ease: relaxed; comfortable
chatted familiar things: talked about everyday things
ere long: before long; soon
definitiveness: clarity
heightened: increased; louder
vehemently: strongly
trifles: small, unimportant things
gesticulations: rapid movements of the hands and arms; gestures
be gone: go away
to and fro: back and forth
strides: steps
raved: talked in a mad way
grated: rubbed against
making a mockery: making fun of
tolerable: bearable
derision: scorn; to be looked down upon by someone else
hypocritical: insincere; dishonest

smiles no longer! I felt that I must scream or die!—and now—again! Hark! louder! louder! louder! *louder!*—

"**Villains!**" I shrieked, "**dissemble** no more! I admit the deed!—tear up the planks!—here, here!—it is the beating of his hideous heart!"

> This story is frequently anthologized. See, for example, *The Norton Anthology of American Literature,* volume 1, edited by Bruce Michelson. 5th ed. W .W. Norton and Co., 1998.

villains: people who do evil or cruel things

to dissemble: to pretend

Activity 2.7

Now that you've read through "The Tell-Tale Heart," take turns retelling each section of the story with a partner. Use only your drawings to help you. Try not to refer to the text. You can tell the story from either the first-person or third-person point of view but be sure to use the same point of view consistently.

Activity 2.8 ⇨

List at least ten things that the narrator does or says to make you suspect that he is insane. Sequence your list so that it follows the order of the events told in the story. Then, in the right column, list the plot terminology found in activity 1.4e that corresponds to each item in the sequence. The first one has been done for you.

Events	Plot
1. The narrator heard things in heaven and earth.	Exposition

Activity 2.9 ⇨

In "The Tell-Tale Heart," Poe uses stylistic devices such as punctuation to suggest that the narrator's manner of speaking reflects his insanity. Try reading sections 1 and 7 aloud to a classmate. As you read, follow the verbal **cues** given by each of the following.

cues: signs that a person should do something

A dash (—)	→	a pause
An exclamation point (!)	→	excitement, energy
Italicized words	→	emphasized words

1. Now that you've reread sections 1 and 7 explain how the narrator's way of speaking suggests to you that he is mentally unstable and unreliable.

Activity 2.10a

A formalist critic would also be interested in analyzing the types of irony that Poe has used in constructing the narrative of "The Tell-Tale Heart."

1. Use your dictionary to define *irony*. List the adjectival and adverbial forms of the word *irony*.
2. The most common type of irony is called *verbal irony*. This occurs when a character in a story says the opposite of what he or she may actually mean. The audience understands that the speaker's intended meaning is different from what he or she actually says. List two examples of verbal irony that take place when the narrator is talking with the police.
3. Sometimes, a character may say or do something that is **unintentionally** ironic. In this case, the irony is called *situational* or *dramatic irony*. When situational or dramatic irony occurs, the audience knows something that a character in the story does not. When the policemen are in the old man's room, what is ironic about the situation?
4. When a character in the story suffers more than he or she seems to deserve or when a character seems fated or destined to act in a particular way this is described as *cosmic* irony or *irony of fate*. What examples of this type of irony do you see in "The Tell-Tale Heart"? Give at least one example.
5. The type of irony that occurs when the opinions of the author and narrator differ greatly is called an *ironic point of view*. What is ironic about the point of view that Poe has used to create his story? In "The Tell-Tale Heart," what do we know about the narrator that he does not realize?

unintentionally: not done on purpose

cosmic: related to the entire universe; on a large scale

fate: an inescapable end or destiny; an unexplainable force that shapes events

Activity 2.10b

What type of irony does Maugham use in "Appointment in Samarra"? Why is his use of irony so effective?

Activity 2.11

Reread Cleanth Brooks's statements in activity 2.3. Are all of the statements applicable to "The Tell-Tale Heart"? Why or why not?

Activity 2.12

From the point of view of a formalist critic, a literary work is a unity and has a single effect; as a result, it is possible to write a sentence about the author's or the story's main intent—what the story teaches us about life. The moral of a fable is similar to the statement of a story's theme, although the statement of theme is generally more complex than a moral.

The parts of the story provide the concrete details from which the theme is generalized. When you write a theme, make sure that it says something about a topic; otherwise, you will not have written a complete theme. Why is the following theme for "The Tell-Tale Heart" incomplete?

> The theme of the story is about madness.
> (topic)

This sentence doesn't tell us anything *about* the nature of madness, and the theme should have something to say *about* an idea or topic. Start the theme with the main idea or topic and then use a verb to say something about this idea or topic.

> Madness uses reasoning powers for destructive purposes.
> (topic)

Using a clause with *that* in your statement of theme will cause you to write a more complete theme.

> The theme of the story is that madness uses reasoning for destructive purposes.

1. What evidence do you find in "The Tell-Tale Heart" to support this theme?
2. Read the sample essay "The Heart Tells All" in chapter 8. What evidence does the author use to support the stated theme?
3. A story can have more than one theme. Do you see any other themes in "The Tell-Tale Heart"? Write these out and provide evidence from the story to support your ideas.

Activity 2.13a

Although formalist criticism provides insight into how a work is structured to create a particular effect, it cannot explain what motivates a character to behave in a certain way. For example, a formalist critic may have a hard time explaining exactly why the narrator was so obsessed with the old man's eye and why he was terrified of it. To explain such behaviors, literary critics often use ideas based on **psychological theories.**

Imagine that the narrator has been taken to court and that you are his psychologist. His lawyers have asked you to prepare a report about the narrator's mental state. Sometimes, a person who is guilty of a crime is declared "not guilty by reason of insanity." In other words, the criminal is not blamed for his or her actions because he or she has been declared insane by a psychologist. The narrator's lawyers have asked you to give tes-

psychological theories: theories that explain a person's behavior and the structure of human personality

timony explaining why you think the narrator should be declared "not guilty by reason of insanity." Write a brief report in the narrator's defense. If you are familiar with ideas and terms from psychological theories, try to use these in your report.

Activity 2.13b ⇨

The Freudian approach to literature is based on the psychological theories developed by Sigmund Freud (1856–1939). Read the following list of words commonly used in English that are associated with the Freudian theories. On your own, or with a partner, see how many of the words are already familiar to you. Write down their definitions. If you aren't sure of a word's meaning, check your dictionary. Look for definitions related to psychology. If you know other words related to Freudian theories, add these to the list and share them with the class.

1. unconscious
2. latent
3. repress
4. libido
5. phallic
6. therapy
7. associations
8. complex (noun)
9. neurosis (plural: neuroses)
10. id
11. projection
12. ego
13. superego

Activity 2.13c ⇨

Imagine that the narrator of "The Tell-Tale Heart" would like to seek psychiatric help from a Freudian therapist, but, since he can't afford to pay for a psychologist, he has bought a few books on Freudian psychology at a used bookstore. He has been reading the books, and now, the night before he is to kill the old man, he is thinking about how Freud's theories apply to his obsession with the old man's eye.

As you read through his thoughts on Freud's theories, notice the words taken from activity 2.13b. (These words have been underlined.) If the reading gives you more information about a word listed in activity 2.13b, add it to your definition. For example, if you had only written that *unconscious* means *not conscious,* then, after reading the summary, you could add that the *unconscious* refers to the part of the psyche that influences a person's actions even though he or she is not aware of its influence. You may need to change your original definitions.

A Tell-Tale View of Freudian Psychology

What does Freud mean by the unconscious? I think he means that there is an unconscious part of the **psyche** that contains powerful

psyche: the self; the makeup of the human personality

psychic forces and instincts. Such forces can cause people to act in ways they cannot explain. Perhaps that is my problem: I cannot say what it is about the old man's eye that makes me want to kill him. My motivation must be unconscious, as yet unknown. Freud would tell me that I could better understand my desire to kill the old man if I were aware of the forces that influence the unconscious part of my personality. But, no, this cannot be true in my case. After all, if I think about it, I know why I must kill the old man—it is because of *his* Evil Eye! So you see, my motivations are conscious after all!

As I understand Freud, he argues that even thoughts that were once conscious can disappear into the unconscious over time. He uses the term <u>latent</u> to refer to thoughts and emotions that were once conscious but then become unconscious. Thus, latent, unconscious memories from my childhood are able to influence my behavior as an adult. Exactly! That's why the smell of rose-damask perfume reminds me of sitting on my mother's lap. But how to explain my obsession with the old man's eye? Maybe his eye does remind me of some latent image in my unconscious. But what *could* it be?

Freud claims that symbolism in art and literature is often an expression of <u>repressed</u> sexual energy called the <u>libido</u>. Symbols associated with the male sexual organs are called <u>phallic</u> symbols. Symbols with concave or circular shapes are generally associated with female sexuality and the womb. In <u>therapy</u>, Freud would have his patients make free <u>associations</u> between objects in order to release their subconscious feelings, particularly as they related to sexuality. So, is the old man's eye a symbol of feminine sexuality? Wouldn't I be mad to suggest it? It couldn't be true, could it? To me, the eye is like that of a vulture; it is not in any way associated with sexuality, or is it? But the knife I will use to dismember his body—the knife is undoubtedly phallic—ha! ha!

Freud's **premise** that human behavior is motivated primarily by sexual desire intrigues me: I love the old man but like a father. To Freud, however, such love is not innocent. Freud explains that a son's sexual desire for his mother is given expression in the ancient Greek myth of King Oedipus. In this myth, a man unknowingly kills his father and then marries and makes love to his own mother. So, Freud concludes that a man could suffer from what he called an Oedipus <u>complex,</u> the desire to kill his father and sleep with his mother. But, surely, I am too clever to have such a complex—I start to feel mad just thinking about it.

But why should I associate the old man's eye with a vulture? A Freudian psychologist might analyze my dreams to better understand this association, but I cannot recall my dreams; in fact, I have trouble sleeping and sleep only a few hours a night, particularly these past six

premise: the main argument or idea behind a concept

nights! If I dream, I am not aware of it. Perhaps the old man's eye reminds me of death or of some unnamed evil just as a vulture's eye. Certainly, it is an Evil Eye! But what evil? My childhood was uneventful. My parents cared for me, sent me to school; I took music lessons; I have always been well behaved, even too good; what unconscious evil could reside in me? Freud **hypothesizes** that the underlying structure of an individual's personality—his or her emotional responses, self-esteem, motivations, etc.—is basically formed by the age of four or five and determines adult behavior. So, was it determined by fate that I should kill the old man? As a small child, was I filled with murderous rage? Is this the mortal terror that envelops me in the night?

to hypothesize: to make an educated guess about the cause or effect of something

But see how cleverly I can explain and then **refute** Freud's response to my questions: if I do not think about my unconscious desires, then, in Freud's view, I repress them. At the same time, I repress my sexual energy, or libido. Perhaps I have also repressed painful memories that could be recalled through hypnosis. In any case, as Freud explains it, this sexual and psychic energy that has been repressed can influence my behavior in strange ways and can even cause physical illnesses. Since such ills originate in the mind, Freud calls them neuroses, literally, "illnesses of the mind." He says that forms of neurosis can be traced to events that take place in early childhood, especially to those times when parents caused their children to feel ashamed about their sexuality. But again, I say, I am *not* neurotic, merely nervous—very, very nervous. I have always been nervous. My excited speech, my painstaking efforts to prepare for the old man's murder, the repetitive ritual of putting my head in the door, always at midnight: these are simply evidence of my nervous state and of my cunning, not neurosis. They are not **compulsive** behaviors, or are they? After all, I'm not repressed, am I? No, it is not me, it is the old man's eye. His eye is evil, *not* me—not even Freud could call me mad!

to refute: to prove that something is not true; to deny something

compulsive: Obsessive, uncontrollable behavior. Freud claimed that compulsive behaviors such as repeatedly washing one's hands have psychic causes.

But let Freud present his arguments, and I will prove that he would be wrong to call me mad. He would say that my psyche is divided into three areas that have come to be known as the id, ego, and superego. According to this division, the id—the unconscious part of the personality—is where the libido is stored. The id is amoral—it does not distinguish between good and evil, nor does it regard social rules or ethics but seeks its own pleasure and satisfaction. If the id's "pleasure principle" is not controlled, it can lead to destructive behavior. It seems that the concept of the id is in many ways similar to many religions' concept of the devil and that wars are an expression of a society's repressed id coming to the surface in a destructive way. Freud maintains that because people are afraid to deal with the power of the id, they unconsciously project their ids, and thus their own evil, onto

scapegoating: when a person blames another innocent individual or group of people for his or her faults or bad experiences

to articulate: to give voice to one's thoughts

other people. He uses the term projection to describe such a psychic event. Historically, witch trials, racism, and **scapegoating** are examples of projections. Now, I would ask, am I not too intelligent, too cunning and **articulate,** to project my own evil onto the old man's eye? How could I be using him as a scapegoat when I love him so? I will not kill him because of a base desire for his gold or because he has somehow insulted me, *no,* I will kill him for a higher end—to rid the world of his Evil Eye! The world will thank me for my wise decision to kill the old man.

Even people whom I have told about the old man must admit that my ego is healthy. The ego—the second division of the psyche, as Freud sees it—protects the individual and the society from the id's negative power. The ego uses the power of reason to overcome the id. Unlike the id, which acts unconsciously and follows its own primitive instincts, the ego acts consciously—for the most part—and bases its actions on reality. Truly, one must admit that I use my reasoning powers to the fullest. My plan to kill the old man has proceeded logically and systematically. These last six nights, he has not even become aware of my presence at his door. Why would anyone say that my ego is unhealthy, that my actions are not based in reality? Of course, just the opposite is true. Besides, by killing the old man, I will protect others and myself from his Evil Eye, and, did not Freud himself say that the ego's function is to protect society from the id?

Freud goes on to claim that the third part of the psyche, the superego, is the part of the self that functions to keep society under the rule of law. Like the id, the superego is largely unconscious and is made up of the morals and rules that we have learned from society. For this reason, people may not commit murder or other crimes because society has taught them that such actions are wrong. Freud calls this powerful shaping force of society the morality **principle:** it is the superego that makes us conform to social rules and **norms.** But Freud's definition is incomplete, for, clearly, if one kills intelligently and for good reasons, then one's superego is functioning well and benefits society, right? That is the way I see it. Only someone like me—who can hear all things in heaven and earth—can have a fully developed superego and, at the same time, be fully aware of the id's powers. Despite Freud's claim, *my* superego is *fully* conscious—I know why I must kill the old man. My highly developed intelligence, my acute sensitivity to my environment, these testify to the **innate** superiority of my superego. Who could judge me for being insane when I have only followed the desire of my superego to rid the world of evil? So you see, I am even more cunning than Freud—ha! ha!

I see that I am not the first to challenge Freud. Some psychologists have argued that Freud **pathologizes** the family, making it the source of too many evils. For example, **Jungian** psychologists examine how

principle: a belief or rule that influences a person's behavior

norms: behaviors that are accepted by society

innate: inborn; natural

pathologizes: makes the source of a person's problems

Jungian: a term used to describe ideas and techniques developed by Carl Jung (see chap. 9, *Jung, Carl*)

societal mores and **archetypal** patterns have shaped the human psyche. Jung and others have argued against Freud's idea that sexuality is the motivating force of the human personality and against Freud's belief that the human personality is determined by the age of four. Freud has also been criticized by feminists for having a narrow view of women. In spite of such criticisms, I can see that Freud's exploration of the unconscious opened the door to the development of modern psychology and that his ideas have shaped Western society's views on human sexuality. His ideas have been used to explain the actions of real individuals as well as to describe the motivations of fictional characters, and Freudians will analyze my actions as well, but clearly they will misunderstand my motivations. I know what I must do tonight at midnight, and I am fully conscious of my actions. How could they claim that I am neurotic?—again, I say, I am simply nervous, not murderous. How could a murderer prove himself to be too clever for Freud?

archetypal: the original pattern for something (see chap. 9, *Jung, Carl*)

© 2000 University of Michigan

1. Having read "A Tell-Tale View of Freudian Psychology," what more can you say about the words listed in activity 2.13b?
2. What about Freudian psychology do you find especially interesting, useful, surprising, unbelievable, confusing? Use the prompts to help you prepare your responses.

    a. What I find interesting is . . .
    b. I think the idea of _____ is especially useful because . . .
    c. I was surprised to learn that . . .
    d. It's hard to believe that . . .
    e. I am confused by . . .

3. Use Freud's theories of the superego, ego, and id to draw a diagram that you think represents Freud's "picture" of the human psyche. Be prepared to explain your diagram.
4. In his summary of Freudian theories, the narrator claims that they do not apply to him. Do you agree or disagree with him? Why?
5. Why do you think it might be difficult to apply Freud's theories to a character in a fictional work?

Activity 2.13d

Write a report on the narrator's psychological state. Try to use ideas and terms common to Freudian psychology. Imagine that your report will be used in court to prove that the narrator should be declared "not guilty by reason of insanity." If you have already completed activity 2.13b, rewrite your analysis to include Freud's theories and terminology.

Activity 2.14 ⇨

Poe's story is told by an unreliable narrator, so why do you think he chose to name his story "The Tell-Tale Heart"?

Activity 2.15 ⇨

1. Do you think that the narrator's experiences in "The Tell-Tale Heart" could have been a dream? Why?
2. If the story is a dream and not a "real" event, how does this change your view of the narrator?

Activity 2.16

Now that you have considered the theme of "The Tell-Tale Heart," take a moment to analyze how Poe has communicated this theme to his audience. Imagine that you are a film director and think about how you would use the camera to express the narrator's point of view and Poe's theme. Keep the following questions in mind.

setting: the place where the action of a story occurs

a. What type of **setting** would you use?
b. How could you use auditory and visual effects to communicate the narrator's mental state?
c. Would your film include the voice of the narrator? Think of the different narrative techniques that you can use.
d. How would you show the different kinds of irony Poe has used?
e. How would you communicate the story's theme to your audience?

With your instructor and classmates discuss the meanings of the following terms that are related to filmmaking. Can you think of any other terminology related to filming? Try to use the terms listed below and any other terms that may come up in a class discussion as you describe your approach to filming the story. Use your dictionary to define unfamiliar terms.

wide angle	background
depth of field	foreground
close-up shot	side view
pan left/right	front view
a frame	to transpose an image

If you have access to recording equipment, think about making an actual film. Your instructor may also ask you to think about how you would shoot a film of "Appointment in Samarra."

Chapter 3

"Young Goodman Brown," by Nathaniel Hawthorne

Photograph courtesy of Marco Fenaroli

"Had Goodman Brown fallen asleep in the forest, and only dreamed a wild dream of a witch-meeting? Be it so, if you will. But alas! It was a dream of evil omen for young Goodman Brown."
—Nathaniel Hawthorne, "Young Goodman Brown"

Activity 3.1 ⇨

Whereas a formalist critic concentrates his or her analysis on the form of a literary work, a historical-biographical critic would be interested in understanding how an author's life and/or a particular historical period influenced a work. When reading the story "Young Goodman Brown," by Nathaniel Hawthorne (1804–64), an American author who was a contemporary of Poe, such a critic would be interested to know how Hawthorne's life experiences might have influenced his writings.

Hawthorne, who was born in New England, was interested in analyzing **Puritan** society through his fictional works. "Young Goodman Brown" is a story about a Puritan man living in the northeast New England colonies in the early 1600s before America was actually a nation. Below you will find information about the Puritans and about Hawthorne's family. Match up each date from the time line with the corresponding information. Write the appropriate date in each blank. Use the time expressions in each passage to help you.

> **Puritan:** A religious group that wanted to "purify" the Christian faith and to practice its faith as it chose. The Puritans left England, where they had been treated unfairly because of their religious beliefs, which were based on the Bible, the holy book of the Christian faith.

  1620 1621 1630 1643 1692

_____ A. Near the end of the seventeenth century, one Puritan community in Salem, Massachusetts, feared that some of its members were witches. In the Salem witch trials, fourteen people were accused of being witches and were killed. Hawthorne's great-grandfather was one of the judges at the trial. Keep this in mind as you read "Young Goodman Brown." By the 1700s, the strong heritage of Puritanism in New England had begun to disappear as people of other faiths and backgrounds began to settle in America.

_____ B. After the first difficult year, the Pilgrims celebrated what is known as the first Thanksgiving. Thanks to the Native Americans, who initially were friendly toward the Pilgrims and helped them learn how to survive in the New World, the Pilgrims had a successful harvest that included corn and pumpkins—vegetables that were found on the North American continent and not in Europe.

_____ C. Twenty-three years after the first Puritans had landed on the shores of the "new land," the various Puritan colonies decided to link themselves together politically and economically to increase their strength by forming the New England Confederation. The thirteen New England states in the United States, have the names of the original colonies, such as Rhode Island and Connecticut.

_____ D. Ten years after the first Puritans had founded Plymouth Colony, over ten thousand Puritans had settled in America. They established small, enclosed communities to keep themselves safe in what they perceived as a wild, unsettled land. Some communities had stricter codes than others did. If a person broke the rules of a community, he or she was banished—sent out into the wilderness.

_____ E. A group of a hundred and one Puritans—people who wanted to "purify" the Christian faith and to practice their faith as they chose—decided to leave England, where they had been treated unfairly because of their religious beliefs. After they landed in America, or the New World, they founded Plymouth Colony. These first Puritans are often called the *pilgrims* because they made a long journey to a new place for religious reasons. During the first winter, fifty of the Puritans died from the hard conditions and because they did not know how to survive in their new environment.

Activity 3.2

As a community, the Puritans followed strict rules that affected their behavior. From a historical perspective, it is important to be aware of the Puritan worldview to more fully understand Hawthorne's "Young Goodman Brown." Jonathan Edwards (1703–58), a Puritan preacher, wrote "A Young Puritan's Code," in which he listed the rules by which a good Puritan should live. (You can find this in the anthology *The American Puritans*, edited by Perry Miller [1956].) A key word in this code is *resolved,* meaning *to make a conscious decision to do something.*

As you read the excerpts from "A Young Puritan's Code," list the values each item suggests were **privileged** in Puritan society as well as the values that the code suggests should be **subverted**. Keep in mind that the Puritans believed in an afterlife wherein a person would be given a reward for "good" behavior in heaven or punished for "bad" behavior in hell. The first one has been done for you.

privileged: given the advantage; put first; admired

subverted: repressed; held down

a. "Resolved, never to lose one moment of *time;* but to improve it in the most profitable way I can."

Privileged values: It's important to use your time productively and to improve yourself.

Subverted values: "Wasting time" is not allowed, so relaxing, doing whatever you feel like doing for no reason at all, is discouraged.

b. "Resolved, never to do anything which I should be afraid to do if it were the last hour of my life."

Privileged values:

Subverted values:

58 · Literary Odysseys

temperance: the practice of controlling one's desires

c. "Resolved, to maintain the strictest **temperance** in eating and drinking."

Privileged values:

Subverted values:

1. Does the society that you were raised in share any similar values with the Puritans? If so, what values are these? If not, how do the values of the society differ?
2. In what ways could a society such as that of the Puritans privilege the values found in its code? In what ways could it subvert opposing values? How does the society you are most familiar with privilege or subvert values?
3. Why do you think a Puritan would have approved of the fable "The Little Red Hen" found in activity 1.4b?

Resolution

Photograph courtesy of Rafael Kapelinski

Activity 3.3 ⇨

Because the characters and the setting in "Young Goodman Brown" are used as symbols to express truths or generalizations about human life, the story is called an *allegory*. In an allegory, the characters themselves symbolize general truths about life. Answer the following questions about the allegorical characteristics of "Young Goodman Brown."

1. In "Young Goodman Brown," the main characters have names that are allegorical. *Goodman* was an everyday sign of respect that the Puritans used. What does the name *Goodman* suggest about Brown's character? What might the adjectives *young* and *brown* suggest about his character?
2. The name of Brown's wife is also used allegorically. Her name is Faith. What are the characteristics of faith? What does this suggest about her character?

Activity 3.4 ⇨

As the names of Goodman Brown and his wife suggest, the nature of good and evil is a question that Hawthorne explores in the story. Before you read "Young Goodman Brown," consider what your answers would be to the following questions about good and evil. Then think about how a Puritan might have answered the following questions.

1. What is the nature of goodness?
2. What is the nature of evil?
3. Are people basically good or evil?
4. How is the balance between good and evil maintained?
5. In your culture, or in cultures with which you are familiar, what images symbolize good and evil?

Activity 3.5a ⇨

Since many of the images and characters in "Young Goodman Brown" have symbolic significance, it is helpful to understand the different ways such symbols can be interpreted. When you analyze the symbols in a story to understand how they contribute to the story's meaning, then you are using what is called a *mythic approach* to the literature. A mythic critic looks for symbols that have special significance within a given society. Such a critic also looks for symbols that have a universal significance among the majority of cultural traditions in the world—such symbols are called *archetypal symbols* because the term *archetype* means *the original model from which other images or ideas come.*

Literary critics adopted the term *archetype* from the ideas of Carl Jung (1875–1961), a Swiss psychologist. Jung studied archetypal images, characters, and story patterns in myths and in religions from around the world in order to discover how the symbols were used and what they might mean. For example, in the case of "Young Goodman Brown," a mythic critic would argue that the archetypal symbols found in the story portray the character of Puritan society. An author such as Hawthorne may or may not use such symbols consciously when writing a story. Often symbols appear in a work spontaneously as an author is involved in the act of creation. Mythic critics analyze the symbols found in the work to better understand how the story is constructed and why the story affects the reader.

The following archetypal symbols are found in Hawthorne's story. Think about the possible meanings that each of the symbols might have. If you are aware of interpretations that may differ from culture to culture, include these interpretations as well. The answer key gives an explication of these symbols. Be prepared to discuss your responses in class. The first one has been done for you.

1. Sunrise and sunset—The sunrise can symbolize rebirth while the sunset symbolizes death. Together they represent a complete cycle.

2. A pink ribbon

3. A town

4. The forest

5. A snake or serpent

6. A witch or wizard

7. The number four

Activity 3.5b

When discussing the symbols in activity 3.5a, you may have noticed that some of the symbols are in opposition to each other, such as *the town* versus *the forest*. The oppositions can be stated or implied, as in the opposition between the number four and the number three.

Such contrasts are often called **binary** oppositions. The prefix *bi-* meaning *two*, refers to the opposition between two things. The term *polar opposites* is also used because the North and South Poles are at opposite "ends" of the earth. Try to list at least three more pairs of binary opposites—stated or implied—found in 3.5a 1–7.

binary: made up of two different parts that "balance" one another

Activity 3.5c ⇨

Generally, a mythic critic tries to interpret each symbol individually or to show how a given story shares the characteristics of myths. However, when you analyze how symbols are contrasted and compared to form an entire narrative, then you are looking at the text as a structuralist critic would. Structuralist criticism first originated in linguistics at the turn of the twentieth century as linguists focused on the study of language structures. Structuralism developed through the 1950s and was applied to other disciplines, such as **anthropology** and literary criticism.

> anthropology: the study of different cultures and their behaviors

Just as linguists study how a language is made up of phonemes—small units of sound—that are set in contrast to one another to create meaningful elements, so structuralists consider symbols to be like a language an author can use to create a literary work. For example, from a linguistic point of view, if you replace the *m* in *mouse* with an *h* you get *house*: the contrasting sounds give you different meanings. This use of contrast in language systems was originally noted by the linguist Ferdinand de Saussure (1857–1913). From a structuralist point of view, the contrasting symbols in "Young Goodman Brown," whether stated directly or implied, such as the implied opposition of the numbers three and four, set up a contrast that gives meaning to the narrative. A structuralist critic examines the contrastive symbols that shape a text. He or she would ask why the symbols combine and contrast in the forms they do by analyzing values that are privileged and subverted in the culture from which the text originates, just as you did in activity 3.2.

Take a look at the cultural values expressed in activity 3.2. How do they correspond to the symbols used in the story? For example, the town could be associated with the value of purposeful work, whereas the forest could represent uncontrolled instincts that are normally subverted in Puritan society. The sunrise could symbolize the privileged value of reason, whereas the sunset could symbolize the unreason and chaos of darkness. Structuralists call the symbols in a text *mythemes*—a combination of the word *myth* and the ending *-eme,* meaning a small unit. The term *mytheme* was coined by the anthropologist Claude Lévi-Strauss (b. 1908), who used this term to describe the contrasting cultural myths of a given society. Although this chapter focuses on the use of symbols to create meaning in a text, a structuralist critic could also look at how events, characters, and word patterns create meaning in a text.

Think of yourself as a structuralist and list some privileged and subverted Puritan values that could be associated with the following symbols used in "Young Goodman Brown."

1. A pink ribbon
2. A witch or wizard

Activity 3.5d

After Lévi-Strauss had written his book *Structural Anthropology* in 1958, structuralism evolved, over a period of thirty years, into poststructuralism and deconstructionism. In general, poststructuralists and deconstructionists examine the philosophical implications of structuralism. Such critics are interested in the apparent **arbitrariness** of sounds. By extension, they wonder how symbols are given their meanings. For example, why should speakers of English accept that *mouse* means a small rodent who likes to eat cheese rather than using the word *house* for *mouse*? In the case of "Young Goodman Brown," such critics would ask why the symbol of a witch has negative **connotations** in society. They might argue that a witch is a neutral symbol until society puts it in binary opposition to a religious figure such as a **saint**. They would also examine how the symbols work together to form the narrative.

Poststructuralists and deconstructionists are interested in understanding whether meaning is found in the symbols themselves or if meaning is **randomly** associated with a given symbol. They are also interested in how a writer uses language to construct reality. Deconstructionism will be discussed in more detail in chapters 6 and 7. For now, take a moment to consider why you think the symbols used in this story have positive or negative connotations. Refer to the list of symbols found in activity 3.5a as you answer the following questions.

> **arbitrariness:** chosen by chance, without a logical reason for the choice
>
> **connotations:** the associations made with a word; e.g., *winter* is associated with cold, snow, and/or death
>
> **saint:** a religious figure, man or woman, who is considered to be holy
>
> **randomly:** without a definite plan or pattern

1. Do these symbols have positive or negative connotations?
2. Do you think these connotations are found in the symbols themselves, or do you think that these meanings are put on the symbols by society? For example, in Western society, the serpent is often considered to be a symbol of evil, whereas in Eastern societies it is a symbol of wisdom and wholeness.
3. How is it possible that two different cultures can give a symbol such as the snake different meanings?

Activity 3.6

In this activity, you will read about the events in "Young Goodman Brown" that are associated with the symbols you have already interpreted. As you read, think about how these events and symbols might be organized to form a narrative.

A. "Young Goodman Brown" begins at sunset. The main action in the story takes place before the sun has risen.
B. The pink ribbon is associated with Faith, who wore it in her hair. When the story takes place, Brown and his wife have been married for only three months. Brown finds a pink ribbon in the forest.

C. In the story, Brown leaves the safety of the town to take a journey into the forest at night.
D. In the forest, Brown meets a man who is never named. This man, who looks like Brown, carries a **staff** that makes Brown think of a snake. Like a wizard, this man has magical powers.   staff: a walking stick
E. While Goodman Brown is in the forest, he meets a group of witches and wizards. He finds that many of them are people from his village.
F. He then comes to a clearing where four pine trees are on fire and a Black Sabbath ceremony is taking place. In this ceremony, men and women are initiated into a community of witches and wizards. The term *Sabbath* means *holy day*.

Before you read the original version of "Young Goodman Brown," use the symbols and the events in the story to help you write your own version of the story. Keep in mind the ways in which the symbols Hawthorne uses could be used to set up contrasts within the story. You can choose to write as an omniscient or selective narrator. Try to include some dialogue in your story. Follow the plot outline described in activity 1.4e.

Before you begin writing, think about how your answers to the following questions might help to shape your version of "Young Goodman Brown."

1. Why do you think Brown goes into the forest? Does Faith go with him? Why or why not? What do he and Faith say to one another?
2. What happens while he is in the forest? Who is/are his antagonist(s)? What events might make up the story's rising action? What might the climax of the story be?
3. What happens when Goodman Brown returns to the town? Has his experience changed him?

Activity 3.7

The Puritans used expressions that are rarely used in modern English. Hawthorne uses many of these expressions in "Young Goodman Brown." For example, the Puritans said *nay* for *no*, *verily* for *truly*, and *thee* or *thou* as a familiar form of *you*. Also, verbs ending in *st* such as *wouldst* are in the second-person familiar form as in *you would*. Try to match up each expression from the 1600s with its modern equivalent. The first one has been done for you.

After you have completed the list and checked your answers, revise your version of "Young Goodman Brown" so that it includes some of the expressions used by the Puritans. You can simply insert the additional words using arrows to show where they would go.

1. tarry with me
2. Howbeit?
3. as thou sayest
4. betake you there
5. with your leave
6. methought
7. 'twixt now and then
8. Sabbath
9. 'twould kill her
10. whither
11. to return from whence I came
12. I pray thee
13. to come forth
14. thou knowest
15. hath
16. forsooth

___ a. to go back to where I came from
___ b. it would kill her
___ c. to come forward or out of something
___ d. with your permission
___ e. as you say
___ f. I ask you
___ g. go there
___ h. I thought
___ i. in truth; indeed
___ j. How can it be?
_1_ k. stay with me/wait with me
___ l. where
___ m. you know
___ n. has
___ o. Sunday
___ p. between now and then

Activity 3.8

Read "Young Goodman Brown." Your instructor may divide the story into sections and have small groups of students or individuals be responsible for summarizing their section for the class.

Young Goodman Brown

Young Goodman Brown came forth, at sunset, into the street of Salem village, but put his head back, after crossing the **threshold**, to exchange a parting kiss with his young wife. And Faith, as the wife was **aptly named,** thrust her own pretty head into the street, letting the wind play with the pink ribbons of her cap, while she called to Goodman Brown.

"Dearest heart," whispered she, softly and rather sadly, when her lips were close to his ear, "pray thee, put off your journey until sunrise, and sleep in your own bed tonight. A woman alone is troubled with such

threshold: the plank of wood at the bottom of a door; the entranceway

aptly named: well named; appropriately named

dreams and such thoughts, that she's afraid of herself, sometimes. Pray, tarry with me this night, dear husband, of all nights in the year!"

"My love and my Faith," replied young Goodman Brown, "of all nights in the year, this one night must I **tarry away** from thee. My journey, as thou callest it, forth and back again, must be done 'twixt now and sunrise. What, my sweet, pretty wife, do you doubt me already, and we but three months married!"

"Then, God bless you!" said Faith, with the pink ribbons, "and may you find all well, when you come back."

"Amen!" cried Goodman Brown. "Say thy prayers, dear Faith, and go to bed at dusk, and no harm will come to thee."

So they parted; and the young man **pursued** his way, until, being about to turn the corner by the meeting-house, he looked back, and saw Faith still looking after him sadly, in spite of her pink ribbons.

"Poor little Faith!" thought he, for his heart **smote** him. "What a **wretch** am I, to leave her on such an **errand**! She talks of dreams, too. Methought, as she spoke, there was trouble on her face, as if a dream had warned her what would happen tonight. But, no, no! 'twould kill her to know about it. Well, she's a blessed angel on earth; and after this one night, I'll **cling** to her skirts and follow her to Heaven."

With this excellent resolve for the future, Goodman Brown thought he was right to hurry on his present evil purpose. He had taken a **dreary** road, darkened by all the **gloomiest** trees of the forest through which he could hardly find the path. It was all as lonely as could be; and there is this **peculiarity** in such a solitude, that the traveller knows not who may be **concealed** by the innumerable trunks and the thick boughs overhead; so that, with lonely footsteps, he may yet be passing through an unseen **multitude**.

"There may be a **devilish** Indian behind every tree," said Goodman Brown to himself; and he glanced fearfully behind him, as he added, "What if the devil himself should be **at my very elbow**!"

His head being turned back, he passed a **crook** of the road, and looking forward again beheld the figure of a man, in **grave** and decent **attire**, seated at the foot of an old tree. He arose at Goodman Brown's approach, and walked onward, side by side with him.

"You are late, Goodman Brown," said he. "The clock of the Old South was ringing as I came through Boston and that is full fifteen minutes **agone**."

"Faith kept me back awhile," replied the young man, with a **tremor** in his voice, caused by the sudden appearance of the man, though not **wholly** unexpected.

It was now deep dusk in the forest, and deepest in that part these two were journeying. As nearly as could be **discerned**, the second traveller was about fifty years old, apparently of the same **rank of life**

---

tarry away: go away for a short time

pursued: followed intently

smote: struck; attacked

wretch: a miserable person or a person who is unkind and evil

errand: a short trip to take care of some business

to cling: To hold on tightly. Puritan women wore long, ankle-length skirts.

dreary: sad; depressing and gray

gloomiest: the darkest; the most depressing

peculiarity: strangeness

concealed: hidden

multitude: a large crowd

devilish: to be full of mischief and to cause trouble like the devil

at my very elbow: standing next to me

crook: a small turn; a bend

grave: serious

attire: clothing

agone: Ago. The speaker has traveled from Salem to the woods, sixteen miles, in fifteen minutes.

tremor: a small quiver or shakiness caused by fear

wholly: Completely. Brown had expected to meet this man in the forest.

discerned: recognized

rank of life: social class

as Goodman Brown, and **bearing a considerable resemblance** to him, though perhaps **more in expression than features**. Still, they might have been taken for father and son. And yet, the elder person was as simply **clad** as the younger, and as simple in **manner** too, he had the indescribable **air** of someone who knew the world and who would not have felt **abashed** at the governor's dinner table, or in **King William's** court. But the only remarkable thing about him, that could be fixed upon as remarkable, was his staff, which **bore** the likeness of a great black snake, so curiously wrought, that it might almost be seen to twist and wriggle itself, like a living serpent. This, of course, must have been an **ocular deception**, assisted by the uncertain light.

"Come, Goodman Brown," cried the man, "this is a **dull pace** for the beginning of a journey. Take my staff if you are so soon **weary**."

"Friend," said Brown, exchanging his slow pace for a full stop, "having **kept covenant** by meeting thee here, it is now my purpose to return from whence I came. I have **scruples**, touching the matter thou **wot'st** of."

"Sayest thou so?" replied he of the serpent, smiling apart. "Let us walk on nevertheless, **reasoning** as we go, and if I convince thee not, thou **shalt** turn back. We are but a little way in the forest yet."

"Too far! Too far!" exclaimed the goodman, unconsciously **resuming** his walk. "My father never went into the woods on such an errand, nor his father before him. We have been a race of honest men and good Christians, since the days of the **martyrs**. And I shall be the first of the name of Brown that ever took this path and kept—"

"Such company, thou wouldst say," observed the elder person, interpreting his pause. "Well said, Goodman Brown! I have been as well acquainted with your family as any other family among the Puritans; and that's no **trifle** to say. I helped your grandfather, the **constable**, when he **lashed** the **Quaker** woman so **smartly** through the streets of Salem. And it was I who brought your father a **pitch-pine knot**, kindled at my own **hearth**, to set fire to an Indian village in **King Philip's** war. They were my good friends, both; and many a pleasant walk we have had along this path, and returned merrily after midnight. I would **fain** be friends with you for their sake."

---

bearing a considerable resemblance: they looked similar, like father and son.

more in expression than features: more in the look on their faces than the nose, eyes, mouth, etc.

clad: dressed

manner: way of being

air: attitude

abashed: embarrasssed

King William's: William III of England, who ruled from 1689 to 1702

bore: carried

ocular deception: a visual trick

dull pace: slow speed

weary: tired

kept covenant: kept a promise

scruples: doubts; second thoughts; ethical considerations

wot'st: you know of

reasoning: talking the matter over; discussing the idea

shalt: you shall; you will

resuming: starting

martyrs: those Puritans who were killed for their beliefs

trifle: a small thing

constable: a public officer who usually works in the legal courts

lashed: whipped

Quaker: a religious group that broke off from the Puritans

smartly: painfully

pitch-pine knot: a torch with a cloth covered in the sap of a pine tree so that it will burn

hearth: fireplace

King Philip's: chief of the Wampanoag Indians, whom the Puritans called King Philip

fain: try to

"If it be as thou sayest," replied Goodman Brown, "**I marvel** that they never spoke to me of these matters. Or, verily, I marvel not, seeing that the least rumor of the sort would have **driven them from** New England. We are a people of prayer and good works, **to boot**, and **abide** no such wickedness."

"Wickedness or not," said the traveller with the twisted staff, "I have a very **general acquaintance** here in New England. The **deacons** of many churches have drunk the **communion wine** with me; **the selectmen, of divers towns**, made me their chairman; and a majority of the Great and General Court are firm supporters of my interest. The governor and I, too—but these are state-secrets."

"Can this be so!" cried Goodman Brown with a stare of amazement at his undisturbed companion. "Howbeit, I have nothing to do with the governor and council; they have their own ways, and are no rule for a simple **husbandman**, like me. But were I to go on with thee, how should I meet the eye of that good man, our minister, at Salem village? Oh, his voice would make me tremble, both Sabbath-day and **lecture-day**!"

Thus far, the elder traveller had listened with **due gravity**, but now burst into a fit of **irrepressible mirth**, shaking himself so violently that his snake-like staff seemed to wriggle in sympathy.

"Ha! ha! ha!" he laughed, again and again; then he said, "Well, go on, Goodman Brown, go on; but pray thee, Don't kill me with laughing!"

"Well, then, to end the matter at once," said Goodman Brown, considerably **nettled**, "there is my wife, Faith. It would break her dear little heart; and I'd rather break my own!"

"Nay, if that be the case," answered the other, "**e'en** go thy ways, Goodman Brown. I would not, for twenty old women like the one **hobbling** before us, that Faith should come to any harm."

As he spoke, he pointed his staff at a female figure on the path, in whom Goodman Brown recognized a very **pious** and exemplary dame, who had taught him his **catechism**, in youth, and was still his moral and spiritual adviser, **jointly** with the minister and Deacon Gookin.

"A marvel, truly, that **Goody** Cloyse should be so far in the wilderness, at night-fall!" said he. "But, with your leave, friend, I shall **take a cut** through the woods, until we have left this Christian woman behind. Being a stranger to you, she might ask whom I was **consorting with**, and whither I was going."

"Be it so," said his fellow-traveller. "Betake you to the woods, and let me keep the path."

Accordingly, the young man turned aside, but took care to watch his companion, who advanced softly along the road, until he had

---

I marvel: I am surprised; I wonder why.

driven them from: They would have been chased out of Salem for meeting the man in the forest.

to boot: a slang expression meaning *in addition* or *besides*

to abide: to put up with something

general acquaintance: an acquaintance with many people

deacons: leaders of the church

communion wine: wine used in a Christian ceremony to symbolize the blood of Christ

the selectmen, of divers towns: the important people in many towns

husbandman: simple working man

lecture-day: a day during the week when the townspeople went to church

due gravity: with seriousness; with respect

irrepressible: unstoppable

mirth: joy; laughter

nettled: upset; bothered

e'en: then

hobbling: walking with difficulty; limping

pious: marked by showing great respect for religious rituals

catechism: religious teachings

jointly: together with

Goody: a shortened version of the title *Goodwife* given to a married woman

to take a cut: To take another short path; a shortcut. (Brown does not want to be seen.)

consorting with: socializing with; spending time with

come within a staff's length of the old dame. She, meanwhile, was making the best of her way, with **singular** speed for so aged a woman, and mumbling some **indistinct** words, a prayer, doubtless, as she went. The traveller put forth his staff, and touched her **withered** neck with what seemed the serpent's tail.

"The devil!" screamed the woman.

"Then Goody Cloyse knows her old friend?" observed the traveller, confronting her, and leaning on his **writhing** stick.

"Ah, forsooth, and is it your worship, indeed?" cried the good dame. "Yea, truly is it, and in the very same image of my old **gossip**, the grandfather of the **silly fellow** that now is. But—would your worship believe it?—my broomstick hath strangely disappeared, stolen, as I suspect, by that unhanged witch, Goody Cory, and that, too, when I was all **anointed** with the juice of smallage and cinquefoil and wolf's bane—"

"Mingled with fine wheat and the fat of a newborn babe," said the shape of old Goodman Brown.

"Ah, master knows the **receipt**," cried the old lady, **cackling** aloud. "So, as I was saying, being all ready for the meeting, and no horse to ride upon, I made up my mind to foot it; for they tell me, there is a nice young man to be taken into communion tonight. But now your good worship will lend me your arm, and we shall be there **in a twinkling**."

"That can hardly be," answered her friend. "I may not spare you my arm, Goody Cloyse, but here is my staff, if you will."

So saying, he threw it down at her feet, where, perhaps, it assumed life, being one of the rods which its owner had formerly lent to the **Egyptian Magi**. Of this fact, however, Goodman Brown could not take **cognizance**. He had cast up his eyes in astonishment, and looking down again, beheld neither Goody Cloyse nor the serpentine staff, but his fellow-traveller alone, who waited for him as calmly as if nothing had happened.

"That old woman taught me my catechism!" said the young man; and there was a world of meaning in this simple comment.

They continued to walk onward, while the elder traveller **exhorted** his companion to make good speed and **persevere** in the path, **discoursing** so aptly, that his arguments seemed rather **to spring up in the bosom** of his **auditor**, than to be suggested by himself. As they went, he plucked a branch of a maple, to serve for a walking-stick, and began to strip it of the twigs and little boughs, which were wet with evening dew. The moment his fingers touched them, they became strangely withered and dried up, as with a week's sunshine. Thus the pair proceeded, at a good free pace, until suddenly, in a

---

singular: noticeable; unusual

indistinct: unclear

withered: wrinkled and dry

writhing: twisting and turning violently

gossip: friend or relative

silly fellow: foolish man. She refers to Brown.

anointed: covered with a substance; in this case, the ingredients of a witch's brew

receipt: the items that are in the recipe for the witch's brew

cackling: high, unpleasant laughter

in a twinkling: in a moment

Egyptian Magi: the court magicians of Pharaoh, who were said to be able to turn rods into serpents

cognizance: conscious notice of something

exhorted: encouraged

to persevere: to keep on doing something even though it is difficult; to not give up

discoursing: talking

to spring up in the bosom: to come from within one's own heart or thoughts

auditor: the person listening; in this case, Brown

gloomy hollow of the road, Goodman Brown sat himself down on the stump of a tree, and refused to go any farther.

"Friend," said he, stubbornly, "my mind is made up. Not another step will I **budge** on this errand. What if a wretched old woman do choose to go to the devil, when I thought she was going to heaven! Is that any reason why I should **quit** my dear wife Faith, and go after her?"

"You will think better of this **by-and-by**," said his acquaintance, **composedly**. "Sit here and rest for awhile; and when you feel like moving again, there is my staff to help you along."

Without more words, he threw his companion the maple stick, and was speedily out of sight, as if he had vanished into the deepening gloom. The young man sat a few moments by the road-side, applauding himself greatly, and thinking with how clear a **conscience** he should meet the minister, in his morning walk, nor **shrink from** the eye of good old Deacon Gookin. And what calm sleep would be his, that very night, which was to have been spent so wickedly, but now would be spent purely and sweetly in the arms of Faith! Amidst these pleasant and praiseworthy meditations, Goodman Brown heard the **tramp** of horses along the road and **deemed** it advisable to conceal himself within the **verge** of the forest, conscious of the guilty purpose that had brought him thither, though now so happily turned from it.

On came the **hoof-tramps** and the voices of the riders, two grave old voices, conversing **soberly** as they drew near. These mingled sounds appeared to pass along the road, within a few yards of the young man's hiding-place; but owing, doubtless, to the depth of the gloom at that particular spot, neither the travellers nor their **steeds** were visible. Though their figures brushed the small boughs by the way-side, it could not be seen that they **intercepted**, even for a moment, the faint gleam from the strip of bright sky, athwart which they must have passed. Goodman Brown alternately **crouched** and stood on tip-toe, pulling aside the branches, and thrusting forth his head as far as he **durst**, without **discerning** so much as a shadow. It **vexed** him the more, because he could have sworn, were such a thing possible, that he recognized the voices of the minister and Deacon Gookin, jogging along quietly, as they **were wont to do,** when **bound** to some **ordination** or **ecclesiastical** council. While yet within hearing, one of the riders stopped to pluck a switch.

"Of the two, **reverend** Sir," said the voice like the deacon's, "I had rather miss an ordination-dinner than to-night's meeting. They tell me that some of our community are to be here from Falmouth and beyond, and others from Connecticut and Rhode-Island; besides

to budge: to move

to quit: to leave

by-and-by: with time
composedly: without being upset; calmly

conscience: the awareness that one's actions are right or wrong
to shrink from: to hide from
tramp: heavy steps
deemed: judged
verge: edge

hoof-tramps: the sound of horses' hoofs
soberly: seriously
steeds: horses
intercepted: blocked (the light)
crouched: bent
durst: dared
discerning: being able to recognize something
vexed: bothered; upset
were wont to do: were used to doing; liked to do
bound: heading to; going to
ordination: a ceremony in which a person is legally recognized as a minister
ecclesiastical: having to do with the church
reverend: title of respect used to address a minister

powows: Native American medicine men. (Hawthorne's spelling differs from the modern word *powwows*.)

deviltry: mischief; causing trouble

spur up: to use sharp, metal devices attached to a rider's heel to make a horse go faster

heathen: An uncivilized person or a person lacking religious beliefs. The Puritans referred to the Native Americans as heathens because the Native Americans did not share their faith and the Puritans did not recognize the religions of the Native American people or their form of civilization.

brightening: shining

firmament: the heavens; the sky

zenith: highest point

aloft: up high; above

fancied: imagined

tavern: a place where people meet to socialize and drink

aught: nothing

lamentations: sad words and sounds

entreating: asking

mocked: made fun of

bewildered: confused

piercing: cutting through

several of the Indian **powows,** who after their fashion, know as much **deviltry** as the best of us. Moreover, there is a goodly young woman to be taken into communion."

"Mighty well, Deacon Gookin!" replied the solemn old tones of the minister. "**Spur up,** or we shall be late. Nothing can be done, you know, until I get on the ground."

The hoofs clattered again, and the voices, talking so strangely in the empty air, passed on through the forest, where no church had ever been gathered, nor solitary Christian ever prayed. Whither, then, could these holy men be journeying, so deep into the **heathen** wilderness? Young Goodman Brown caught hold of a tree for support, being ready to sink down on the ground, faint and overburdened with the heavy sickness of his heart. He looked up to the sky, doubting whether there really was a heaven above him. Yet, there was the blue arch, and the stars **brightening** in it.

"With Heaven above and Faith below, I will yet stand firm against the devil!" cried Goodman Brown.

While he still gazed upwards into the deep arch of the **firmament,** and had lifted his hands to pray, a cloud, though no wind was stirring, hurried across the **zenith,** and hid the brightening stars. The blue sky was still visible, except directly overhead, where this black mass of cloud was sweeping swiftly northward. **Aloft** in the air, as if from the depths of the cloud, came a confused and doubtful sound of voices. Once, the listener **fancied** that he could distinguish the accents of the town's-people of his own, men and women, both pious and ungodly, many of whom he had met at the communion-table, and had seen others rioting at the **tavern.** The next moment, so indistinct were the sounds, he doubted whether he had heard **aught** but the murmur of the old forest, whispering without a wind. Then came a stronger swell of those familiar tones, heard daily in the sunshine, at Salem village, but never, until now, from a cloud of night. There was one voice, of a young woman, uttering **lamentations,** yet with an uncertain sorrow, and **entreating** for some favor, which, perhaps, it would grieve her to obtain. And all the unseen multitude, both saints and sinners, seemed to encourage her onward.

"Faith!" shouted Goodman Brown, in a voice of agony and desperation; and the echoes of the forest **mocked** him, crying "Faith! Faith!" as if **bewildered** wretches were seeking her, all through the wilderness.

The cry of grief, rage, and terror, was yet **piercing** the night, when the unhappy husband held his breath for a response. There was a scream, drowned immediately in a louder murmur of voices, fading into far-off laughter, as the dark cloud swept away, leaving the clear and silent sky above Goodman Brown. But something fluttered lightly down through the air, and caught on the branch of a tree. The young man seized it, and beheld a pink ribbon.

"My Faith is gone!" cried he, after one **stupefied** moment. "There is no good on earth; and **sin is but a word**. Come, devil! for to thee is the world given."

And maddened with despair, so that he laughed loud and long, did Goodman Brown grasp his staff and set forth again, at such a rate, he seemed to fly along the forest-path, rather than to walk or run. The road grew wilder and drearier, and more faintly traced, and vanished at length, leaving him in the heart of the dark, still rushing onward with that instinct that guides mortal man to evil. The whole forest was **peopled** with frightful sounds; the creaking of the trees, the howling of wild beasts, and the yell of Indians; while, sometimes, the wind **tolled** like a distant church-bell, and sometimes gave a broad roar around the traveller, as if all Nature were laughing him to scorn. But he was himself **the chief horror of the scene**, and **shrank not** from its other horrors.

"Ha! ha! ha!" roared Goodman Brown, when the wind laughed at him. "Let us hear which will laugh louder! Think not to frighten me with your deviltry! Come witch, come wizard, come Indian powow, come devil himself! and here comes Goodman Brown. You may as well fear him as he fear you!"

In truth, all through the haunted forest, there could be nothing more frightful than the figure of Goodman Brown. On he flew, among the black pines, **brandishing** his staff with **frenzied** gestures, now giving vent to an inspiration of horrid blasphemy, and now shouting forth such laughter, as set all the echoes of the forest laughing like **demons** around him. The **fiend** in his own shape is less **hideous**, than when he rages in the breast of man. Thus sped the **demoniac** on his **course**, until, quivering among the trees, he saw a red light before him, as when the **felled** trunks and branches of a clearing have been set on fire, and throw up their blaze against the sky, at the hour of midnight. He paused, in a **lull of the tempest** that had driven him onward, and heard the swell of what seemed a **hymn**, rolling solemnly from a distance, with the weight of many voices. He knew the tune; it was a familiar one in the choir of the village meeting-house. The verse died heavily away, and was lengthened by a chorus, not of human voices, but of all the sounds of the **benighted** wilderness, **pealing** in awful harmony together. Goodman Brown cried out; and his cry was lost to his own ear, by its unison with the cry of the desert.

In the interval of silence, he **stole** forward, until the light glared full upon his eyes. At one **extremity** of an open space, **hemmed in** by

---

stupefied: shocked; unable to speak

sin is but a word: The idea of sin no longer exists. The word *sin* has no meaning.

peopled: filled with

tolled: made a ringing sound

the chief horror of the scene: The most frightening thing in the forest was Brown.

shrank not: did not turn away

brandishing: waving something (in this case a staff) threateningly

frenzied: mad; wild

demons: spirits or fallen angels who follow the devil

fiend: the devil; an evil person

hideous: terrible

demoniac: one who is controlled by a demon

course: way

felled: cut down

lull of the tempest: a pause in the storm

hymn: a song sung in church; a religious song

benighted: covered by darkness

pealing: ringing out like bells

stole: moved toward something very slowly and quietly

extremity: the far end

hemmed in: closed in

the dark wall of the forest, arose a rock, bearing some **rude**, natural resemblance either to an altar or a **pulpit**, and surrounded by four blazing pines, their tops aflame, their **stems** untouched, like candles at an evening meeting. The mass of **foliage**, that had overgrown the summit of the rock, was all on fire, blazing high into the night, and **fitfully** illuminating the whole field. Each **pendent** twig and leafy **festoon** was in a blaze. As the red light arose and fell, a numerous **congregation** alternately shone forth, then disappeared in shadow, and again grew, as it were, out of the darkness, peopling the heart of the solitary woods at once.

"A grave and dark-clad company!" **quoth** Goodman Brown.

In truth, they were such. Among them, quivering to-and-fro, between gloom and splendor, appeared faces that would be seen, next day, at the council-board of the province, and others which, Sabbath after Sabbath, looked **devoutly** heavenward, and **benignantly** over the crowded **pews**, from the holiest pulpits in the land. Some affirm that the lady of the governor was there. At least, there were **high dames** well known to her. And wives of honored husbands, and widows, a great multitude, and ancient maidens, all of excellent **repute**, and **fair** young girls, who trembled, **lest** their mothers should **espy** them. Either the sudden gleams of light, flashing over the **obscure** field, bedazzled Goodman Brown, or he recognized a score of the church-members of Salem village, famous for their especial **sanctity**. Good old Deacon Gookin had arrived, and waited **at the skirts** of the **venerable** saint, his **revered** pastor. But, **irreverently** consorting with these grave, **reputable,** and pious people, these elders of the church, these **chaste** dames and **dewy** virgins, there were men of **dissolute** lives, and women of **spotted** fame, wretches given over to all mean and filthy vice, and suspected even of horrid crimes. It was strange to see, that the good shrank not from the wicked, nor were the sinners abashed by the saints. Scattered, also, among their pale-faced enemies, were the Indian priests, or powows, who had often scared their native forest with more hideous **incantations** than any known to English witchcraft.

"But, where is Faith?" thought Goodman Brown; and, as hope came into his heart, he trembled.

Another verse of the hymn arose, a slow and **mournful strain**, such as the pious love, but joined to words which expressed all that our nature can conceive of sin, and darkly hinted at far more. **Unfathomable** to mere mortals is the **lore** of fiends. Verse after verse

---

rude: rough; unfinished

pulpit: a place from which a minister gives a sermon

stems: tree trunks

foliage: plants

fitfully: stopping and then starting again

pendent: hanging

festoon: decoration

congregation: a group of people gathered together for a religious purpose

quoth: quoted; said

devoutly: with an attitude of devotion to religion

benignantly: with good feelings toward something or someone

pews: long rows of wooden benches upon which a congregation sits

high dames: women of the upper class

repute: reputation

fair: pretty

lest: for fear that

to espy: to see

obscure: hidden

sanctity: holiness; purity

at the skirts: at the side of; close to

venerable: worthy of great respect

revered: highly respected

irreverently: without respect

reputable: of a good reputation

chaste: pure

dewy: fresh

dissolute: corrupt; uncontrolled

spotted: not pure

incantations: spells that are spoken

mournful: extremely sad

strain: tune

unfathomable: can not be understood

lore: a body of knowledge or stories associated with a tradition

was sung, and still the chorus of the desert swelled between, like the deepest tone of a mighty organ. And, with the final peal of that dreadful **anthem,** there came a sound, as if the roaring wind, the rushing streams, the howling beasts, and every other voice of the **unconverted** wilderness, were mingling and **according** with the voice of guilty man, **in homage to the prince of all.** The four blazing pines threw up a **loftier** flame, and obscurely discovered shapes and **visages** of horror on the smoke-**wreaths,** above the **impious assembly.** At the same moment, the first on the rock shot redly forth, and formed a glowing arch above its base, where now appeared a figure. With reverence be it spoken, the figure bore no slight **similitude,** both in **garb** and manner, to some grave **divine** of the New England churches.

"Bring forth the **converts!**" cried a voice that echoed through the field and rolled into the forest.

At the word, Goodman Brown stepped forth from the shadow of the trees and approached the congregation, with whom he felt a **loathful** brotherhood, by the sympathy of all that was wicked in his heart. He could have **well nigh** sworn, that the shape of his own dead father **beckoned** him to advance, looking downward from a smoke-wreath, while a woman, with dim features of despair, threw out her hand to warn him back. Was it his mother? But he had no power **to retreat** one step, nor to resist, even in thought, when the minister and the good old Deacon Gookin seized his arms, and led him to the blazing rock. **Thither** came also the slender form of a veiled female, led between Goody Cloyse, that pious teacher of catechism, and Martha Carrier, who had received the devil's promise to be queen of hell. A **rampant hag** was she! And there stood the **proselytes** beneath the **canopy** of fire. The deacon grabbed his arm and led him to the rock. Then came a thin woman, wearing a veil, led by Goody Cloyse.

"Welcome my children," said the dark figure, "to the **communion** of your race! Ye have found, **thus young,** your nature and your destiny. My children look behind you!"

They turned; and flashing forth, as it were, in a sheet of flame, the fiend-worshippers were seen; the smile of welcome gleamed darkly on every visage.

"There," resumed the **sable** form, "are all whom ye have reverenced from youth. Ye deemed them holier than yourselves, and ye shrank from your own sin, contrasting it with their lives of **righteousness,** and prayerful **aspirations** heavenward. Yet, here are they all, in my worshipping assembly! This night it shall be granted you to know their secret **deeds;** how **hoary-bearded** elders of the church

---

anthem: a song of praise

unconverted: not having been persuaded to believe in a religion

according: agreeing with

in homage to: in praise of

the prince of all: the devil

loftier: higher

visages: faces

wreaths: things woven into a circular shape; in this case, the smoke

impious: not respecting or believing in anything

assembly: gathering of people

similitude: similarity

garb: clothing

divine: a holy person

converts: people who decide to believe in something they did not believe in before

loathful: hateful

well nigh: nearly

beckoned: signaled

to retreat: to move backward; to move away

thither: there

rampant: running wild

hag: a witch; a negative term for an old woman

proselytes: new converts to a faith

canopy: a covering

communion: people sharing a common faith; an act that symbolizes membership in a community

thus young: at so young an age

sable: dark; black

righteousness: holiness

aspirations: strong desires to achieve something great or important

deeds: actions

hoary-bearded: white-bearded

have whispered **wanton** words to the young maids of their households; how many a woman, eager for widow's **weeds**, has given her husband a drink at bed-time, and let him sleep his last sleep in her bosom; how beardless youths have **made haste** to inherit their fathers' wealth; and how fair damsels—blush not, sweet ones!—have dug little graves in the garden, and **bidden** me, the sole guest, to an infant's funeral. By the sympathy of your human hearts for sin, ye shall **scent out** all the places—whether in church, bed-chamber, street, field, or forest—where crime has been committed, and shall **exult** to behold the whole earth one stain of guilt, one mighty blood-spot. Far more than this! It shall be yours **to penetrate**, in every bosom, the deep mystery of sin, the fountain of all wicked arts, and which **inexhaustibly** supplies more evil **impulses** than human power—than my power, at its **utmost**!—can make manifest in deeds. And now, my children, look upon each other."

They did so, and by the blaze of the **hell-kindled** torches, the wretched man beheld his Faith, and the wife her husband, trembling before that **unhallowed** altar.

"**Lo**! There ye stand, my children," said the figure, in a deep and solemn tone, almost sad, with its despairing awfulness, as if his once **angelic nature** could yet mourn for our miserable race. "Depending upon one another's hearts, ye had still hoped that **virtue** were not all a dream. Now ye are undeceived! Evil is the nature of mankind. Evil must be your only happiness. Welcome, again, my children, to the communion of your race."

And they stood there, the only pair, it seemed, who were yet hesitating on the verge of wickedness, in this dark world. A basin was hollowed, naturally, in the rock. Did it contain water, reddened by the **lurid** light? Or was it blood? **Herein** did the Shape of Evil dip his hand, and prepare to lay the **mark of baptism** upon their foreheads, that they might be partakers of the mystery of sin, more conscious of the secret guilt of others, both in deed and thought, than they could now be of their own. The husband **cast one look** at his pale wife, and Faith at him. What **polluted** wretches would the next glance show them to each other, shuddering alike at what they **disclosed** and what they saw!

"Faith! Faith!" cried the husband, "Look up to Heaven and resist the Wicked one."

Whether Faith obeyed, he knew not. Hardly had he spoken, when he found himself amid calm night and solitude, listening to a roar of the wind, which died heavily away through the forest. He **staggered** against the rock and felt it chill and damp, while a hanging twig, that had been all on fire, **besprinkled** his cheek with the coldest dew.

The next morning, young Goodman Brown came slowly into the street of Salem village, staring around him like a bewildered man. The good old minister was taking a walk along the grave-yard, to get an appetite for breakfast and meditate his sermon, and **bestowed** a blessing, as he passed, on Goodman Brown. He shrank from the venerable saint, as if to avoid an **anathema**. Old Deacon Gookin was at **domestic worship,** and the holy words of his prayer were heard through the open window. "What God doth the wizard pray to?" quoth Goodman Brown. Goody Cloyse, that excellent old Christian, stood in the early sunshine, at her own **lattice,** catechizing a little girl, who had brought her a pint of morning's milk. Goodman Brown snatched away the child, as from the grasp of the fiend himself. Turning the corner by the meeting-house, he spied the head of Faith, with the pink ribbons, gazing anxiously forth, and bursting into such joy at the sight of him, that she **skipt** along the street, and almost kissed her husband before the whole village. But, Goodman Brown looked **sternly** and sadly into her face, and passed on without a greeting.

Had Goodman Brown fallen asleep in the forest, and only dreamed a wild dream of a witch-meeting?

Be it so, if you will. But **alas!** It was a dream of evil **omen** for young Goodman Brown. A stern, a sad, a darkly meditative, a distrustful, if not a desperate man, did he become, from the night of that fearful dream. On the Sabbath, when the congregation were singing a holy **psalm,** he could not listen because an anthem of sin rushed loudly upon his ear, and drowned all the blessed strain. When the minister spoke from the pulpit, with power and **fervid** eloquence, and, with his hand on the open Bible, of the sacred truths of our religion, and of saint-like lives and triumphant deaths, and of the future bliss or misery **unutterable,** then did Goodman Brown turn pale, dreading lest the roof should thunder down upon the gray **blasphemer** and his hearers. Often awaking suddenly at midnight, he shrank from the bosom of Faith, and at morning or eventide, when the family knelt down at prayer, he **scowled,** and muttered to himself, and gazed sternly at his wife, and turned away. And when he had lived long, and was **borne** to his grave, a hoary corpse, followed by Faith, an aged woman, and children and grandchildren, a goodly procession, besides neighbors, not a few, they carved no hopeful verse upon his tombstone for his dying hour was gloom.

staggered: fell against

besprinkled: sprinkled

bestowed: gave

anathema: a curse that banishes a person from the church

domestic worship: worship done in the home

lattice: a framework of crossed wood or metal; at a door or window

skipt: skipped

sternly: unkindly; with a serious, unpleasant manner

alas: sadly

omen: a sign of something that will happen in the future

psalm: a sacred song or poem; a biblical hymn from the Book of Psalms

fervid: burning; urgent

unutterable: cannot be said or uttered

blasphemer: one who says things that are said disrespectfully, particularly against religious beliefs

scowled: frowned

borne: carried

This story is anthologized in many places. See, for example, *Harper's Single Volume American Literature,* edited by Donald McQuade. Longman, 1999.

1. What is your reaction to Young Goodman Brown's behavior? Choose one response or write your own in a single short sentence. Be prepared to discuss the reasons for your response.

   a. Young Goodman Brown imagined everything.
   b. Even if the story is true, Young Goodman Brown overreacted.
   c. Young Goodman Brown was right to be suspicious of others after he returned home.
   d. Young Goodman Brown should have listened to Faith and stayed home.

2. Which event would you say is the climax of the story?
3. Three times, Goodman Brown tries to turn back, but each time, he is compelled to stay with the elder man. How does the man in the forest convince him to stay?
4. Faith's name is used allegorically throughout the story; for example, when Brown is late to meet the man in the forest, he tells him: "Faith kept me back awhile." In this sentence, Faith can be both his wife and his belief in God. Find other examples of Faith's name being used allegorically.
5. In what ways is "Young Goodman Brown" similar to a tale?
6. How do the events in the original version of "Young Goodman Brown" differ from the events in your version of the story?

Activity 3.9 ⇨

1. Who do you think is narrating the story? Look in the final paragraph of the story for clues.
2. What narrative techniques has Hawthorne used?
3. How would you describe the narrator's attitude toward young Goodman Brown? Is the narrator judgmental or nonjudgmental? Supply evidence from the story to support your answer.

Activity 3.10 ⇨

1. Like Poe, Hawthorne uses irony effectively in his story. For example, Goodman Brown says of Goody Cloyse, "That woman taught me my catechism!" Brown's statement is ironic because the woman who taught him his religious beliefs is a witch. Give three examples of verbal irony that you find in the story. Explain why these statements are ironic. (See 2.10a for a review of irony.)
2. What examples do you find of situational irony in "Young Goodman Brown"?
3. What examples of cosmic irony do you find in the story?

Activity 3.11 ⇨

At the end of "Young Goodman Brown," the narrator says,

> Had Goodman Brown fallen asleep in the forest, and only dreamed a wild dream of a witch-meeting?
> Be it so, if you will. But alas! It was a dream of evil omen for young Goodman Brown.

1. Have you ever had a dream that left a strong impression upon you or changed your behavior? What was it?
2. Are you convinced that Goodman Brown's experience was a dream? Why or why not?
3. What events in the story seem unreal or dreamlike?

Activity 3.12

For Faith, Brown's journey into the forest changes her fate ironically as well. How might Faith explain the change in her husband's behavior? Write a paragraph or two narrated by Faith in which she explains her understanding of the events that so changed her husband.

Activity 3.13 ⇨

How might you reinterpret the symbols found in "Young Goodman Brown" based on a Freudian point of view? Which symbols might represent the parts of the psyche? Which symbols might be associated with repression or latent desires? Which symbols could represent projection? Review activities 2.13a and 2.13b for ideas related to Freudian psychology. The first one has been done for you. Be prepared to discuss your ideas in class.

a. Sunrise and sunset—The sunrise symbolizes consciousness, whereas the sunset symbolizes the unconscious.

b. A pink ribbon

c. A town

d. The forest

e. A snake or serpent

f. A witch or wizard

g. The number four

Activity 3.14

Imagine that Goodman Brown has gone to see a Freudian psychologist for therapy. He wants to discuss the events that took place in the forest. Even if what happened was a dream, Brown is upset because the dream seemed so real and has influenced his behavior for the worst. He would like to be the way he was before he went into the forest. Write a dialogue between a Freudian psychologist and Goodman Brown. In the dialogue, have Brown explain his problem to the psychologist and receive advice from the psychologist. Use details from the story to make your point. A portion of such a conversation has been provided as an example.

Mr. Brown: Why was I so attracted to the darkness of the forest?
Dr. Jones: It's a result of your strict Puritan education. You were taught that everything that is natural in human life is full of evil and sin. You were also forced to live in a moral system that did not permit you to talk about sexual life and natural impulses. As a consequence of this, you have a very strict superego. Your repressed id felt a strong desire to go into the forest.

If you have not learned about the Freudian approach, you could simply imagine that you are a psychologist discussing Brown's experience with him.

Activity 3.15 ⇨

Review the questions about good and evil that you previously discussed in activity 3.4 and answer the following questions.

1. Having read "Young Goodman Brown," how do you think Hawthorne might have answered the question, "Are people basically good or evil"? Use details from the story to support your point of view.
2. How do you think Freud would have answered the question, "Are people basically good or evil"?
3. Do you think Hawthorne would agree with a Freudian analysis of his story? Why or why not?

Activity 3.16 ⇨

The following statement of theme for "Young Goodman Brown" is incomplete. Rewrite the statement to make it complete. (See 2.12 to review the concept of theme.)

The theme of the story is about good and evil.

Do you think that Hawthorne's story contains other themes as well? If so, what might these be? Your instructor may have you write an essay in which you state and explain the theme of "Young Goodman Brown." In your essay, include details from the story to support your ideas.

Activity 3.17

Although Hawthorne wrote his story in the 1800s, stories about witches and wizards are popular even now. Discuss any such stories you have read or seen as movies. Include your responses to the following questions in your discussions:

1. What kinds of themes are in these stories?
2. What is the attitude toward the nature of evil and goodness?
3. How is the image that popular culture has of witches and wizards similar to or different from the Puritan perspective? How would you explain the reasons for these similarities and/or differences?

Activity 3.18 ⇨

On the tombstone of a young Puritan woman who died in 1776, there is an engraving of a skeleton encircled by a snake. The skeleton holds the sun in one bony hand and the moon in the other. There are carvings of angels in the top left and right corners, while carvings of demons are in the lower left and right corners. Based on the historical and cultural information provided in this chapter, why would you expect to find such symbols on a Puritan's tombstone?

Chapter 4
"On the Road," by Langston Hughes

Photograph courtesy of Marco Fenaroli

"I have a dream that my four little children will one day live in a nation where they will not be judged by the color of their skin but by the content of their character."—Dr. Martin Luther King, Jr.

"In the face of one's victim, one sees himself."—James Baldwin

Activity 4.1

In 1952, the African American writer Langston Hughes (1902–67) wrote "On the Road." In this story, an unemployed, homeless, black man named Sargeant who lives in the United States during the mid-1930s finds himself in a dreamlike situation. But, as with Goodman Brown, the question remains, how real was his dream? As with Brown, Sargeant's dream says much about his own character and even more about the society in which he lives. To more fully understand "On the Road," you will approach this story as a sociological critic. A sociological critic analyzes the social influences—the cultural, economic, and political values—that a given text reflects. Such a critic might also consider how the social position of an author and his or her audience might have influenced the writing of a text. To more fully appreciate Sargeant's position in society and the import of his dream, it is helpful to understand the social context in which he finds himself, a context that reflects the legacy of slavery in America and the social context that set the stage for the **Civil Rights movement** of the 1960s.

Even though the United States is often considered to be a place of freedom and equality, Africans were originally brought to America as slaves and were not protected by the laws that guaranteed the rights of citizens. The ideals of freedom and equality expressed in the United States Constitution and the Bill of Rights—a list of ten **amendments** added to the Constitution in 1791 to clarify the rights of the individual in relation to the state—generally did not apply to African Americans.

Read through the three (of the original ten) constitutional amendments that are listed below. Then, write what each amendment suggests about the rights of the individual in relation to the state and why you think it is necessary for such rights to be protected by the United States Constitution. The first one has been done for you.

> **Civil Rights movement:** A social protest to ensure the civil rights of all citizens regardless of race. In this case, the movement is associated with the efforts of African Americans to gain civil rights.
>
> **amendments:** changes or additions made to an official document

1. *The First Amendment*
   Congress shall make no law in respect to the establishment of a religion, or prohibiting the free **exercise** of a religion; or restricting the freedom of speech or the press; or the right of the people peaceably **to assemble,** and **to petition** the government to right wrongs that have been done.

   Civil rights: A person has the right to express himself or herself freely.
   Necessity: Sometimes the state may try to limit freedom of expression to increase its own power.

   > **to exercise:** In this sense, *exercise* means to practice one's faith.
   >
   > **to assemble:** to join with other people to form a group
   >
   > **to petition:** to ask; to collect names of people to show that they support an idea

2. *The Fourth Amendment*
   The right of people to be secure in their persons, houses, papers, and effects, against unreasonable searches and **seizures,** shall not be violated.

   > **seizures:** In this sense, *seizures* refers to the government's attempt to take away someone or something illegally.

Civil rights:

Necessity:

3. *The Sixth Amendment*
   In all **criminal prosecutions**, the accused shall enjoy the right to a speedy, public trial.

   criminal prosecutions: trials of persons who are charged with crimes

   Civil rights:

   Necessity:

Activity 4.2 ⇨

In the following excerpt from *Incidents in the Life of a Slave Girl*, you will read an autobiographical account of slavery as it was experienced by Harriet Jacobs (1813–97), a woman who was born into slavery in North Carolina and who escaped. In this excerpt, she describes the slaveholder, whom she referred to as Dr. Flint, and their relationship. She also appeals to her audience to stop slavery.

From Incidents in the Life of a Slave Girl

I turned from him with disgust and hatred. But he was my master. I was compelled to live under the same roof with him—where I saw a man forty years my senior daily violating the most sacred **commandments** of nature. He told me I was his property; that I must be subject to his will in all things. My soul revolted against the mean **tyranny**. But where could I turn for protection? No matter whether the slave girl be as black as ebony or as fair as her **mistress**. In either case, there is no shadow of law to protect her from insult, from violence, or even from death; all these are inflicted by fiends who bear the shape of men. . . .

Oh, what days and nights of fear and sorrow that man caused me! Reader, it is not to awaken sympathy for myself that I am telling you truthfully what I suffered in slavery. I do it **to kindle a flame** of compassion in your hearts for my sisters who are still in **bondage**, suffering as I once suffered.

I once saw two beautiful children playing together. One was a fair white child; the other was her slave, and also her sister. When I saw them embracing each other, and heard their joyous laughter, I turned sadly away from the lovely sight. I foresaw the **inevitable blight** that would fall on the little slave's heart. I knew how soon her laughter would be changed to sighs. The fair child grew up to be a still fairer woman. From childhood to womanhood her pathway was blooming

commandments: laws; order

tyranny: evil, corrupt rule or power that harms others

mistress: a female slaveholder

to kindle a flame: to start a small fire that will grow; to get someone interested in something; in this case, the antislavery, or abolition, movement

bondage: the condition of being kept in slavery or in chains; being kept against one's will

inevitable: not able to be avoided

blight: Something that causes damage or stains. In this case, slavery is a blight on American ideals and the child's inocence.

with flowers, and overarched by a sunny sky. Scarcely one day of her life had been clouded when the sun rose on her happy bridal morning.

How had those years dealt with her slave sister, the little playmate of her childhood? She also was very beautiful; but the flowers and sunshine of love were not for her. She drank the cup of sin, and shame, and misery whereof her **persecuted** race are compelled to drink.

In view of these things, why are ye silent, ye free men and women of the north? Why do your tongues **falter** in maintenance of the right? Would that I had more ability! But my heart is so full, and my pen is so weak! There are noble men and women who plead for us, striving to help those who cannot help themselves. God bless them! God give them strength and courage to go on! God bless those, everywhere who are laboring for the cause of humanity!

persecuted: unfairly punished for something

falter: hesitate

From *Incidents in the Life of a Slave Girl* by Harriet Jacobs. Copyright © 1987 by the President and Fellows of Harvard College. Reprinted by permission of Harvard University Press.

1. The slaveholder does not view Jacobs as an individual with rights. To him, what is Harriet's status in society?
2. Why do you think that there was "no shadow of a law" to protect Jacobs even though the Bill of Rights had been written many years before?
3. What is the "maintenance of the right" for which Jacobs asks? How does she think it can be achieved?

Activity 4.3 ⇨

Shortly after the **Civil War** ended in 1865, two more amendments were added to the Bill of Rights. What rights do these amendments protect? Why do you think it was necessary to add these amendments to the Constitution?

Civil War: the American Civil War fought between the northern States, the Union, and the southern states, the Confederacy, from 1861 to 1865

1. *(1868) The Fourteenth Amendment*
   People born or naturalized as citizens of the United States shall have equal protection under the law.

   Civil rights:

   Necessity:

2. *(1870) The Fifteenth Amendment*
   A citizen shall not be denied the right to vote on account of race, color, or previous condition of servitude.

   Civil rights:

   Necessity:

Activity 4.4

Americans are known for their idealism—their positive beliefs and hopes, which are known collectively as the *American dream*. The American writer John Steinbeck (1902–68) analyzed the **paradoxical** nature of the American dream in his nonfiction work *America and Americans*. Read the excerpt from the chapter "A Paradox and a Dream" and complete the activities that follow.

paradoxical: contrary to expectations and yet true

From "A Paradox and a Dream"

Americans seem to live and breathe and function by paradox, but in nothing are we as paradoxical as in our passionate belief in our own myths. We truly believe ourselves to be natural-born mechanics and **do-it-yourself-ers.** We spend our lives in motor cars, yet most of us—a great many of us at least—do not know enough about a car to look in the gas tank when the motor fails. Our lives as we live them would not function without electricity, but it is a rare man or woman who, when the power goes off, knows how to look for a burned-out **fuse** and replace it. We believe **implicitly** that we are the **heirs** of the pioneers; that we have inherited self-sufficiency and the ability to take care of ourselves, particularly in relation to nature. There isn't a man among us in ten thousand who knows how to butcher a cow or a pig and cut it up for eating, let alone a wild animal. . . . Americans treasure the knowledge that they live close to nature, but fewer and fewer farmers feed more and more people; and as soon as we can afford to we eat out of cans, buy frozen TV dinners. . . .

The **inventiveness** once necessary for survival may also be a part of the national dream. . . . For Americans too the wide and general dream has a name. It is called "the American Way of Life." No one can define it or point to any one person or group who lives it, but it is very real nevertheless. . . . These dreams describe our **vague yearnings** toward what we wish we were and hope we may be: wise, just, compassionate, and noble. The fact that we have this dream at all is perhaps an indication of its possibility.

do-it-yourself-ers: Steinbeck has made up this word by adding the suffix *-ers* to the expression *do-it-yourself*, which means *to make or do something yourself, without help.*

fuse: part of an electrical device that helps to control the strength of an electrical current

implicitly: being naturally characteristic of something though not consciously perceived

heirs: the people who will inherit something from their parents or other relatives

inventiveness: the ability to come up with new ideas

vague: unclear

yearnings: strong desires

America and Americans, by John Steinbeck. Viking, 1966.

Part 1

Refer to Steinbeck's analysis to complete the outline that follows. This outline lists American cultural myths and paradoxical behaviors. Be prepared to discuss your responses in class.

American Cultural Myths	Paradoxical Behaviors
a. Americans are natural-born do-it-yourself-ers.	1. _____
b. Americans have a pioneer spirit of self-sufficiency	2. _____
c. _____	3. There are fewer farmers, and Americans often eat packaged foods.

Part 2

1. How do you understand what Steinbeck refers to as "the American Way of Life"? What does this way of life mean to you in terms of political, economic, and individual power?
2. Although Americans act paradoxically, why does Steinbeck still think that the American dream is possible?
3. What paradox could be suggested by the following picture?

Photograph courtesy of Mary Ziemer

4. Would you say that only Americans are paradoxical in their behavior, or are people generally full of paradoxes whether or not they are American? Are you aware of paradoxes that are held by other nations? What are some paradoxes in your own behavior or in the behavior of people you know?

Activity 4.5

emancipation: the state of being freed from slavery

proclamation: An official declaration. In 1863 President Lincoln declared that all slaves were legally free.

bypassed: went around; avoided

segregation: the separation of people and public institutions by color or race

discrimination: to treat someone unfairly or unequally because of his or her race

derogatory: done or said in a way that lowers the value of another person

minstrel shows: traveling shows of musical entertainment and comedy

ethics: the moral codes or beliefs that govern a society

assumptions: unspoken beliefs

Black Belt: the area where blacks lived

remote: distant; far away from where most people are

optical: having to do with the eyes

Paradoxically, in spite of amendments to the Constitution and the **Emancipation Proclamation,** the majority of African Americans did not enjoy the protection of their rights and were restricted from having economic and political power. Societal codes that **bypassed** constitutional laws and were either written or unspoken continued to cause repression in the lives of African Americans. Such laws were called *black codes.* They emerged after the Civil War ended in 1865, and they resulted in **segregation** and **discrimination.** Unofficially, these codes were also called *Jim Crow laws.* The name *Jim Crow* was a **derogatory** term that was used to refer to African Americans. It was taken from a slave character played in **minstrel shows** touring the country. In these shows, white actors painted their faces black to portray the character of a black slave named Jim Crow.

Richard Wright (1908–60), an African American writer, recounts the experience of growing up under black codes in his autobiographical work *The Ethics of Living Jim Crow.* As you read the following excerpt from Wright's book, think about the unspoken social codes and ethical **assumptions** that operate in a segregated society. The passage has been divided into sections followed by questions.

Part 1

From The Ethics of Living Jim Crow

It was a long time before I came in close contact with white folks again. We moved from Arkansas to Mississippi. Here we had the good fortune not to live behind the railroad tracks, or close to white neighborhoods. We lived in the very heart of the local **Black Belt.** There were black churches and black preachers; there were black schools and black teachers; black groceries and black clerks. In fact, everything was so solidly black that for a long time I did not ever think of white folks, save in **remote** and vague terms. But this could not last forever. As one grows older one eats more. One's clothing costs more. When I finished grammar school, I had to go to work. My mother could no longer feed and clothe me on her cooking job.

1. What does this passage suggest about the ways blacks and whites lived in relation to one another in Mississippi in the 1920s?

Part 2

There is but one place where a black boy who knows no trade can get a job and that's where the houses and faces are white, where the trees, lawns, and hedges are green. My first job was with an **optical** company in Jackson, Mississippi. The morning I applied, I stood straight and neat before the boss, answering all his questions with sharp **yessirs and nosirs**. I was very careful to pronounce my "sirs" distinctly, in order that he might know that I was polite, that I knew where I was, and that I knew he was a white man. I wanted that job badly.

He looked me over as though he were examining **a prize poodle**. He questioned me closely about my schooling, being particularly insistent about how much mathematics I had had. He seemed very pleased when I told him that I had had two years of algebra.

yessirs and nosirs: Wright has changed the expressions *yes sir* and *no sir* into plural nouns to show that he said these words often and that he was expected to say them.

a prize poodle: A poodle is a type (breed) of dog. Many poodles are very intelligent and can be taught to do tricks. A *prize poodle* has received one or more awards either for physical beauty or for performing various tricks.

2. What is the power relationship between the white boss and Richard? How do you know this is so?

Part 3

"Boy, how would you like to try to learn something around here?" he asked me.

"I'd like it fine, sir," I said, happy. I had visions of **"working my way up."** Even Negroes have those visions.

"All right," he said. "Come on."

I followed him to the small factory.

"Pease," he said to the white man of about thirty-five, "this is Richard. He's going to work for us."

Pease looked at me and nodded.

Then I was taken to a white boy of seventeen.

"Morrie, this is Richard, who's going to work for us."

"Whut yuh sayin' there, boy!" Morrie boomed at me.

"Fine!" I answered.

The boss instructed these two to help me, teach me, give me jobs to do, and let me learn what I could in my spare time.

My wages were five dollars a week.

working my way up: slowly getting to a higher position by hard work

What yuh sayin' there, boy: *What are you saying there, boy!* Boy was a derogatory expression that was commonly used to refer to black men, both young and old, rather than calling them by their names.

3. Why do you think the author has put "working my way up" in quotes?
4. What power relationship is established between Richard, Morrie, and Pease? What words reflect this relationship?

Part 4

I worked hard, trying to please. For the first month I got along O.K. Both Pease and Morrie seemed to like me. But one thing was missing. And I kept thinking about it. I was not learning anything and nobody was volunteering to help me. Thinking they had forgotten that I was to learn something about the work, about the mechanics

> **grinding lenses:** shaping lenses using a machine to match an eye prescription from an optometrist
>
> **nigger:** a negative term used to refer to blacks
>
> **bastard:** a derogatory term used to refer to a child without a legal father

of **grinding lenses,** I asked Morrie one day to tell me about the work. He grew red.

"Whut yuh tryin t' do, **nigger?** git smart?" he asked.

"Naw; I ain't tryin t' git smart," I said.

"Well, don't if yuh know whut's good for yuh!"

I was puzzled. Maybe he just doesn't want to help me, I thought. I went to Pease.

"Say, are yuh crazy, you black **bastard?**" Pease asked me, his gray eyes growing hard.

I spoke out, reminding him that the boss had said I was to be given a chance to learn something.

"Nigger, you think you're white, don't you?"

"Naw, sir!"

"Well, you're acting mighty like it!"

"But, Mr. Pease, the boss . . ."

Pease shook his fist in my face.

"This is a white man's work around here, and you better watch yourself!"

5. What unspoken code has Richard violated in this passage? How do you know this?

Part 5

> **son-of-a-bitch:** *Bitch* is a term for a dog, so a *son-of-a-bitch* is a *son-of-a-dog.*
>
> **snitched:** told that someone had done something wrong

From then on they changed toward me. They said good-morning no more. When I was just a bit slow in performing some duty, I was called a lazy black **son-of-a-bitch.**

Once I thought of reporting all this to the boss. But the mere idea of what would happen to me if Pease and Morrie should learn that I had "**snitched**" stopped me. And after all, the boss was a white man, too. What was the use?

The climax came at noon one summer day. Pease called me to his workbench. To get to him I had to go between two narrow benches and stand with my back against the wall.

"Yes, sir," I said.

Morrie came over, blocking the narrow passage between the benches. He folded his arms, staring at me solemnly.

I looked from one to the other, sensing that something was coming.

"Yes, sir," I said for the third time.

Pease looked up and spoke very slowly.

"Richard, Mr. Morrie here tells me you called me Pease."

He meant that I had failed to call him Mr. Pease. I looked at Morrie. He was gripping a steel bar in his hands. I opened my mouth to speak, to protest, to assure Pease that I had never called him simply

Pease, and that I had never had any intentions of doing so, when Morrie grabbed me by the collar, ramming my head against the wall.

"Now, be careful, nigger!" snarled Morrie, baring his teeth. "I heard yuh call 'im Pease! Now if yuh didn't, **yuh're callin' me a lie,** see?" He waved the steel bar threateningly.

yuh're callin' me a lie: *You are calling me a liar.*

6. Why does Richard think to himself, "What was the use?"
7. What would you do if you were in Richard's place? What might be the results of your actions?

Part 6

If I had said: No, sir, Mr. Pease, I never called you Pease, I would have been automatically calling Morrie a liar. And if I had said: Yes, sir, Mr. Pease, I called you Pease, I would have been pleading guilty to having uttered the worst insult that a Negro can utter to a southern white man. I stood hesitating, trying to frame a **neutral** reply.

"Richard, I asked you a question!" said Pease. Anger was creeping into his voice.

"I don't remember calling you Pease, Mr. Pease," I said cautiously. "And if I did, I sure didn't mean . . ."

"You black son-of-a-bitch! You called me Pease, then!" he spat, slapping me till I bent sideways over a bench. Morrie was on top of me, demanding:

"Didn't you call 'im Pease? If yuh say yuh didn't, I'll **rip yo gut string loose** with this bar, yuh black granny dodger! Yuh can't call a white man a lie 'n get away with it, you black son-of-a-bitch!"

I **wilted**. I begged them not to bother me. I knew what they wanted. They wanted me to leave. "I'll leave," I promised. "I'll leave right now."

They gave me a minute to get out of the factory. I was warned not to show up again, or tell the boss.

I went.

When I told the folks at home what had happened, they called me a fool. They told me that I must never again attempt to exceed my boundaries. When you are working for white folks, they said, you got to "**stay in your place**" if you want to keep working.

neutral: *not associated with one particular point of view*

rip yo gut string loose: *I'll rip out your guts. To rip out means to tear something out; guts is a slang term for organs in the stomach area.*

wilted: *weakened like a dying flower*

stay in your place: *to accept your position in life without trying to improve it*

From *Uncle Tom's Children* by Richard Wright. Copyright 1937 by Richard Wright. Copyright renewed 1965 by Ellen Wright. Reprinted by permission of HarperCollins Publishers, Inc.

8. Why do you think it was the "worst insult" to forget to call a white southern man "Mr."?
9. How does Richard try to make his explanation to Pease neutral?

10. In your view, was Richard a "fool" to act the way he did? Why or why not? What "boundaries" had he exceeded? Why did his family tell him to "stay in his place"?
11. Ethics are usually associated with the positive moral codes that govern a society. If this is the case, why is it ironic that Wright chose to entitle his work *The Ethics of Living Jim Crow*?

Activity 4.6 ⇨

While reading the materials in this chapter, you will find that the English used by some of the black characters in the readings follows a pattern that differs from the English you may have been taught. This English is referred to as African American Vernacular (AAV) or Black English Vernacular (BEV) and it developed within the black communities.

In the essay "From Outside, In," Barbara Mellix, an American writer, describes the experience of growing up with two ways of speaking English—black and white. Switching between two ways of speaking is called *code switching*. Read the excerpts from Mellix's essay for a better understanding of the code switching you may see in many stories about African Americans.

Part 1

From Outside, In

Like my children, I grew up speaking what I considered two distinctly different languages—black English and standard English (or as I thought of them then, the ordinary everyday speech of "country" coloreds and "proper" English)—and in the process of acquiring these languages, I developed an understanding of when, where, and how to use them. But unlike my children, I grew up in a world that was primarily black. My friends, neighbors, minister, teachers—almost everybody I associated with every day—were black. And we spoke to one another in our own special language: *That sho is a pretty dress you got on. If she don' soon leave me off I'm gon tell her head a mess. I was so mad I coul'a pissed a blue nail. He all the time trying to low-rate somebody. Aint's that just bout the nastiest thing you ever set ears on?*

1. How would you rephrase the italicized Black English Vernacular into what Mellix calls "standard English"?
2. In what ways do the two types of English differ?
3. Are there situations where you or people you know use code switching between languages? Describe these situations.

Part 2

> My parents never set aside time to drill us in standard English. Their forms of instruction were less formal. When my father was feeling particularly **expansive,** he would **regale** us with tales of his **exploits** in the outside world. In almost flawless English, complete with dialogue and flavored with gestures and **embellishments,** he told us about his attempt to get a haircut at a white barbershop; his refusal to acknowledge one of the town merchants until the man addressed him as "Mister"; the time he refused to step off the sidewalk uptown to let some whites pass; his airplane trip to New York City (to visit a sick relative) during which the stewardesses and porters—recognizing that he was a "gentleman"—addressed him as "Sir." I did not realize then—nor, I think, did my father—that he was teaching us, among other things, standard English and the relationship between language and power.

expansive: characterized by happiness and openness

regale: to entertain; to amuse

exploits: heroic acts

embellishments: additional decorations

4. What is the relationship between language and power to which Mellix refers?
5. In what ways did Mellix's father experience racism?

Part 3

> My mother's approach was different. Often, when one of us said, "I'm gon wash off my feet," she would say, "And what will you walk on if you wash them off?" Everyone would laugh at the victim of my mother's "proper" mood. But it was different when one of us children was in a proper mood. "You think you are so superior," I said to my older sister one day when we were arguing and she was winning. "Superior!" my sister mocked. "You mean I am acting '**biggidy**'?" My sisters and brothers sniggered, then joined in teasing me. Finally, my mother said, "Leave your sister alone. There's nothing wrong with using proper English." There was a half-smile on her face. I had gotten "uppity," had "**put on airs**" for no good reason. I was at home, alone with the family, and I hadn't been prompted by one of my mother's proper moods. But there was also a proud light in my mother's eyes; her children were learning English very well.

biggidy: BEV for *superior*

to put on airs: to act as if you are better than other people

6. How would you say, "I'm gon wash off my feet," in "standard" English?
7. Why do you think it was considered "uppity" to use "proper" English at home?

Part 4

audible: able to be heard

to have something to prove: to have the need to show that you are worthy of respect

As a child I felt this same doubleness in uptown Greeleyville where the whites lived. "Ain't that a pretty dress you're wearing!" Toby, the town policeman, said to me one day when I was fifteen. "Thank you very much," I replied, my voice barely **audible** in my own ears. The words felt wrong in my mouth, rigid, foreign. It was not that I had never spoken that phrase before—it was common in black English, too—but I was extremely conscious that this was an occasion for proper English. I had taken out my English and put it on as I did my church clothes, and I felt as if I were wearing my Sunday best in the middle of the week. It did not matter that Toby had not spoken grammatically correct English. He was white and could speak as he wished. **I had something to prove.** Toby did not.

This material originally appeared in *The Georgia Review*, Volume XLI, No. 2 (Summer 1987). © 1987 by The University of Georgia. © 1987 by Barbara Mellix. Reprinted by permission of Barbara Mellix and *The Georgia Review*.

8. What does the author mean when she says she had a sense of "doubleness"?
9. What did the author "have to prove"? Why didn't Toby have anything to prove?
10. Why do you think Mellix chose the title "From Outside, In" for her article?

Activity 4.7 ⇨

color-blind: unable to see skin "colors"

Judeo-Christian: *Judeo* refers to the Jewish tradition; Europe and the United States are said to share a Judeo-Christian tradition.

In the story "On the Road," the main character, Sargeant, lives in a world dominated by Jim Crow laws. Even though the Fifteenth and Sixteenth Amendments to the Constitution were "**color-blind**" and provided equal protection under the law, Sargeant did not benefit from such protection because of Jim Crow laws and the society's attitudes.

In "On the Road," Hughes presents the paradox of racism existing in a **Judeo-Christian** society. To understand the story better, it is important to understand the following symbols. Briefly write what you associate with these items and discuss them with classmates before you begin reading the story.

a. A church
b. A crucifix
c. Samson

Photograph courtesy of Rafael Kapelinski

Crucifix headstones

The story has been divided into parts followed by questions.

Part 1

On the Road

He was not interested in snow. When he got off the **freight,** one early evening during the depression, Sargeant never even noticed the snow. But he must have felt it **seeping** down his neck, cold, wet, sopping in his shoes. But if you had asked him, he wouldn't have known it was snowing. Sargeant didn't see the snow, not even under the bright lights of the main street, falling white and flaky against the night. He was too hungry, too sleepy, too tired.

The **Reverend** Mr. Dorset, however, saw the snow when he switched on his porch light, opened the front door of his **parsonage,** and found standing there before him a big black man with snow on his face, a human piece of night with snow on his face—obviously unemployed.

Said the Reverend Mr. Dorset before Sargeant even realized he'd opened his mouth: "I'm sorry. No! Go right on down this street four blocks and turn to your left, walk up seven and you'll see the **relief shelter.** I'm sorry. No!" He shut the door. Sargeant wanted to tell the holy man that he had already been to the relief shelter, been to hundreds of relief shelters during the **depression** years, the beds were always gone and supper was over, the place was full, and they drew the color line anyhow. But the minister said, "No," and shut the door. Evidently he didn't want to hear about it. And he *had* a door to shut.

The big black man turned away. And even yet he didn't see the snow, walking right into it. Maybe he sensed it, cold, wet, sticking to his jaws, wet on his black hands, sopping in his shoes. He stopped and stood on the sidewalk hunched over—hungry, sleepy, cold—looking up and down. Then he looked right where he was—in front of a church! Of course! a church! sure, right next to a parsonage, certainly a church.

It had *two* doors.

Broad white steps in the night all snow white. Two high arched doors with slender stone pillars on either side. And way up, a round lacy window with a stone crucifix in the middle and Christ on the crucifix in stone. All this was pale in the street lights, solid and stony pale in the snow.

Sargeant blinked. When he looked up, the snow fell into his eyes. For the first time that night he saw the snow. He shook his head. He shook the snow from his coat sleeves, felt hungry, felt lost, felt not lost, felt cold. He walked up the steps of the church. He knocked at

freight: a train car used to carry goods

seeping: oozing

reverend: The spiritual leader of a church. *A reverend* is trained in theology.

parsonage: The house in which the reverend lives. This house is paid for by the church.

relief shelter: a place the poor or homeless can go to seek shelter and food—relief

depression: the U.S. Great Depression of 1929 to approximately 1939, characterized by business failures and high unemployment

ramrod: a metal rod used for cleaning firearms

grunts: low sounds

chain gang: prisoners or slaves who are joined together by chains to do hard labor

the door. No answer. He tried the handle. Locked. He put his shoulder against the door and his long black body slanted like a **ramrod**. He pushed. With loud rhythmic **grunts**, like the grunts in a **chain-gang** song, he pushed against the door.

"I'm tired... Huh!... Hongry... Uh!... I'm sleepy... Huh! I'm cold... I got to sleep somewheres," Sargeant said. "This here is a church, ain't it? Well, uh!"

He pushed against the door.

Suddenly, with an undue cracking and creaking, the door began to give way to the tall black Negro who pushed ferociously against it.

By now two or three white people had stopped in the street, and Sargeant was vaguely aware of some of them yelling at him concerning the door. Three or four more came running, yelling at him.

"Hey!" they said. "Hey!"

lunge: to make a sudden, forceful move to reach for someone or something

"Uh-huh," answered the big tall Negro, "I know it's a white folks' church, but I got to sleep somewhere." He gave another **lunge** at the door. "Huh!"

And the door broke open.

1. Unlike Sargeant, the reverend immediately notices the snow. Why do you think this is so?
2. Why does the narrator emphasize that the reverend *had* a door to shut?
3. What might it mean to "draw the color line" at a public place?
4. Why does Sargeant say it's a "white folks' church"?
5. What Jim Crow laws has Sargeant violated? What do you predict will be the result of these "violations"?

Part 2

cops: a slang term for the police

But just when the door gave way, two white **cops** arrived in a car, ran up the steps with their clubs, and grabbed Sargeant. But Sargeant for once had no intention of being pulled or pushed away from the door.

Sargeant grabbed, but not for anything so weak as a broken door. He grabbed for one of the tall stone pillars beside the door, grabbed at it and caught it. And held it. The cops pulled. Sargeant pulled. Most of the people in the street got behind the cops and helped them pull.

"A big black unemployed Negro holding onto our church!" thought the people. "The idea!"

The cops began to beat Sargeant over the head, and nobody protested. But he held on.

And then suddenly the church fell down.

Gradually, the big stone front of the church fell down, the walls and the rafters, the crucifix and the cross and the Christ. Then the whole thing fell down, covering the cops and the people with bricks and stones and debris. The whole church fell down in the snow.

Sargeant got out from under the church and went walking on up the street with the stone pillar on his shoulder. He was under the impression that he had buried the parsonage and the Reverend Mr. Dorset who said, "No!" So he laughed, and threw the pillar six blocks up the street and went on.

6. What is the symbolic significance of the church's collapse?
7. When the townspeople think that a black man is holding onto their church, they say, "The idea!" What do you think is meant by this expression?
8. In part 2, what clue tells us that Sargeant may have just begun to dream?

Part 3

Sargeant thought he was alone, but listening to the crunch, crunch, crunch on the snow of his own footsteps, he heard other footsteps, too, doubling his own. He looked around, and there was Christ walking along beside him, the same Christ that had been on the cross on the church—still stone with a rough stone surface, walking along beside him just like he was broken off the cross when the church fell down.

"Well, I'll **be dogged**," said Sargeant. "This here's the first time I ever seed yo off the cross."

to be dogged: to be surprised or confused by something

"Yes," said Christ, crunching his feet in the snow. "You had to pull the church down to get me off the cross."

"You glad?" said Sargeant.

"I sure am," said Christ.

They both laughed.

"I'm **a hell of a fellow**, ain't I?" said Sargeant. "Done pulled the church down!"

a hell of a fellow: a great man

"You did a good job," said Christ. "They have kept me nailed on a cross for nearly two thousand years."

"Whee-ee-e!" said Sargeant. "I know you're glad to get off."

"I sure am," said Christ.

They walked on in the snow. Sargeant looked at the man of stone.

"And you have been up there two thousand years?"

"I sure have," Christ said.

"Well, if I had a little cash," said Sargeant, "I'd show you around a bit."

I've been around: an expression that means that a person has seen much of the world and knows how it works

"**I've been around**," said Christ.

"Yeah, but that was a long time ago."

"All the same," said Christ, "I've been around."

They walked on in the snow until they came to the railroad yards. Sargeant was tired, sweating and tired.

"Where you goin'?" Sargeant said, stopping by the tracks. He looked at Christ. Sargeant said, "I'm just a bum on the road. How about you? Where you goin'?"

"God knows," Christ said, "but I'm leavin' here."

9. Why does Christ say that he's been on the stone cross for two thousand years, and why is he still made of stone?

Part 4

They saw the red and green lights of the railroad yard half veiled by the snow that fell out of the night. Away down the track they saw a fire in a **hobo jungle.**

"I can go there and sleep," Sargeant said.

"You can?"

"Sure," said Sargeant. "That place ain't got no doors."

Outside the town, along the tracks, there were **barren** trees and bushes below the **embankment,** snow-gray in the dark. And down among the trees and bushes there were **makeshift** houses made out of boxes and tin and old pieces of wood and canvas. You couldn't see them in the dark but you knew they were there if you'd ever been on the road, if you had ever lived with the homeless and hungry in a depression.

"I'm **side-tracking,**" Sargeant said, "I'm tired."

"I'm gonna make it on to Kansas City," said Christ.

"O.K," Sargeant said, "So long!"

He went down into the hobo jungle and found himself a place to sleep. He never did see Christ no more. About 6:00 A.M. a freight came by. Sargeant scrambled out of the jungle with a dozen or so more hobos and ran along the track, grabbing at the freight. It was dawn, early dawn, cold and gray.

"Wonder where Christ is by now?" Sargeant thought. "He musta gone on way on down the road. He didn't sleep in this jungle."

Sargeant grabbed the train and started to pull himself up into a moving coal car, over the edge of a wheeling coal car. But strangely enough, the car was full of cops. The nearest cop rapped Sargeant soundly across the knuckles with his nightstick. Wham! Rapped his big black hands for clinging to the top of the car. Wham! But Sargeant did not turn loose. He clung on and tried to pull himself into the car. He hollered at the top of his voice, "Damn it, lemme in this car!"

---

hobo jungle: The place where the hobos lived was called a jungle because the townspeople saw it as being uncivilized and wild, like a jungle.

barren: without life; without leaves

embankment: a raised structure to hold back water or to carry a railway

makeshift: made quickly and not made well; made to last only a short time

side-tracking: taking a side trip off the main routes

10. During the depression, many homeless and unemployed people traveled on trains from town to town. These people were called *hobos*. From the story, what can you tell about their living conditions?
11. Why does Sargeant say that he can sleep in the hobo camp?

Part 5

"Shut up," barked the cop. "You crazy **coon**!" He rapped Sargeant across the knuckles and punched him in the stomach. "You ain't out in no jungle now. This ain't no train. You in jail."

Wham! across his bare black fingers clinging to the bars of his cell. Wham! between the steel bars low down against his shins.

Suddenly Sargeant realized that he really was in jail. He wasn't on no train. The blood of the night before had dried on his face, his head hurt terribly, and a cop outside in the corridor was hitting him across the knuckles for holding onto the door, yelling and shaking the cell door.

"They musta took me to jail for breaking down the door last night," Sargeant thought, "that church door."

Sargeant went over and sat on a wooden bench against the cold stone wall. He was emptier than ever. His clothes were wet, clammy cold wet, and shoes sloppy with snow water. It was just about dawn. There he was, locked up behind a cell door, nursing his bruised fingers. The bruised fingers were his but not the *door*.

Not the *club* but the fingers.

"You wait," mumbled Sargeant, black against the jail wall. "I'm gonna break down this door, too."

"Shut up—or I'll **paste you one**," said the cop.

"I'm gonna break down this door," yelled Sargeant as he stood up in his cell.

Then he must have been talking to himself because he said, "I wonder where Christ's gone? I wonder if he's gone to Kansas City?"

coon: a derogatory slang term used for blacks

paste you one: hit you

From *Something in Common* by Langston Hughes. Copyright © 1963 by Langston Hughes. Copyright renewed © 1991 by Arnold Rampers and Ramona Bass. Reprinted by permission of Hill and Wang, a division of Farrar, Straus, & Giroux, Inc., and by Harold Ober Associates Incorporated.

12. How do we know that Sargeant's dream has ended?
13. What is the power relationship between Sargeant and the cops? What details tell you this? Why do you think the words *door* and *club* are emphasized?
14. In the Old Testament story of Samson and Delilah, Samson's destruction of the temple results in the destruction of the Israelites' enemies. What happens as a result of Sargeant's "destruction" of the church? Why is this difference significant?

15. Based on the last line of the story, who is "on the road?" Why is this point significant?

Activity 4.8

Langston Hughes wrote "On the Road" six years before the Civil Rights movement underwent its most active period—from 1958 until the assassination of Martin Luther King Jr., the movement's leader, in 1968. Dr. King, who was a minister, used religious values to appeal to the white population to change the unequal power structures in the United States. He fought for the rights that were guaranteed by the Constitution to be applied to African Americans, and he wanted all Americans to practice the ideals of equality and freedom that are part of the American dream. In 1963, King was arrested for having organized sit-ins against restaurants in Birmingham, Alabama, that refused to serve African Americans. During a sit-in, civil rights protesters would simply refuse to leave a restaurant or an office until they'd been served or had been arrested. While in prison, Dr. King wrote an open letter to Christian ministers who did not agree with his methods of obtaining rights for blacks.

The Civil Rights movement presented Americans with a question: When a society's laws are unjust and treat people unfairly, should they be obeyed? King thought not. He argued that people should join together to disobey unjust laws in acts of nonviolent civil disobedience. In his work entitled "Letter from Birmingham Jail," King gives the following arguments in support of civil disobedience.

> ... A law is unjust if it is inflicted on a minority that, as a result of being denied the right to vote, had no part in enacting or **devising** the law. Who can say that the legislature of Alabama which set up that state's segregation laws was democratically elected?

devising: shaping; creating

He explains:

> Sometimes a law is just **on its face** and unjust in its application. For instance, I have been arrested on a charge of parading without a permit. Now, there is nothing wrong in having an **ordinance** which requires a permit for a parade. But such an ordinance becomes unjust when it is used to maintain segregation and to deny citizens the First Amendment privilege of peaceful assembly and protest.

on its face: on the surface; at first glance

ordinance: a law or legal decree made by a government or legal body

He adds:

> ... One who breaks an unjust law must do so openly, lovingly, and with a willingness to accept the penalty. I submit that an individual who breaks a law that his conscience tells him is unjust, and who willingly accepts the penalty of imprisonment in order **to arouse** the conscience of the community over its injustice, is in reality expressing the highest respect for the law.

to arouse: to wake up

From *Why We Can't Wait,* by Martin Luther King Jr. Harper and Row, 1964.

1. In these excerpts, which two constitutional amendments does King allude to?
2. What are some of the paradoxes that King points out to his readers?
3. Are you aware of laws that seem to be just but are used unjustly?
4. What paradox is seen in the following picture? What does it suggest about the American dream?

Photograph courtesy of Rafael Kapelinski

Los Angeles, California

Activity 4.9

In his "Letter from Birmingham Jail," King explains that nonviolent civil disobedience has a long history and that it should be undertaken in four steps:

> collection of the facts to determine whether injustices exist; negotiation; self-purification; and direct action.

1. List some historical examples of times when civil disobedience has been practiced or when you think it should have been practiced. Have such acts of civil disobedience been predominantly violent or nonviolent? Are there current unjust situations in the world that you think could be resolved through nonviolent civil disobedience?

Activity 4.10

King credited the American writer and philosopher Henry David Thoreau (1817–62) with having introduced him to the idea of nonviolent civil disobedience as a tool for political change. Here are a few of Thoreau's ideas found in his essay "Civil Disobedience," which was first given as a lecture entitled "Resistance to Civil Government" in 1848. (a) "Under a government which imprisons unjustly, the true place for a just man is also a prison." (b) "Can there be a government in which majorities do not virtually decide right and wrong but conscience? . . . Must the citizen ever for a moment, or in the least degree, **resign** his conscience to the legislator? Why has every man a conscience then? I think that we should be men first and subjects afterward. It is not desirable to cultivate a respect for the law, so much as for the right." (c) "**Confucius** said: If a state is governed by the principles of reason, poverty and misery are subjects of shame; if a state is not governed by the principles of reason, riches and honors are subjects of shame."

to resign: to give up (in this case, to give up one's choice to decide what is right and wrong); to accept a situation without struggling

Confucius: a Chinese philosopher (551–479 B.C.), also known as K'ung Fu-Tzu

1. Based on the information and excerpts in activities 4.8–4.10, what parallels, or similar ideas, do you see between Thoreau and King?
2. Thoreau has included a quote from Confucius. How might this quote apply to U.S. society?

Activity 4.11

James Baldwin (1924–87), an African American writer, preferred to live in France because he experienced less racial discrimination there than he did in the United States. In his work *The Fire Next Time,* written in 1963, Baldwin calls for more aggressive action to break down racial discrimination.

From The Fire Next Time

The Negroes of this country may never be able to rise to power, but they are very well placed indeed **to precipitate** chaos and **ring down** the curtain on the American dream.

This has everything to do, of course, with the nature of that dream and with the fact that we Americans, of whatever color, do not dare examine it and are far from having made it a reality. There are too many things we do not wish to know about ourselves. People are not, for example, terribly anxious to be equal (equal, after all, to what and to whom?) but they love the idea of being superior. And this human truth has an especially grinding force here, where identity is almost impossible to achieve and people are **perpetually** attempting to find their feet on the shifting sands of status. . . .

to precipitate: to start something

to ring down the curtain on: to cause the end of something, as when the curtain is lowered at theater performance

perpetually: continually

And I submit, then, that the racial tensions that **menace** Americans today have little to do with real **antipathy**—on the contrary, indeed—and are involved only symbolically with color. These tensions are rooted in the very same depths as those from which love springs, or murder. The white man's unadmitted—and apparently, to him, unspeakable—private fears and longings are projected on to the Negro. The only way he can be released from the Negro's tyrannical power over him is **to consent,** in effect, to become black himself, to become a part of that suffering and dancing country that he now watches **wistfully** from the heights of his lonely power. . . . The only thing white people have that black people need, or should want, is power—and no one holds power forever.

> **to menace:** to threaten someone or something
>
> **antipathy:** strong feelings of dislike
>
> **to consent:** to agree to something
>
> **wistfully:** thoughtfully sad; with longing

The Fire Next Time, by James Baldwin. Random House, 1995.

1. Based upon Baldwin's arguments, what is it that Pease and Morrie in *The Ethics of Living Jim Crow* really fear?
2. What is it that the Reverend Dorset in "On the Road" really fears when he sees Sargeant? According to Baldwin, what would he have to do to overcome this fear?
3. How do you understand the quote from Baldwin that is found in the caption to the picture at the beginning of this chapter?
4. Like Steinbeck, Baldwin sees paradoxes in Americans' attitudes toward the American dream. What are some of the paradoxes that Baldwin notes? In your opinion, why does he say that both black and white Americans dare not examine the American dream too closely?
5. What idea from Freudian psychology does Baldwin use to describe the relationship of whites to blacks?
6. Compare these brief excerpts with those by King. On which points do they differ?
7. Baldwin wrote *The Fire Next Time* in 1963. If he were writing today do you think he would still have the same views on race relations?

Activity 4.12

On August 28, 1963, one hundred years after President Lincoln signed the Emancipation Proclamation, civil rights leaders organized a march for freedom in Washington, DC. The march was organized to show support for the Civil Rights movement and for civil rights legislation. Two hundred and fifty thousand people gathered together at the foot of the Lincoln Memorial to hear Martin Luther King give a speech. Here are two of the dreams that King mentions in his speech.

> I have a dream that one day on the red hills of Georgia the sons of former slaves and the sons of former slave owners will be able to sit down together at the table of brotherhood.

> I have a dream that my four little children will one day live in a nation where they will not be judged by the color of their skin but by the content of their character.

1. What powerful American ideal is Dr. King alluding to when he uses the word *dream*?
2. Do you think King's dreams have come true? Why or why not? Are there dreams that have not yet been realized by the society in which you live?
3. Look at the picture at the beginning of this chapter. How would you explain this picture based on King's speech and the material you have read in this chapter? How does the picture contrast with the one below?
4. Write a short speech in which you describe your dream for your local community, your nation, or the world. If possible, read a copy of King's speech first and try to use a style similar to his.

Photograph courtesy of Marco Fenaroli

Activity 4.13 ⇨

Use the dates referred to in this chapter to complete the following time line about the Civil Rights movement. A few dates have been added to the time line to make it more complete. You may find that you need to add more events for dates that already have information listed.

1863–

1865–

1868–

1870–

1896– The U.S. Supreme Court rules that "separate but equal" facilities are legal, thus legalizing segregation.

1952–

1954– The Supreme Court rules that public school segregation is illegal.

1955– Rosa Parks, an elderly African American woman, refuses to give up her seat on the bus to a white person as the black codes required her to do. She is arrested, and her arrest inspires the **boycott** of buses in the south. Martin Luther King leads the boycott and is arrested for the first time. In 1956, bus segregation is ruled unconstitutional. The boycott makes a powerful statement about the unity of the Civil Rights movement. If possible, listen to a recording of the song "Sister Rosa" by the Neville Brothers (© 1989 A&M Records).

1957– The courts move to desegregate schools.

1963– President John F. Kennedy is assassinated on November 22.

1964– Martin Luther King receives the Nobel Peace Prize. The Civil Rights Act is passed by Congress and signed by President Lyndon Johnson. The bill had been initiated by the Kennedy administration to eliminate segregation in public institutions.

1965– Voting Rights Act. This act **repealed** laws that said that a person had to be able to read to vote. Before the act was passed, blacks had been required to pass a **literacy** test before they were allowed to vote. However, such tests were designed so that no one, black or white, could pass them. They were used against blacks to keep them from participating in the political process and from gaining political power.

1968–

1983– The third Monday in January is designated as Martin Luther King Day, a federal holiday.

to boycott: to refuse to use a service or product as a form of protest

repealed: removed or changed a law or decision

literacy: having to do with the ability to read

1. What examples of individual and collective or group nonviolent civil disobedience do you find on this time line. What were the end results of such actions?

Activity 4.14

When we place "On the Road" in the social context of the issues related to the African American experience, this helps us to better understand the story. How might Hughes's story have helped to inspire the Civil Rights movement in America?

Activity 4.15

"On the Road" can also be placed in the social context of issues related to homelessness. Sargeant speaks for the homeless when he points out that the Reverend Mr. Dorset "*had* a door to shut."

Although "On the Road" is set in the 1930s, homelessness in the United States continues to exist. The National Coalition for the Homeless (NCH), a U.S.-based charity, cites a federal government study in which it is estimated that approximately 12 million people, including adults and children, experienced homelessness between 1989 and 1994.

NCH also cites studies that argue that homelessness has a number of causes, such as a lack of affordable housing and health care; a lack of full-time jobs in the service industry; domestic violence, which forces primarily women and children to leave their homes; and mental illness, which accounts for 20–25 percent of the single adult homeless population. (See http://nch.ari.net/causes.html.) And, as Sargeant's experience demonstrates, unjust societal codes can help to create homelessness.

Whereas Sargeant represents the experience of the homeless, Reverend Dorset can, in turn, represent a common reaction that people have toward the homeless: one of fear or of simply ignoring the problem. What do you think could be done to eradicate homelessness? If possible, access Internet sites such as the National Coalition for the Homeless for more information about homelessness and what is being done to help the homeless.

Activity 4.16

If the former slave Harriet Jacobs could visit the United States now, what would be her reaction to the history of the Civil Rights movement? What would she say still needs to be done?

Chapter 5
"I Stand Here Ironing," by Tillie Olsen

Photograph courtesy of Marco Fenaroli

"You ought to do something about her with a gift like that—but without money or knowing how, what does one do? . . . Let her be. So all that is in her will not bloom—but in how many does it? There is still enough left to live by."—"I Stand Here Ironing," by Tillie Olsen

Activity 5.1a ⇨

In this chapter, you will be introduced to feminist criticism, a critical approach that examines the historical and social inequalities between men and women as they are reflected in literature. Because feminist critics, both male and female, believe that the lives and works of women authors are often overlooked in a patriarchal or male-dominated society, they attempt to focus attention on the contributions women have made to the arts and to society.

As an introduction to this approach, study the picture of an American quilt and then answer the questions found below. Be prepared to discuss your answers.

Quilt and photograph courtesy of Lucile Leister

1. How are quilts made, and who makes them? Do you know anyone who makes quilts? If so, how much work is involved in creating a handmade quilt?
2. How do you think quilt making could possibly be connected to feminist criticism?

Activity 5.1b

The feminist writer Alice Walker (b. 1944), an African American, asked herself the same questions as those you responded to in activity 5.1a. In her nonfiction book *In Search of Our Mothers' Gardens: Womanist Prose* (1983) Walker asks, "What did it mean for a black woman to be an artist in our grandmothers' time? In our great-grandmothers' day? It is a question with an answer cruel enough to stop the blood."

Walker addressed her question to other black women. Keeping in mind that the grandmothers and great-grandmothers of Alice Walker's generation were most likely slaves or the daughters of slaves, how do you think Walker's question would be answered by these women? Write out your ideas. You may want to refer to the writings found in chapter 4 for additional information, particularly *Incidents in the Life of a Slave Girl,* by Harriet Jacobs, found in activity 4.2.

Activity 5.1c ⇨

Walker asks if her readers had a "genius of a great-great-grandmother who died under some **ignorant** and **depraved white overseer's lash**" and if this woman was required to bake biscuits for some "lazy **backwater tramp**" even though in her heart she wanted to paint or to write. She wonders if this woman was forced to have children—ten to twenty children who were then used as slaves or sold to other slaveholders—when she was meant to be a sculptor. Given such terrible conditions—in which it was illegal for blacks to read and to write and to develop their thoughts, let alone to be artists—Walker wonders how the creativity of black women was **sustained**.

Looking at black women in the early twentieth century, she points to singers such as Billie Holiday, Roberta Flack, and Aretha Franklin as examples of black women who managed to express their creativity through one of the few outlets allowed to them: music. She also suggests that black women who were labeled "crazy" or "**sainted**" were probably frustrated artists who died with their talents unrealized. Based on this summary of Walker's essay, answer the following questions.

ignorant: without knowledge or understanding

depraved: uncivilized; corrupt; evil

white overseer: the person who supervised the slaves

lash: a whip

backwater tramp: a woman of suspect morals who lives in an isolated area

sustained: to keep something going

sainted: literally, a person who has the characteristics of a holy person; in this context, a person who is somehow different from others

1. In your own words, explain why it was impossible for many black slave women to become artists.
2. What do the quotation marks around the adjectives *crazy* and *sainted* signify?
3. Walker lists a number of African American female vocalists. If possible, listen to a tape of one of these artists, or of another black female singer with whom you are familiar, and imagine what might have happened to this woman if she hadn't been allowed to sing. Write down your thoughts.

Activity 5.1d ⇨

In her book, *In Search of Our Mothers' Gardens,* Walker describes her mother's life. She married at seventeen and had nine children. She made the family's clothes, canned fruits and vegetables in the summer. Winter evenings, she made quilts. Days, she spent working in the fields with her husband. Between her children and her other responsibilities, she had no time for herself. When, Walker asks, did her mother have the opportunity to be creative?

In answer to this question, Walker points to a quilt that she saw hanging in the **Smithsonian Institution** in Washington, DC. This quilt, said to "have been made by an anonymous black woman one hundred years ago," was an exquisite work of art, made from rags into a imaginative and **finely wrought** quilt. Walker says, "If we could locate this 'anonymous' black woman from Alabama, she would turn out to be one of our grandmothers—an artist who left her mark in the only materials she could afford, and in the only **medium** her position in society allowed her to use."

> **Smithsonian Institution:** a collection of museums
>
> **finely wrought:** something that is made very well with attention to detail
>
> **medium:** the material that is used to make and/or to express something, e.g., paint, music, writing

1. Why does Walker see the quilt as a symbol of the creative spirit found in black women?
2. Even though Walker's mother was not a slave, both Walker's mother and the "anonymous" black slave who made the quilt found in the Smithsonian Institution shared similar positions in society. How would you describe those positions? What caused these women to be in such positions?
3. How does the life of Walker's mother differ from your own mother's or from the lives of other women you know who are mothers? How is it similar? How is it like or unlike your own life? Why is this so?

Activity 5.1e ⇨

> **everyday use:** daily use of something

In a short story by Walker entitled **"Everyday Use"** (published in her book *In Love and Trouble: Stories of Black Women,* [1973]), she has an African American mother tell a story about the relationship between her two daughters, Dee and Maggie. In the story, Dee, who is fashionable and quick minded, comes from her home in the city to visit her mother and sister at their farm in the country. Maggie, who is slow and shy, still lives at home and helps out on the farm.

The end of the story focuses on some quilts that Dee wants to take back home with her even though her mother had already promised them to her sister, Maggie, for when she gets married. At first, Dee asks if she can have the "old quilts" that were made by her mother, aunt, and grandmother. The quilts were all stitched by hand and were made from clothes that her grandmother had worn. Although Dee had called the quilts "old-fashioned" before she went away to college, she now thinks they are "**priceless**," and she wants to hang them on her walls. She doesn't want her sister, Maggie, to have them because she says that Maggie will put them to "everyday use." Even though Maggie wants the quilts herself, she offers them to her sister, saying that she can remember her grandmother without the quilts. Besides, her grandma had taught her the art of quilt making and she could make more if she wanted. In the end, though, the mother decides that Maggie should have the grandmother's quilts after all.

As Dee is leaving, she tells Maggie and her mother that they don't understand their "**heritage**." She tells her sister "**to make something of** [**herself**]" because it's "a new day" for black women. Then she puts on enormous sunglasses that nearly cover her face, gets into her car, and drives off, leaving Maggie and her mom on the porch, where they sit down, **dip some snuff**, and enjoy the afternoon together.

priceless: without price; precious; can't be copied

heritage: history; background; roots

to make something of one's self: to improve one's skills and knowledge so that one can be someone important

to dip some snuff: Snuff is a kind of crushed tobacco. *To dip some snuff* means to put a pinch of snuff between the gums and the cheek or to sniff the snuff through the nose.

1. On the basis of the previous discussion of Walker's feminist ideas that relate to quilt making and what it symbolizes, why do you think the grandmother's quilts have now become so important to Dee?
2. Why do you think the mother in the story finally decides that Maggie and not her sister, Dee, should have the quilts?
3. Why is Dee angry that Maggie might put them to "everyday use"?
4. What do you think about the mother's decision to give Maggie the quilts?
5. What might Dee mean when she says to her mother and sister that they don't understand their heritage? What does she mean when she says that it's a "new day"?
6. On the surface, this story would appear to be about two sisters who want the same family quilts, but what larger social theme is the story also about?

Activity 5.1f

Write or retell the summary of "Everyday Use" from the mother's point of view. Imagine that you are the mother and use the first-person point of view for your narrative. As a narrator who is also a participant in the story, you know only what you are thinking, but, as a mother, you are good at describing your daughters' thoughts and feelings. Include dialogue in your story. Add imaginative details that weren't included in the summary. Share your writing with a classmate.

If possible, after you've written your own story, read the original version of Walker's "Everyday Use." As you read, note down what has been left out of the summary of the story. Also note down what information you have learned about the two sisters and their mother from the actual story. Be prepared to discuss your notes in class.

Activity 5.1g

Look back at the picture of the quilt in activity 5.1. After having read about Walker's views, do you look at the quilt differently? What do you think now that you may not have thought when you first answered the questions in activity 5.1?

Activity 5.2 ⇨

In 1929, the English writer Virginia Woolf (1882–1941), famous for her novels and critical essays, wondered what life must have been like for a creative woman living in the seventeenth century. She researched the lives of women living in the seventeenth century to find out what their living conditions were like. The following *True/False* statements about the quality of a woman's life in England during the 1700s are based on Woolf's research. Write *T* next to the statements you think are true and *F* next to those that you think are false.

1. ___ Wife beating was considered a husband's right.

2. ___ Marriages were generally arranged by parents.

3. ___ All women could own property.

4. ___ Most women were sent to school.

5. ___ In general, women could not earn their own money.

6. ___ Women married in their twenties.

7. When reviewing **Renaissance** literature, Woolf wonders why "no woman wrote a word of that extraordinary literature when every other man, it seemed, was capable of song or **sonnet**." Given the correct answers to the preceding true and false questions, how would you respond to Woolf's question?

> **Renaissance:** the "rebirth" of ideas from ancient Greek and Roman cultures in Europe in the fifteenth–seventeenth centuries
>
> **sonnet:** a verse form of fourteen lines that follows a set rhyme and rhythm

Activity 5.3a

Perhaps you are already familiar with William Shakespeare, an English writer of the sixteenth century who wrote many well-known plays such as *Hamlet* and *Romeo and Juliet*. Imagine that he had a sister who was just as talented as he was at writing. What do you think would have happened to his sister? Would she have been able to use her abilities? Why or why not? (Keep in mind that until the mid–twentieth century it was generally considered improper for women to work in the theater. And, in fact, in some countries, it is still considered improper.) Write a paragraph describing what you think the life of Shakespeare's talented sister might have been like. Give her a name and describe how she might have felt.

Activity 5.3b ⇨

Woolf also thought about what might have happened to Shakespeare's talented sister. In her book *A Room of One's Own* (1929), she argues that women need privacy and an independent source of income if they want to create the conditions necessary to become artists. To illustrate this need, Woolf writes about Shakespeare's imaginary sister, Judith. She uses Judith's life to illustrate how difficult it was for women to produce art in the 1500s. In the following excerpt, Woolf describes what might have happened to Judith. The excerpt has been divided into three sections followed by questions. Note that Woolf uses British spelling.

Part 1

From A Room of One's Own

Let me imagine, since facts are so hard to come by, what would have happened had Shakespeare had a wonderfully gifted sister, called Judith, let us say. Shakespeare himself went, very probably—his mother was **an heiress**—to the grammar school, where he may have learnt Latin—**Ovid, Virgil, Horace**—and the elements of grammar and logic. He was, it is well known, a wild boy who **poached** rabbits, perhaps shot a deer, and had, rather sooner than he should have done, to marry a woman in the neighbourhood, who bore him a child rather quicker than was right. That **escapade** sent him to seek his fortune in London. He had, it seemed, a taste for theatre: he began by holding horses at the stage door. Very soon he got work in the theatre, became a successful actor, and lived at the **hub of the universe**, meeting everybody, knowing everybody, practising his art on the **boards**, exercising his **wits** in the streets, and even getting **access** to the palace of the queen.

an heiress: a woman who inherits money from her family

Ovid: a Roman poet (43 B.C.–17 A.D.)

Virgil: a Roman poet (70–19 B.C.)

Horace: a Roman poet (65–8 B.C.)

poached: caught an animal, bird, or fish illegally or without permission

escapade: an adventure; something that is done without the approval of others

hub of the universe: The center of the universe. A *hub* is the center part of a wheel.

boards: stage

wits: cleverness; intelligence

access: having the ability or the permission to meet the people you need to meet or to get the information you need

1. As Woolf imagines Shakespeare's life, what experiences did he have that helped him as a writer?
2. Shakespeare apparently got a young woman pregnant before they were married. How did this change Shakespeare's life? How would the woman have been treated if she hadn't married Shakespeare?

Part 2

Meanwhile his extraordinarily gifted sister, let us suppose, remained at home. She was as adventurous, as imaginative, as **agog** to see the world as he was. But she was not sent to school. She had no chance of learning grammar and logic, let alone of reading Horace and Virgil. She picked up a book now and then, one of her brother's

agog: to be full of excitement

to mend the stockings: to sew up the holes in socks

to mind the stew: to supervise the cooking of a meat dish

to moon about: to go about with dreamy, sad thoughts

the apple of her father's eye: her father's favorite child; one who is shown great affection

on the sly: in secret

betrothed: when a marriage contract has been prepared

petticoat: a slip worn under a dress

parcel: a small package or bundle

perhaps, and read a few pages. But then her parents came in and told her **to mend the stockings** or **mind the stew** and not **moon about** with books and papers. They would have spoken sharply but kindly, for they were substantial people who knew the conditions of life for a woman and loved their daughter—indeed more likely than not she was **the apple of her father's eye**. Perhaps she scribbled some pages up in the apple loft **on the sly**, but was careful to hide them or set fire to them. Soon, however, before she was out of her teens, she was to be **betrothed** to the son of a neighbouring wool-stapler. She cried out that marriage was hateful to her, and for that she was severely beaten by her father. Then he ceased to scold her. He begged her instead not to hurt him, not to shame him in this matter of her marriage. He would give her a chain of beads or a fine **petticoat,** he said, and there were tears in his eyes. How could she disobey him? How could she break his heart? The force of her own gift drove her to it. She made up a small **parcel** of her belongings, let herself down by a rope one summer's night and took the road to London. She was seventeen.

Photograph courtesy of Rafael Kapelinski

"She was as adventurous, as imaginative, as agog to see the world as he was."—Virginia Woolf, *A Room of One's Own*

3. As Woolf imagines Judith's upbringing, what circumstances kept Judith from becoming a writer?
4. Why do you think Judith resisted getting married?
5. What do you think about her father's reaction to her resistance?

Part 3

> The birds that sang in the hedge were not more musical than she was. She had the quickest **fancy,** a gift like her brother's for the tune of words. Like him, she had a taste for the theatre. She stood at the stage door; she wanted to act, she said. Men laughed in her face. The manager—a fat, loose-lipped man—**guffawed.** He bellowed something about **poodles** dancing and women acting—no woman, he said, could possibly be an actress. He hinted—you can imagine what. She could get no training in her **craft.** Could she even seek her dinner in a tavern or roam the streets at midnight? Yet her genius was for fiction and **lusted** to feed abundantly upon the lives of men and women and the study of their ways. At last—for she was very young, oddly like Shakespeare the poet in her face, with the same grey eyes and rounded brows—at last Nick Green the actor-manager took pity on her; she found herself with child by that gentleman and so—who shall measure the heat and violence of the poet's heart when caught and **tangled** in a woman's body?—killed herself one winter's night and lies buried at some cross-roads where the omnibuses now stop outside the Elephant and Castle.
>
> That, more or less, is how the story would run, I think, if a woman in Shakespeare's day had had Shakespeare's genius.

fancy: imagination

guffawed: laughed loudly in surprise and disbelief

poodles: A breed of small dogs that can be trained to do tricks, including to "dance" on their hind legs. Woolf alludes to the idea that watching a woman act was considered to be like watching a poodle dance.

craft: a skill or trade

lusted: desired something greatly

tangled: caught up in something as in a knot

From *A Room of One's Own* by Virginia Woolf, copyright 1929 by Harcourt Brace & Company and renewed 1957 by Leonard Woolf. Reprinted by permission of the publisher and The Society of Authors as the Literary Representative of the Estate of Virginia Woolf.

6. How does Judith's experience in London differ from her brother's? Why do you think this is the case?
7. Do you know of any women or men who were (or are) not able to fully develop their talents because of their position in society and/or because of family responsibilities? Who were they? What were their talents? What specific circumstances kept them from realizing their artistic potential?
8. During his lifetime, Shakespeare had a daughter, Susanna. The **epigraph** on her tombstone says that she was "**witty** above her sex." Yet, in spite of her wit, Susanna, who married a doctor, did not become a writer. Based on the ideas presented in Woolf's *A Room of One's Own*, why do you think Susanna did not become a writer? Why is the epigraph ironic?

epigraph: the words written on a tombstone

witty: able to see amusing or ironic relationships

Activity 5.4 ⇨

What commonalities do you find in Walker's and Woolf's views of women and their creativity? How do they differ?

Activity 5.5a

Even though women of today generally have more rights than women of the seventeenth century (in the majority of countries), their many responsibilities both at home and in the workplace often keep them from becoming writers or artists.

In the nonfiction work *Silences* (1965), the American feminist writer Tillie Olsen (b.1913) wonders what conditions are necessary for the creation of art. In her own life, Olsen often had to "let writing die over and over within her" because of her familial and professional responsibilities. In *Silences,* she considers the social positions of women writers in England and the United States during the last two centuries. Before you read the excerpt from *Silences,* take the following minisurvey. Circle whether you agree or disagree with each statement. Be prepared to explain your choices.

1. During the nineteenth century and the early twentieth century, most of the well-known women writers married during their lifetimes.

    Agree   Disagree

2. If married, these same women writers tended to have many children.

    Agree   Disagree

3. Whether or not they were married, women writers during the nineteenth and twentieth centuries had servants or some form of household help.

    Agree   Disagree

4. Women don't need to create art because they can give birth to babies.

    Agree   Disagree

5. When men and women don't create, it's only because they do not want to.

    Agree   Disagree

6. Young boys are generally raised to have more confidence in themselves than girls.

    Agree   Disagree

7. When you are raising four children, you can find time to write if you really want to make the time.

   Agree   Disagree

8. In family life, women are expected to care for the needs of others before their own needs.

   Agree   Disagree

Activity 5.5b ⇨

Read the following excerpt from Olsen's *Silences*. As you read think about how your responses to the survey compare to the responses that Tillie Olsen provides in the following excerpted passages from *Silences*. Also, think about how the following picture reflects the ideas found in the text.

Photograph courtesy of Rafael Kapelinski

Silence

From Silences

In the nineteenth century, of the women whose achievements endure for us in one way or another, nearly all never married (Jane Austen, Emily Brontë, Christina Rossetti, Emily Dickinson, Louisa May Alcott, Sarah Orne Jewett) or married late in their thirties (George Eliot, Elizabeth Barrett Browning, Charlotte Brontë, Olive Schreiner). I can think of only four (George Sand, Harriet Beecher Stowe, Helen Hunt Jackson, and Elizabeth Gaskell) who married and had children as young women. All had servants.

In our century [the twentieth century], until very recently, it has not been so different. Most did not marry (Selma Lagerlof, Willa Cather, Ellen Glasgow, Gertrude Stein, Gabriela Mistral, Elizabeth Madox Roberts, Charlotte Mew, Eudora Welty, Marianne Moore) or, if married, have been childless (Edith Wharton, Virginia Woolf, Katherine Mansfield, Dorothy Richardson, H. H. Richardson, Elizabeth Brown, Isak Dinesen, Katherine Anne Porter, Lillian Hellman, Dorothy Parker). Colette had one child (when she was forty). If I include Sigrid Undset, Kay Boyle, Pearl Buck, Dorothy Canfield Fisher, that will make a small group who had more than one child. All had household help or other special **circumstances**.

Am I resaying the **moldy theory** that women have no need, some say no capacity, to create art, because they can "create" babies? And the additional proof is precisely that the few women who have created it are nearly all childless? No.

The power and the need to create, over and beyond **reproduction**, is native in both women and men. Where the gifted among women (*and men*) have remained **mute**, or have never attained full capacity, it is because of circumstances, inner or outer, which oppose the needs of creation.

Wholly surrendered and dedicated lives; time as needed for the work; totality of self. But women are traditionally trained to place others' needs first, to feel these needs as their own (**the "infinite capacity"**); their **sphere**, their satisfaction to be making it possible for others to use their abilities. This is what Virginia Woolf meant when, already a writer of achievement, she wrote in her diary:

> Father's birthday. He would have been 96, 96, yes, today; and could have been 96, like other people one has known; but mercifully was not. His life would have entirely ended mine. What would have happened? No writing, no books;—inconceivable . . .

If I talk now quickly of my own silences—almost **presumptuous** after what has been told here—it is that the individual experience may add.

In the twenty years I bore and reared my children, I usually had to work on a paid job as well, the simplest circumstances for creation did not exist. Nevertheless writing, the hope of it, was "the air I breathe, as long as I shall breathe at all." In that hope, there was **conscious storing, snatched reading,** beginnings of writing, and always "the secret **rootlets of reconnaissance.**"

Bliss of movement. A full extended family life; the world of my job (**transcriber** in a dairy-equipment company); and the writing, which I was somehow able to carry around within me through work, through home. Time on the bus, even when I had to stand, was enough; the stolen moments at work, enough; the deep night hours for as long as I could stay awake, after the kids were in bed, after the household tasks were done, sometimes during. It is no accident that the first work I considered publishable began: "I stand here ironing, and what you asked me moves tormented back and forth with the iron."

In such snatches of time I wrote what I did in those years, but there came a time when this triple life was no longer possible. The fifteen hours of daily realities became too much distraction for the writing. I lost **craziness of endurance.** What might have been, I don't know; but I applied for, and was given, eight months' writing time. There was still full family life, all the household responsibilities, but I did not have to hold an eight-hour job. I had continuity, three full days, sometimes more—and it was in those months I made the mysterious turn and became a writing writer. . . .

. . . How much it takes to become a writer. Bent (far more common than we assume), circumstances, time, development of craft—but beyond that: how much **conviction** as to the importance of what one has to say, one's right to say it. And the will, the measureless store of belief in oneself to be able to come to, **cleave to,** find the form of one's own life's **comprehensions.** Difficult for any male not born into that class that **breeds** such confidence. Almost impossible for a girl, a woman.

The **leeching** of belief, of will, the damaging of capacity begin so early. **Sparse** indeed is the literature on the way of denial to small girl children of the development of their **endowment** as born human: active, **vigorous** bodies; exercise of the power to do, to make, to investigate, to invent, to conquer obstacles, to resist violations of the self; to think, create, choose; **to attain** community, confidence in self. Little has been written on the harms of **instilling** constant concern with appearance; the need to please, to support; the training in acceptance, **deference.**

conscious storing: purposefully remembering something for later use

snatched reading: reading for a moment here and there whenever one can for short periods of time

the rootlets of reconnaissance: the beginnings of making the effort to reach out to the world or to try to write

bliss of movement: the happiness of having the freedom to do something

transcriber: one who writes out something that has been dictated

craziness of endurance: the ability to survive in a difficult situation

conviction: a deeply held belief

to cleave to: to hold onto someone, to an idea, or to a belief

comprehensions: understanding

breeds: produces a certain kind of animal, plant, or feeling, e.g., to breed discontent

leeching: Slowly sucks something away. A leech is a freshwater worm that sucks the blood of mammals.

sparse: When something is sparse there is not much of it.

endowment: a natural ability

vigorous: energetic; powerful

attain: to reach a goal

instilling: putting an idea or feeling "into" someone

deference: the quality of being submissive; giving into others; following authority

From *Silences* by Tillie Olsen. © 1965, 1972, 1978 by Tillie Olsen. Used by permission of Delacorte Press/Seymour Lawrence, a division of Bantam Doubleday Dell Publishing Group, Inc., and Elaine Markson.

1. Based on this reading, how do you think Tillie Olsen would complete the survey in activity 5.5a? What evidence can you use from the reading to support the choices she would have made?
2. Why does Olsen include Woolf's quotation about her father's death? What is your reaction to what Woolf wrote about her father?
3. In her essay, Olsen writes, "Little has been written on the harms of instilling constant concern with appearance; the need to please, to support; the training in acceptance, deference." What do you think she means by this statement? How do the dolls in the photograph of a store window in Brugge, Belgium, reflect the "instilling of constant concern with appearance"?

Dolls in a shop window

Photograph courtesy of Rafael Kapelinski

4. Discuss how the photograph at the beginning of the excerpt reflects the ideas expressed in the text?
5. In *Silences,* Olsen refers to her first published work of fiction, a short story entitled "I Stand Here Ironing." Based on this title, who do you assume will narrate the story? What does your assumption suggest about the roles of men and women in society?
6. You may have noticed that Olsen uses incomplete sentences in her writing. For example,

   A. "Wholly surrendered and dedicated lives; time as needed for the work; totality of self."

B. "Bliss of movement."
C. "Almost impossible for a girl, a woman."

Why do you think she does this? What is the effect?

Activity 5.5c ⇨

The following excerpt is from the preface to *Incidents in the Life of a Slave Girl*, by Harriet Jacobs, who, as discussed in chapter 4, was a slave who escaped to the North and wrote of her experiences. In the preface to her diary, Jacobs writes:

> I wish I were more **competent** to the task I have undertaken. But I trust my readers will excuse **deficiencies** in consideration of circumstances. I was born and reared in Slavery; and I remained in a Slave State twenty-seven years. Since I have been at the North, it has been necessary for me to work diligently for my own support, and the education of my children. This has not left me much leisure to make up for the loss of early opportunities to improve myself, and it has compelled me to write these pages at irregular intervals, whenever I could snatch an hour of time.

competent: skilled
deficiencies: weaknesses; areas where someone is lacking in skill

From *Incidents in the Life of a Slave Girl* by Harriet Jacobs. Copyright © 1987 by the President and Fellows of Harvard College. Reprinted by permission of Harvard University Press.

1. How are Jacobs's difficulties as a writer similar to Olsen's? How do they differ?
2. In what way do Jacobs's experiences support Walker's views on the creativity of slaves?

Activity 5.6a ⇨

In "I Stand Here Ironing," the narrator's daughter has a gift for being a comedian. Name some female comedians with whom you are familiar. You may notice that such women only began to gain acceptance in the mid–nineteenth century. Why do you think this is the case? What difficulties might a woman comedian face in her career?

Activity 5.6b

Before reading the story "I Stand Here Ironing," study the following list of vocabulary terms found in the text. Look up any new words in a dictionary and/or discuss them with a partner. How do you think these words might be related to the experience of being a parent? What might the expectant mother in the photograph be thinking about? Be prepared to discuss your thoughts in class.

icebox	motherhood
social worker	child care
to comfort	chicken pox
affection	pockmarks
nursery school	to nurse (a baby)
convalescent home	measles
Christmas stockings	

Photograph courtesy of Rafael Kapelinski

Expectancy

Activity 5.6c ⇨

Read "I Stand Here Ironing" and answer the questions that follow each section. As you read, think about how Olsen has used the story to express her feminist ideas.

Part 1

I Stand Here Ironing

tormented: in great emotional pain

I stand here ironing and what you asked me moves **tormented** back and forth with the iron.

"I wish you would manage the time to come in and talk with me about your daughter. I'm sure you can help me understand her. She's a youngster who needs help and whom I'm deeply interested in helping."

"Who needs help." Even if I came, what good would it do? You think because I am her mother **I have a key**, or that in some way you could use me as a key? She has lived for nineteen years. There is all that life that has happened outside of me, beyond me.

And when is there time to remember, **to sift**, to weigh, **to estimate**, to total? I will start and there will be an interruption and I will have to gather it all together again. Or I will become **engulfed** with all I did or did not do, with what should have been and what cannot be helped.

She was a beautiful baby. The first and only one of our five that was beautiful at birth. You do not guess how new and uneasy her **tenancy** in her now-loveliness. You did not know her all those years she was thought homely, or see her **poring over** her baby pictures, making me tell her over and over how beautiful she had been—and would be, I would tell her—and was now, to **the seeing eye**. But the seeing eyes were few or nonexistent. Including mine.

I nursed her. They feel that's important nowadays. I nursed all the children, but with her, with all the fierce **rigidity** of first motherhood, I did like the books then said. Though her cries battered me to trembling and my breast ached with swollenness, I waited till the clock **decreed**.

Why do I put that first? I do not even know if it matters, or if it explains anything.

She was a beautiful baby. She blew shining bubbles of sound. She loved motion, loved light, loved color and music and textures. She would lie on the floor in her blue overalls patting the surface so hard in ecstasy her hands and feet would blur. She was a miracle to me, but when she was eight months old I had to leave her daytimes with the woman downstairs to whom she was no miracle at all, for I worked or looked for work and for Emily's father, who "could no longer **endure**" (he wrote in his good-bye note) "sharing want with us."

I was nineteen. It was the **pre-relief, pre-WPA** world of the **depression**. I would start running as soon as I got off the streetcar, running up the stairs, the place smelling sour, and awake or asleep to startle awake, when she saw me she would break into a clogged weeping that could not be comforted, a weeping I can hear yet.

After a while I found a job **hashing** at night so I could be with her days, and it was better. But it came to where I had to bring her to his family and leave her.

I have a key: I have the answer to something or have what is needed to do something.

to sift: to go through something carefully

to estimate: to determine the value of something

engulfed: overwhelmed

tenancy: the act of inhabiting or living in something; a *tenant* is a person who lives in a building

poring over something: looking over something carefully

the seeing eye: the ability to see beyond physical appearances

rigidity: stiffness; tenseness

decreed: said something should be done; mothers were told not to feed their babes in between the specified feeding times, even if they cried for food

endure: to manage to deal with a situation even when it is difficult to do so

pre-relief: the time before the government provided aid to those in need of financial help

pre-WPA: The Works Progress Administration was a federal program that helped nine million jobless people from 1935 to 1943. "Pre-WPA" refers to the time before this program was begun.

depression: the U.S. Great Depression of the 1929 to approximately 1939, characterized by business failures and high unemployment

hashing: chopping something into small pieces; in this sense, hashing means waiting tables

1. With whom is the narrator talking? Why?
2. When the narrator sums up her daughter's life, she first talks about breast-feeding her as a baby and keeping her to a tight schedule. Then she asks, "Why did I put that first?" How might you answer her question?

3. Based on this introduction, in what ways is the narrator's situation similar to that of Walker's mother? How does it differ?
4. Why isn't Emily a "miracle" for the woman who takes care of her? What does the narrator do so that she can stay with her daughter? In the end, why does she have to send her daughter to live with family?
5. In this first excerpt, where do you find ideas similar to those Olsen later expressed in *Silences*?

Part 2

fare: the money one needs to use a means of transportation

shoddy: not well made; something that is cheaply made

pockmarks: scars left on the face from sores

fatigue: extreme tiredness

laceration: a deep cut which may be physical or emotional

curdled: gone bad; i.e., curdled milk is rotten milk

rasp: a rough sound like scratching; a dry sound

scaredy: a slang expression that children use when they want to tease someone for being afraid of something

to clutch: to hold onto something tightly

to implore: to beg someone to do something

rebellion: going against what is accepted

denunciations: accusations that someone has done something wrong

tightness: tenseness

somber: serious in a sad way

fluid: flexible; coming easily to someone

pantomimes: the acting out of something without words

rouses: awakens a feeling in someone

It took a long time to raise the money for her **fare** back. Then she got chicken pox and I had to wait longer. When she finally came, I hardly knew her, walking quick and nervous like her father, looking like her father, thin, and dressed in a **shoddy** red that yellowed her skin and glared at the **pockmarks.** All the baby loveliness gone.

She was two. Old enough for nursery school they said, and I did not know what I know now—the **fatigue** of the long day, and the **laceration** of group life in the kinds of nurseries that are only parking places for children.

And even without knowing, I knew. I knew the teacher that was evil because all these years it has **curdled** into my memory, the little boy hunched in the corner, her **rasp,** "why aren't you outside, because Alvin hits you? That's no reason, go out, **scaredy.**" I knew Emily hated it even if she did not **clutch** and **implore** "don't go Mommy" like the other children, mornings.

She always had a reason why we should stay home. Momma, you look sick. Momma, I feel sick. Momma, the teachers aren't there today, they're sick. Momma, we can't go, there was a fire there last night. Momma, it's a holiday today, no school, they told me.

But never a direct protest, never **rebellion.** I think of our others in their three-, four-year-oldness—the explosions, the tempers, the **denunciations,** the demands—and I feel suddenly ill. I put the iron down. What in me demanded that goodness in her? And what was the cost, the cost to her of such goodness?

The old man living in the back once said in his gentle way: "You should smile at Emily more when you look at her." What *was* in my face when I looked at her? I love her. They were all the acts of love.

It was only with the others I remembered what he said, and it was the face of joy, and not of care or **tightness** or worry I turned to them—too late for Emily. She does not smile easily, let alone almost always as her brothers and sisters do. Her face is closed and **somber,** but when she wants, how **fluid.** You must have seen it in her **pantomimes,** you spoke of her rare gift for comedy on the stage that **rouses** laughter out of the audience so dear they applaud and applaud and do not want to let her go.

Where does it come from, that comedy? There was none of it in her when she came back to me that second time, after I had to send her away again. She had a new daddy now to learn to love, and I think perhaps it was a better time.

Except when we left her alone nights, telling ourselves she was old enough.

"Can't you go some other time, Mommy, like tomorrow?" she would ask. "Will it be just a little while you'll be gone? Do you promise?"

The time we came back, the front door open, the clock on the floor in the hall. She rigid awake. "It wasn't just a little while. I didn't cry. Three times I called you, just three times, and then I ran downstairs to open the door so you could come faster. The clock talked loud. I threw it away, it scared me what it talked."

6. Why do you think the narrator asks, "And what was the cost, the cost to [Emily] of such goodness?"
7. The narrator says that she showed the face of joy and not of care or tightness or worry, to her other children. Why do you think the mother was more relaxed with her other children than she was with Emily?

Part 3

She said the clock talked loud again that night I went to the hospital to have Susan. She was **delirious** with the fever that comes from red measles, but she was fully conscious all the week I was gone and the week after we were home when she could not come near the new baby or me.

delirious: a feeling of mental confusion caused by a high fever

She did not get well. She stayed skeleton thin, not wanting to eat; and night after night she had nightmares. She would call for me, and I would rouse from exhaustion to sleepily call back: "you're all right, darling, go to sleep, it's just a dream," and if she still called, in a sterner voice, "now go to sleep, Emily, there's nothing to hurt you." Twice, only twice, when I had to get up for Susan anyhow, I went in to sit with her.

Now when it is too late (as if she would let me hold and comfort her like I do the others) I get up and go to her at once at her moan or restless **stirring**. "Are you awake, Emily? Can I get you something?" And the answer is always the same: "No, I'm all right, go back to sleep, Mother."

stirring: moving slightly, like someone just beginning to wake up

They persuaded me at the clinic to send her away to a **convalescent** home in the country where "she can have the kind of food and care you can't manage for her, and you'll be free to concentrate on the new baby." They still send children to that place. I see pictures on the society page of **sleek** young women planning affairs to raise money

convalescent: recovering from a severe illness; a convalescent home is where one can stay while recovering

sleek: slim and stylish

for it, or dancing at the affairs, or decorating Easter eggs or filling Christmas stockings for the children.

They never have a picture of the children so I do not know if the girls still wear those gigantic red bows and the ravaged looks on the every other Sunday when parents can come to visit "unless otherwise **notified**"—as we were notified the first six weeks.

Oh it is a handsome place, green lawns and tall trees and **fluted** flower beds. High up on the balconies of each cottage the children stand, the girls in their red bows and white dresses, the boys in white suits and giant red ties. The parents stand below shrieking up to be heard and the children shriek down to be heard, and between them the invisible wall: "Not to Be **Contaminated** by Parental **Germs** or **Physical Affection**."

There was a tiny girl who always stood hand in hand with Emily. Her parents never came. One visit she was gone. "They moved her to Rose Cottage," Emily shouted in explanation. "They don't like you to love anybody here."

She wrote once a week, the labored writing of a seven-year-old. "I am fine. How is the baby. If I write my letter nicely I will have a star. Love." There never was a star. We wrote every other day, letters she could never hold or keep but only hear read—once. "We simply do not have room for children to keep any personal possessions," they patiently explained when we pieced one Sunday's shrieking together **to plead** how much it would mean to Emily, who loved so to keep things, to be allowed to keep letters and cards.

Each visit she looked **frailer**. "She isn't eating," they told us.

(They had runny eggs for breakfast or **mush with lumps,** Emily said later, I'd hold it in my mouth and not swallow. Nothing ever tasted good, just when they had chicken.)

It took us eight months to get her released home, and only the fact that she gained back so little of her seven lost pounds convinced the social worker.

I used to try to hold and love her after she came back, but her body would stay stiff, and after a while she'd push away. She ate little. Food sickened her, and I think much of life too. Oh she had physical lightness and brightness, twinkling by on skates, bouncing like a ball up and down up and down over the jump rope, skimming over the hill; but these were momentary.

8. Where was Emily sent to and why? What was the place like?
9. The narrator says that Emily's letter never had a star. What does she mean by that? Why do you think she includes this detail?

---

notified: informed or told about something

fluted: hollowed like the grooves in a classical style column

contaminated: no longer safe to eat, to drink, or to use because it can make a person sick

germs: Microscopic organisms that cause illnesses. The idea here is that parents were considered germs.

physical affection: physical signs that a person cares for someone else such as holding hands and hugging

to plead: to beg someone to do something

frailer: weaker; thinner

mush with lumps: Mush is a milky, soft cereal. *With lumps* means that the texture of the cereal was spoiled by lumps that weren't supposed to be there.

Part 4

She **fretted** about her appearance, thin and dark and foreign-looking at a time when every little girl was supposed to look or thought she should look a chubby blond **replica of Shirley Temple.** The doorbell sometimes rang for her, but no one seemed to come and play in the house or be a best friend. Maybe because we moved so much.

There was a boy she loved painfully through two school semesters. Months later she told me how she had taken pennies from my purse to buy him candy. "**Licorice** was his favorite and I brought him some every day, but he still liked Jennifer **better'n** me. Why, Mommy?" The kind of question for which there is no answer.

School was a worry to her. She was not **glib** or quick in a world where glibness and quickness were easily confused with ability to learn. To her overworked and exasperated teachers she was an **overconscientious** "slow learner" who keeps trying to catch up and was absent entirely too often.

I let her be absent, though sometimes the illness was imaginary. How different from my now-strictness about attendance with the others. I wasn't working. We had a new baby, I was home anyhow. Sometimes, after Susan grew enough, I would keep her home from school, too, to have them all together.

Mostly Emily had **asthma,** and her breathing, harsh and labored, would fill the house with a curiously **tranquil** sound. I would bring the two old dresser mirrors and boxes of collections to her bed. She would select beads and single earrings, bottle tops and shells, dried flowers and pebbles, old postcards, and scraps, all sorts of **oddments**; then she and Susan would play Kingdom, setting up landscapes and furniture, peopling them with action.

Those were the only times of peaceful companionship between her and Susan. I have edged away from it, that poisonous feeling between them, that terrible balancing of hurts and needs I had to do between the two, and did so badly, those earlier years.

Oh, there are conflicts between the others too, each one human, needing demanding, hurting, taking—but only between Emily and Susan, no, Emily toward Susan that **corroding** resentment. It seems so obvious on the surface, yet it is not obvious. Susan, the second child, Susan, golden-and-curly-hairdo and chubby, quick and articulate and assured, everything in appearance and manner Emily was not; Susan, not able to resist Emily's precious things, losing or sometimes clumsily breaking them; Susan telling jokes and riddles to company for applause while Emily sat silent (to say to me later: that was my riddle, Mother, I told it to Susan); Susan, who for all the five years' difference in age was just a year behind Emily in developing physically.

---

fretted: worried

replica of Shirley Temple: a copy of the famous child film star, Shirley Temple, who had thick curls and dimples

licorice: a type of candy
better'n: better than
glib: able to speak quickly and uncaringly

overconscientious: too careful and thoughtful

asthma: a respiratory illness in which a person has trouble breathing
tranquil: peaceful
oddments: a collection of small and varied objects

corroding: wearing; destroying by slow means

vulnerable: easily hurt or wounded

preening: dressing up and making oneself look nice

I am glad for that slow physical development that widened the difference between her and her contemporaries, though she suffered over it. She was too **vulnerable** for that terrible world of youthful competition, of **preening** and parading, of constant measuring of yourself against every other, of envy, "If I had that copper hair," "If I had that skin. . . ." She tormented herself enough about not looking like the others, there was enough of the unsureness, the having to be conscious of words before you speak, the constant caring—what are they thinking of me? Without having it all magnified by the merciless physical drives.

puberty: the "teen" years, from 11–15

10. In this section, Emily enters **puberty**. What concerns her most at this stage of her life?
11. List the contrasts between Emily and Susan.
12. Why are the differences between Emily and Susan so significant?
13. Although Emily's mother wants her to be happy and loves her very much, she says that she cannot protect her from everything. Why not?

Part 5

to be racked: to be stretched violently as though on a torture rack

seal: the characteristic mark or sign of someone

coherent: understandable; forming a logical whole

hysteria: the state of being emotionally out of control

stammering: speaking with stops and starts

Ronnie is calling. He is wet and I change him. It is rare there is such a cry now. That time of motherhood is almost behind me when the ear is not one's own but must always be **racked** and listening for the child cry, the child call. We sit for a while and I hold him, looking out over the city spread in charcoal with its soft aisles of light. "*Shoogily,*" he breathes and curls closer. I carry him back to bed, asleep. *Shoogily.* A funny word, a family word, inherited from Emily, invented by her to say: *comfort.*

In this and other ways she leaves her **seal,** I say aloud. And startle at my saying it. What do I mean? What did I start to gather together, to try and make **coherent**? I was at the terrible, growing years. War years. I do not remember them well. I was working, there were four smaller ones now, there was not time for her. She had to help be a mother, and housekeeper, and shopper. She had to set her seal. Mornings of crisis and near **hysteria** trying to get lunches packed, hair combed, coats and shoes found, everyone to school or Child Care on time, the baby ready for transportation. And always the paper scribbled on by a smaller one, the book looked at by Susan and then mislaid, the homework not done. Running out to that huge school where she was one, she was lost, she was a drop; suffering over the unpreparedness, **stammering** and unsure in her classes.

There was so little time left at night after the kids were bedded down. She would struggle over books, always eating (it was in those years she developed her enormous appetite that is legendary in our family) and I would be ironing, or preparing food for the next day, or writing **V-mail** to Bill, or tending the baby. Sometimes, to make me laugh, or out of her despair, she would imitate **happenings** or **types** at school.

I think I said once: "Why don't you do something like this in the school **amateur show**?" One morning she phoned me at work, hardly understandable through the weeping: "Mother, I did it. I won, I won; they gave me first prize; they clapped and clapped and wouldn't let me go."

> **V-mail:** mail sent using a special photographic process to soldiers fighting during World War II
>
> **happenings:** events
>
> **types:** the different people at school
>
> **amateur show:** a talent show for people who are not professional entertainers

Part 6

14. What family circumstances keep Emily's mother from spending time with her?
15. Emily's mother says that Emily would perform for her to make her laugh or because of Emily's own despair. Why was Emily in despair?
16. How is Emily's comic gift finally realized?

Part 7

Now suddenly she was Somebody, and as **imprisoned** in her difference as she had been in anonymity.

She began to be asked to perform at other high schools, even in colleges, then at city and statewide affairs. The first one we went to, I only recognized her that first moment when thin, shy, she almost drowned herself into the curtains. Then: Was this Emily? The control, the command, the convulsing and deadly clowning, the spell, then the roaring, stamping audience, unwilling to let this rare and precious laughter out of their lives.

Afterwards: You ought to do something about her with a gift like that—but without money or knowing how, what does one do? We have left it all to her, and the gift has as often **eddied** inside, **clogged** and **clotted**, as been used and growing.

She is coming. She runs up the stairs two at a time with her light graceful step, and I know she is happy tonight. Whatever it was that occasioned your call did not happen today.

"Aren't you ever going to finish the ironing, Mother? **Whistler** painted his mother in a rocker. I'd have to paint mine standing over an ironing board." This is one of her communicative nights and she tells me everything and nothing as she fixes herself a plate of food out of the icebox.

She is so lovely. Why did you want me to come in at all? Why were you concerned? She will find her way.

She starts up the stairs to bed. "Don't get me up with the rest in the morning." "But I thought you were having midterms." "Oh,

> **imprisoned:** trapped
>
> **eddied:** moved like water that runs against the main current
>
> **clogged:** filled with matter so that water can not flow freely
>
> **clotted:** formed into lumps
>
> **Whistler:** An American painter, James Whistler (1834–1903). Olsen alludes to Whistler's famous painting of his mother, *Arrangement in Grey and Black No. 1: Portrait of the Artist's Mother.*

> those," she comes back in, kisses me, and says quite lightly, "in a couple of years when we'll all be atom-dead they won't matter a bit."
>
> She has said it before, She *believes* it. But because I have been **dredging** the past, and all that **compounds** a human being is so heavy and meaningful in me, I cannot endure it tonight.
>
> I will never total it all. I will never come in to say: She was a child seldom smiled at. Her father left me before she was a year old. I had to work her first six years when there was work, or I sent her home and to his relatives. There were years she had care she hated. She was dark and thin and foreign-looking in a world where the prestige went to blondeness and curly hair and dimples, she was slow where glibness was prized. She was a child of **anxious**, not proud, love. We were poor and could not afford for her the soil of easy growth. I was a young mother, I was a **distracted** mother. There were other children pushing up demanding. Her younger sister seemed all that she was not. There were years she did not want me to touch her. She kept too much in herself, her life was such she had to keep too much in herself. My wisdom came too late. She has much to her and probably little will come of it. She is a child of her age, of depression, of war, of fear.
>
> Let her be. So all that is in her will not bloom—but in how many does it? There is still enough left to live by. Only help her to know—help make it so there is cause for her to know—that she is more than this dress on the ironing board, helpless before the iron.

© 1956, 1957, 1960, 1961. From *Tell me a Riddle* by Tillie Olsen. Introduction by John Leonard. Used by permission of Delacorte Press/Seymour Lawrence, a division of Bantam Doubleday Dell Publishing Group, Inc., and Elaine Markson.

dredging: to bring up something from the bottom of a body of water; the narrator is dredging up her memories

compounds: makes up (in this instance, makes up a person)

anxious: nervous; worried

distracted: unable to pay attention or to concentrate on something or someone

17. Emily's mother says that Emily is now "as imprisoned in her difference as she had been in anonymity." What do you think she means by this?
18. At the very end of the story, the mother asks that the listener help her daughter to realize her talents. How would you help Emily develop her talents given the circumstances of her family life?

Activity 5.6d

Dr. Mary Pipher, a psychologist and author of the book *Reviving **Ophelia**: Saving the Selves of Adolescent Girls* (Putnam Publishers, 1994), focuses on the problems facing teenage girls. She helps them to realize their **authentic** selves through psychological analysis. How do you imagine Emily would answer the following questions that Pipher often asks her patients?

Ophelia: a female character in Shakespeare's play *Hamlet* who kills herself when Hamlet appears to have rejected her love

authentic: real; true

a. "How would I describe myself to myself?"
b. "What are my strengths and weaknesses?"

c. "What goals do I have for myself as a person?"
   d. "What would I be proud of on my **deathbed**?"

> deathbed: the bed on which one lies when about to die

1. No matter what your age or sex, imagine how you might have answered the questions found in items a–d when you were in your early teens? How would you answer the questions now? If the answers differ, why is this so? If they are similar, why do you think this is the case?
2. Why do you think it's important for both adolescent boys and girls to answer the questions found in items a–d?
3. In her book, Pipher quotes the French writer Marie-Henri Beyle, "Stendhal" (1783–1842), who said, "All geniuses born women are lost to the public good." What would have caused Stendhal to make such a statement? Do you think this statement is still true today? Why or why not?
4. How does the picture at the beginning of this chapter relate to "I Stand Here Ironing"?

Activity 5.7

Walker, Woolf, and Olsen all try to answer a similar question: In what circumstances can a person, particularly a woman, be creative? Write your own answer using information from this chapter to help you. Discuss the importance of feminist criticism in answering such a question. Your instructor may ask you to write a short paragraph or a more developed essay on this topic.

Activity 5.8

Walker **aligns** the image of a handmade quilt with the feminist movement. However, quilts have taken on symbolic importance in other movements as well. In the fight against **AIDS**, people have been making a quilt in memory of those who have died of AIDS. The Quilt, as it is referred to, began as one panel in 1987 and has grown to over forty-two thousand panels in memory of those who have suffered and died from AIDS. As of 2000, if The Quilt were laid end to end, it would be nearly fifty miles (80.6 kilometers) long. The names of over eighty-thousand people, representing 21 percent of all AIDS victims in the United States, have been stitched onto The Quilt. For this reason, the project is also called the NAMES Project.

> aligns: associates one thing with another
>
> AIDS: acquired immune deficiency syndrome, a disease in which a person's immune system breaks down and no longer protects him or her from germs

One of the names on The Quilt is that of Jessica Hazard. As an infant, Jessica contracted AIDS from a blood transfusion that was contaminated with the AIDS virus. People who did not know her made a panel in her memory. The panel has been made to look like a child's bed that is covered with toys—a stuffed rabbit, a teddy bear, and a panda. The words *Baby Jessica* have been stitched onto the panel. People have used love letters, leather, pearls, car keys, and cowboy boots when making panels in memory of those who have died. If possible, look up the NAMES project on the Internet to see some sample quilt panels (http://www.aidsquilt.org).

If you were to make a quilt that represented your own life, what symbols, images, and/or patterns would you include as symbols of your life? What kind of fabrics would you use? You can draw or write out your ideas.

Chapter 6

"A Clean, Well-Lighted Place," by Ernest Hemingway

Photograph courtesy of Marco Fenaroli

"You have youth, confidence, and a job," the older waiter said. "You have everything."—Ernest Hemingway, "A Clean, Well-Lighted Place"

Activity 6.1

Since the development of literature is closely tied to philosophy, literary critics may also be interested in analyzing how a given literary work reflects a philosophical movement in history. Such critics consider not only the historical **milieu** that influenced the creation of a text but also the philosophical **trends** that are reflected in it. In this chapter, you will consider how ideas related to the philosophical movement called *existentialism* are brought to life in the story "A Clean, Well-Lighted Place," written, in 1933 by the American writer Ernest Hemingway (1899–1961). As the name *existentialism* suggests, existentialists are concerned with the question of existence: How should one live in a world that can not be explained?

In preparation for an introduction to existentialism, write a brief response to the following question. Discuss your responses in groups and/or as a class.

milieu: a given time and its characteristics

trends: developments in society that are long lasting, e.g., jeans, computers

1. How would you feel and what would you do if you knew that you were going to die tonight at midnight?

For a summary of the precepts related to existentialism, read the following scenario that describes how an existentialist might have responded to the question, "How would you feel and what would you do if you knew that you were going to die at midnight?"

acutely: strongly

alienated: separated

> If I knew that I were going to die, my first reaction would likely be "No." I would probably respond more powerfully to my emotions than to my reasoning powers, and I would feel the pressure of my existence **acutely**. At this point, it would be important to ask myself, "Who am I?" and to decide what actions would be the most important for me to take in the short amount of time I had left to live. If I were to walk down a street full of people who were unaware of their death, I would feel **alienated** from them, unable to explain my feelings. Finally, in spite of death's absurdity and its irrational approach, I could assert my freedom to live my last few hours of life as I chose to do in a meaningful and morally responsible way.

© 2000 University of Michigan.

Activity 6.2

In the Mahabharata, a holy book of the Hindu tradition, a prince named Yudhisthira is asked the question, "Of all the world's wonders, which is the most wonderful?" (Yudhisthira is asked this question by the Dharma, the personification of virtue and duty, who appears to him in the form of a crane.) He answers, "That no man believes that he himself will die, though he sees others dying around him." What do you think about Yudhisthira's answer?

Like Yudhisthira, an existentialist is aware of death and is interested in answering the question, "How should the individual live in the face of death?" How would you answer this question?

Activity 6.3

Albert Camus (1913–60), a French writer and philosopher, lived through World War II, an experience that caused him to ask, "Since life has lost all meaning, why shouldn't a person commit suicide?" In his writings and life, he explored the philosophical **implications** of such a question. Although he did not label himself an existentialist, he has been aligned with existential philosophy. Before you read the excerpt, answer the following question.

implications: the logical conclusions that can be made about something

1. How would you feel if you were **condemned** to roll a heavy stone up a steep hill, and then, once it was at the top of the hill, the stone would roll down again? This process would be repeated endlessly, and there would be no way to escape your fate.

condemned: made to do something as punishment

In this excerpt, Camus answers a similar question by analyzing the life of Sisyphus, a mythical Greek man who was accused of showing disrespect to the gods. Sisyphus stole their secrets, and he bound the god of death in chains. As long as death was bound in chains, no one died.

To punish Sisyphus for his **defiance**, the gods condemned him to **ceaselessly** roll a large rock up a steep hill only to have it roll down again. Camus examines Sisyphus's feelings and describes him as a kind of existential or absurd hero. He is called an *absurd hero* because he acts heroically even though he has been placed in a strange and seemingly meaningless situation. As you read the excerpt, underline the portions of the writing that reflect the **tenets** of existentialism.

defiance: the act of challenging or disobeying something or someone

ceaselessly: without end

tenets: beliefs; the main principles of something

From The Myth of Sisyphus

You have already grasped that Sisyphus is the absurd hero. . . . His **scorn** of the gods, his hatred of death, and his passion for life won him that unspeakable penalty in which the whole being is exerted toward accomplishing nothing. This is the price that must be paid for the passions of this earth. . . . As for this myth, one sees merely the whole effort of a body straining to raise the huge stone, to roll it and push it up a slope a hundred times over; one sees the face screwed up, the cheek tight against the stone, the shoulder **bracing** the clay-covered mass, the foot **wedging** it, the fresh start with arms out-

scorn: the act of showing that one has a low opinion of someone or something

bracing: set strongly against something

wedging: forcing something into a narrow space

earth-clotted: filled with dirt

stretched, the wholly human security of two **earth-clotted** hands. At the very end of this long effort.... the purpose is achieved. Then Sisyphus watches the stone rush down in a few moments toward that lower world whence he will have to push it up again toward the summit. He goes back down to the plain.

It is during that return, that pause, that Sisyphus interests me. A face that **toils** so close to stones is already stone itself! I see that man going back down with a heavy yet **measured** step toward the torment of which he will never know the end.... The rock is still rolling.

toils: works hard
measured: carefully thought out

fidelity: faithfulness

I leave Sisyphus at the foot of the mountain! One always finds one's burden again. But Sisyphus teaches the higher **fidelity** that negates the gods and raises rocks. He too concludes that all is well. This universe henceforth without a master seems to him neither sterile nor **futile**. Each atom of that stone, each mineral flake of that night-filled mountain, in itself forms a world. The struggle itself toward the heights is enough to fill a man's heart. One must imagine Sisyphus happy.

futile: without hope or purpose

The Myth of Sisyphus and Other Essays, by Albert Camus, translated by Justin O'Brien. Random House, 1955.

Photograph courtesy of Marco Fenaroli

"One always finds one's burden again."—Albert Camus, *The Myth of Sisyphus*

2. What characterizes Sisyphus as an "absurd hero"?
3. Why do you think Camus writes that Sisyphus must be happy?
4. How might Sisyphus respond to Camus's question: "Since life had lost all meaning, why shouldn't a person commit suicide?"
5. At the end of the myth, Camus writes "One always finds one's burden again." What could the stone represent in everyday life? How could you apply this statement to your own life experiences?
6. If possible, access an online bookstore to find a review of *The Myth of Sisyphus*. Share the review in class.

Activity 6.4

Just as Sisyphus must attempt to find meaning in a seemingly meaningless activity, the protagonist of Hemingway's "A Clean, Well-Lighted Place" must deal with feelings of nothingness and despair. However, unlike Sisyphus, Hemingway's protagonist is not described as being "happy." In "A Clean, Well-Lighted Place," Hemingway shows that an existential awareness of life's purposelessness and absurdity can be **accentuated** by loneliness and aging. He illustrates this idea by contrasting the loneliness of two old men's lives with the hopefulness characterized by a young waiter.

accentuated: emphasized; brought out

The story is set in a Spanish-speaking country and begins in a café where two waiters are waiting for an old man to finish drinking so that they can close up the café and go home. Throughout the story, the two waiters remain unnamed: one is simply called the older waiter and the other the younger waiter. Before you read the story, respond to the following two questions.

A. If you were working late at a café and waiting for one customer to finish drinking so that you could go home, what might you be thinking about that customer? What might you say to him or her?
B. If you were living alone, what kinds of things might you do to avoid being home alone? Where would you go? Why?

As you read "A Clean, Well-Lighted Place," imagine that you are a formalist critic and think about how Hemingway has used narrative techniques and the plot structure to communicate existential themes. The story has been divided into sections followed by questions and/or short activities.

Part 1

A Clean, Well-Lighted Place

It was late and every one had left the café except an old man who sat in the shadow the leaves of the tree made against the electric light. In the daytime the street was dusty, but at night the dew settled the dust and the old man liked to sit late because he was deaf and now at night it was quiet and he felt the difference. The two waiters inside the café knew that the old man was a little drunk, and while he was a good client they knew that if he became too drunk he would leave without paying, so they kept watch on him.

"Last week he tried to commit suicide," one waiter said.

"Why?"

"He was in despair."

"What about?"

"Nothing."

"How do you know it was nothing?"

"He has plenty of money."

They sat together at a table that was close against the wall near the door of the café and looked at the terrace where the tables were all empty except where the old man sat in the shadow of the leaves of the tree that moved slightly in the wind. A girl and a soldier went by in the street. The street light shone on the brass number on his collar. The girl wore no head covering and hurried beside him.

"The guard will pick him up," one waiter said.

"What does it matter if he gets what he's after?"

"He had better get off the street now. The guard will get him. They went by five minutes ago."

1. In the story's introduction, Hemingway does not mention that one of the waiters is old and that one is young. Look back at the dialogue between the two waiters and identify which waiter is saying a given line. (Mark a line O for the older waiter or Y for the younger one.) If possible, work in groups of three. After you have agreed on which waiter is saying a particular line, read the introduction aloud with one person taking on the role of the narrator, one person the role of the older waiter, and another the role of the younger waiter.
2. One of the waiters says that the old man tried to kill himself for "nothing" because he had plenty of money. How do you interpret this statement? Do you agree with the waiter's reasoning?
3. The narrator says of the old man that "at night it was quiet and he felt the difference." What do you think is meant by the word *difference*?

Part 2

The old man sitting in the shadow rapped on his saucer with his glass. The younger waiter went over to him.

"What do you want?"

The old man looked at him. "Another brandy," he said.

"You'll be drunk," the waiter said. The old man looked at him. The waiter went away.

"He'll stay all night," he said to his colleague. "I'm sleepy now. I never get into bed before three o'clock. He should have killed himself last week."

The waiter took the brandy bottle and another saucer from the counter inside the café and marched out to the old man's table. He put down the saucer and poured the glass full of brandy.

"You should have killed yourself last week," he said to the deaf man. The old man motioned with his finger. "A little more," he said. The waiter poured on into the glass so that the brandy slopped over and ran down the stem to the top saucer of the pile. "Thank you," the old man said. The waiter took the bottle back inside the café. He sat down at the table with his colleague again.

"He's drunk now," he said.

"He's drunk every night."

"What did he want to kill himself for?"

"How should I know?"

"How did he do it?"

"He hung himself with a rope."

"Who cut him down?"

"His niece."

"Why did they do it?"

"Fear for his soul."

"How much money has he got?"

"He's got plenty."

"He must be eighty years old."

"Anyway I should say he was eighty."

"I wish he would go home. I never get to bed before three o'clock. What kind of hour is that to go to bed?"

"He stays up because he likes it."

"He's lonely. I'm not lonely. I have a wife waiting in bed for me."

"He had a wife once too."

"A wife would be no good to him now."

"You can't tell. He might be better with a wife."

"His niece looks after him."

"I know. You said she cut him down."

"I wouldn't want to be that old. An old man is a nasty thing."

"Not always. This old man is clean. He drinks without spilling. Even now, drunk. Look at him."

"I don't want to look at him. I wish he would go home. He has no regard for those who must work."

4. How would you describe the young waiter's attitude toward the old man who is drinking in the café? Why does he feel this way about the old man?
5. What is the older waiter's attitude toward the old man? How does it differ from the younger waiter's point of view?
6. Review this section of the story and make a note of which waiter is speaking. Then, as in part 1, read part 2 aloud in groups of three. You may need to make changes in your original response to question 1.

Part 3

The old man looked from his glass across the square, then over at the waiters.

"Another brandy," he said, pointing to his glass. The waiter who was in a hurry came over.

"Finished," he said, speaking with that omission of syntax stupid people employ when talking to drunken people or foreigners. "No more tonight. Close now."

"Another," said the old man.

"No. Finished." The waiter wiped the edge of the table with a towel and shook his head.

The old man stood up, slowly counted the saucers, took a leather coin purse from his pocket and paid for the drinks, leaving half a **peseta** tip. The waiter watched him go down the street, a very old man walking unsteadily but with dignity.

"Why didn't you let him stay and drink?" the unhurried waiter asked. They were putting up the shutters. "It is not half-past two."

"I want to go home to bed."

"What is an hour?"

"More to me than to him."

"An hour is the same."

"You talk like an old man yourself. He can buy a bottle and drink at home."

"It's not the same."

"No, it is not," agreed the waiter with a wife. He did not wish to be unjust. He was only in a hurry.

"And you? You have no fear of going home before your usual hour?"

"Are you trying to insult me?"

peseta: a Spanish coin

"No, **hombre**, only to make a joke."

"No," the waiter who was in a hurry said, rising from pulling down the metal shutters. "I have confidence. I am all confidence."

"You have youth, confidence, and a job," the older waiter said. "You have everything."

"And what do you lack?"

"Everything but work."

"You have everything I have."

"No. I have never had confidence and I am not young."

"Come on. Stop talking nonsense and lock up."

"I am of those who like to stay late at the café," the older waiter said. "With all those who do not want to go to bed. With all those who need a light for the night."

"I want to go home and into bed."

"We are of two different kinds," the older waiter said. He was now dressed to go home. "It is not only a question of youth and confidence although those things are very beautiful. Each night I am **reluctant** to close up because there may be some one who needs the café."

hombre: Spanish for *man*

reluctant: not wanting to do something; unwilling

7. Again, identify which waiter is saying what and read the section aloud in groups of three.
8. At the end of this section, the older waiter says to the younger waiter, "We are of two different kinds . . ." Complete the list below with the contrasts between the two waiters. The first one has been done for you.

Older Waiter	Younger Waiter
a. not in a hurry, reluctant	in a hurry
b. had never had confidence	_____
c. _____	says the old man can drink at home
d. _____	eager to close the café
e. _____	thinks the old man is a "nasty thing"

9. Why does the younger waiter think the older one is trying to insult him?
10. How does the younger waiter respond when the older one says he lacks confidence and is not young? Why?

Part 4

bodega: Spanish for *a place to drink wine*

"Hombre, there are **bodegas** open all night long."

"You do not understand. This is a clean and pleasant café. It is well lighted. The light is very good and also, now there are shadows of the leaves."

"Good night," the other said. Turning off the electric light he continued the conversation with himself. It is the light of course but it is necessary that the place be clean and pleasant. You do not want music. Certainly you do not want music. Nor can you stand before a bar with dignity although that is all that is provided for these hours. What did he fear? It was not fear or dread. It was a nothing that he knew too well. It was all a nothing and a man was nothing too. It was only that and light was all it needed and a certain cleanness and order. Some lived in it and never felt it but he knew it all was **nada y pues nada** y nada y pues nada. Our nada who art in nada, nada be thy name thy kingdom nada thy will be nada in nada as it is in nada. Give us this nada our daily nada and nada us our nada as we nada our nadas and nada us not into nada but deliver us from nada; pues nada. Hail nothing full of nothing, nothing is with thee. He smiled and stood before a bar with a shining steam pressure coffee machine.

nada y pues nada: Spanish for *nothing and then nothing*

"What's yours?" asked the barman.

"Nada."

"**Otro loco mas,**" said the barman and turned away.

otro loco mas: Spanish for *another crazy person*

"A little cup," said the waiter.

The barman poured it for him.

"The light is very bright and pleasant but the bar is unpolished," the waiter said.

The barman looked at him but did not answer. It was too late for conversation.

"You want another **copita**?" the barman asked.

copita: Spanish for *a small cup*

"No, thank you," said the waiter and went out. He disliked bars and bodegas. A clean, well-lighted café was a very different thing. Now, without thinking further, he would go home to his room. He would lie in the bed and finally, with daylight, he would go to sleep. After all, he said to himself, it is probably only insomnia. Many must have it.

Reprinted with permission of Scribner's, a Division of Simon & Schuster, from *Winner Take Nothing* by Ernest Hemingway. Copyright 1933 by Charles Scribner's Sons. Copyright renewed © 1961 by Mary Hemingway. Copyright © Hemingway Foreign Rights Trust.

Photograph courtesy of Rafael Kapelinski

"A clean, well-lighted café was a very different thing."—Ernest Hemingway, "A Clean, Well-Lighted Place"

11. In this section, the café is contrasted with the bodega. Briefly discuss how the café differs from the bodega based on the information you have in the story.
12. Why do you think it was so important for the old man and the older waiter to have "a clean, well-lighted place" in which to sit?
13. What does the waiter in the bodega think about the older waiter? What makes this situation ironic?
14. The older waiter says to himself that he has insomnia. Why is this ironic?
15. Based on the story's conclusion, what do you think the waiter means when he says that the old man had tried to kill himself for "nothing"?
16. In what ways is the older waiter in "A Clean, Well-Lighted Place" similar to Sisyphus?

Activity 6.5a ⇨

At the end of "A Clean, Well-Lighted Place," the narrator describes the old man's thoughts saying, "he knew it was all nada y pues nada y pues nada y pues nada." The lines that follow in the paragraph are based on the so-called Lord's Prayer, a prayer that Jesus taught his followers to pray to God. The original prayer is found in the New Testament Book of Matthew

6:9–13. When a literary work refers to an event, a place, or a character in another work of literature this is called an *allusion*. Thus, allusions taken from the Bible are referred to as biblical allusions. In this activity, Hemingway's allusion to the Lord's Prayer has been placed line by line beside the original version to highlight their similarities and differences. Read each prayer and then answer the questions that follow.

hallowed: thought of as holy; worthy of praise and worship

debts: what a person owes; sins

Hemingway's Allusion	**The Lord's Prayer**
Our nada who are in nada,	Our Father in heaven,
nada be thy name	**hallowed** be your name.
thy kingdom nada	Your kingdom come.
thy will be nada	Your will be done,
in nada as it is in nada.	on earth as it is in heaven.
Give us this nada	Give us this day
our daily nada	our daily bread.
and nada us our nada	And forgive us our **debts**,
as we nada our nadas	as we forgive our debtors.
and nada us not into nada	And do not lead us into the time of trial,
but deliver us from nada pues nada.	but rescue us from the evil one.

Why do you think Hemingway has chosen to allude to the Lord's Prayer? Why has he used the word *nada*?

Activity 6.5b ⇨

Take a moment to consider the worldview of a person who believes in the original prayer found in activity 6.5a and that of a person who prays Hemingway's version. For the purpose of discussion, let's say that the younger waiter would pray the Lord's Prayer while the older waiter prays the adaptation. Answer the following questions about their worldviews. Try to use terminology from existential philosophy in your response. As you answer the questions, you can use the lists below to help you respond to the first two questions.

1. What does each waiter believe about God? Why do you think this is so?

Younger Waiter

a. God is alive.

b. _____

c. God should be praised.

Older Waiter

<u>God is dead</u>

God isn't anywhere.

_____

d. God's kingdom is coming.   _____

   (There is a sense of purpose.)   _____

e. _____   God's will is not done on earth.

f. _____   No one provides for our needs.

g. God forgives.   _____

h. _____   There is no eternal life.

Other:

2. What does each waiter think about a person's relationship to other people? What causes them to feel this way?

Younger Waiter   *Older Waiter*

a. People should forgive.   _____

b. _____   There is no temptation, no sin.

c. People follow God's will.   God's will is not at work in people's lives.

d. People can communicate with God and with other people.   _____

Other: _____

_____

3. How would each waiter explain the meaning or purpose of daily life and life in general?
4. In which part of the story's plot structure does the prayer appear? Why is this significant?

Activity 6.6a

In "A Clean, Well-Lighted Place," Hemingway uses **universalizing** techniques to make his story appeal to a wider audience. For example, the narrator does not provide many details about the setting. Although we know the story is set in a Spanish-speaking country, we do not know the name of the town or the city. Because of this, in our imaginations, the story can take place in any town we might associate with the story.

When you make your own associations, you personalize or **localize** the events in the story. Think of places that you associate with the feelings that the older waiter associates with the café and with the bodega. Write a paragraph in which you localize these places by giving them names and

universalizing: making something appeal to a wide audience

to localize: to focus on one location

describing in more detail what they are like and how they make you feel. For example, you may feel more comfortable in a café than a disco, or in a library than a gym, or the opposite. Perhaps you prefer a dimly lit place to a clean, well-lighted place. Perhaps you prefer a place outdoors to begin inside. In a paragraph or two, describe these places and the feelings you associate with them.

Activity 6.6b

Hemingway also uses universalizing techniques to identify the characters in "A Clean, Well-Lighted Place." For example, the characters are not named, nor are they described. Because of this, they can stand for "every person." Also, the reader is free to associate these characters with people he or she may have met. Write a brief description of how you imagine the two waiters. Give details about their physical characteristics.

Activity 6.7a ⇨

Although Hemingway uses only the comparatives *older* or *younger* to describe the physical characteristics of the waiters, they both seem lifelike because Hemingway successfully uses other characterization techniques to communicate each character's personality. An author can use characterization techniques such as the following to create a character.

1. The character says things about himself or herself that tell you about the character's personality.
2. Other characters in the story or the narrator say things about a character.
3. The characters do things that tell you about their personalities.

Look back at the list you completed in activity 6.4, question 8. What characterization techniques has Hemingway used to give you the information about the younger waiter found in a–e? The first one has been done for you.

a. In a hurry—the narrator says this

In a–e, Hemingway has used the dialogue between the two waiters as a method of characterization. What are some things the waiters do that suggest what their personalities are like? List three of the older waiter's actions and three of the younger waiter's actions. Then explain what these actions say about their characters. The actions of the old man who was drinking late in the café have been done as an example.

Action	Characterization
1. The old man tried to commit suicide.	1. He is in despair.
2. The old man drinks until late in the café.	2. He doesn't want to go home. He needs the café.

Activity 6.7b

Often, authors tell how a character does something to help the reader better understand that character's personality. For example, the narrator of "A Clean, Well-Lighted Place" says that the young waiter spoke to the old man "with that omission of syntax stupid people employ when talking to drunken people or foreigners." Since Hemingway rarely describes how a character does something, why do you think he includes this detail? Have you ever spoken in a similar manner to someone else, and/or has someone spoken in a similar manner to you? If so, describe the situation.

Activity 6.7c ⇨

When reading "A Clean, Well-Lighted Place," you may have noticed that Hemingway rarely describes how someone says or does something. For example, he does not use adverbs such as *angrily, impatiently,* or *hurriedly* to describe how the old waiter and the young waiter speak aloud. Review the portion of the dialogue in part 2 that begins with "He's drunk now." Rewrite this portion of the story from this line until the lines "I don't want to look at him. I wish he would go home. He has no regard for those who must work." Add adverbs or adverbial phrases to describe how you imagine each line should be said. The first two lines of the dialogue have been rewritten below.

"He's drunk now," he said angrily.
"He's drunk every night," the older waiter said matter-of-factly.

After you have rewritten the dialogue, share your revisions in small groups and then answer the following questions together.

1. Why do you think Hemingway avoids using adverbs?
2. Even though Hemingway rarely uses adverbs, it is easy to imagine how a character might have said a given line. Why is this the case?

Activity 6.8

As you read Hemingway's story, you used your imagination to personalize the story: perhaps, as in activities 6.5a–6.7b, you imagined a more detailed setting and pictured the characters in your mind. Or, as in activity 6.7c, you imagined how a character might have said something. Essentially, by using your imagination, you "completed" Hemingway's story. When you analyze the process whereby a reader helps to "create" a story or text, you are using a critical approach to literature called *reader response criticism.*

Reader response critics believe that a text remains incomplete until it has been read. Such a critic analyzes the strategies a reader uses to understand a text and to bring it to life. The strategies a reader uses to understand a text are called *paradigms* and are based on an understanding of how texts are written. For example, in this chapter, you have used a formalistic approach to analyze the text. Because of the strategies used in formalism, you analyzed the author's use of literary techniques such as plot development, narration, universalization, and characterization.

However, reader response critics such as Stanley Fish (b. 1938), the main proponent of the approach, argue that rather than reading a text to find a theme that has been "hidden" there by the author, the reader reconstructs a given meaning. In fact, the actual form of a work is essentially irrelevant because the "form" a work takes is located in how a reader experiences the text. Fish argues that the structure of the reader's response to a work is more important than how the formal features of a work—its plot, imagery, and observable structure—thus the name reader response criticism.

For a reader response critic, the text itself has no **self-contained** meaning, and, without a reader, it is, in fact, meaningless. When you read a story, you don't just "**decode**" it, you create it. Fish argues that when a person uses different strategies to interpret a text, then he or she will understand that text differently. As an illustration, in this textbook, you have used psychological, sociological, and feminist interpretations of texts; the different approaches may have caused you to interpret the same text in different ways. In his article, "How to Recognize a Poem When You See One," Fish concludes that "all objects are made and not found, and that they are made by the interpretive strategies we set in motion." Because of this, the reader needs "to learn how to see and therefore to make" a text.

Reader response criticism provides a shift in perspective because it breaks down the division between the subject, that is, the person who is reading the text, and the object, the text itself: meanings are not "found" in texts but created by readers. Critics of this approach argue that it is too subjective, and they accuse Fish of having reinstated the "affective fallacy" that was criticized by the New Critics. Reader response criticism has also been criticized because it negates the possibility of a text having a truth that an author wants to communicate. But Fish argues that because people use interpretive strategies that have been conventionalized by their

self-contained: complete in itself; the meaning is built into the story

to decode: to find the meaning of a code (a code being a system of symbols used to represent a secret meaning)

use in society, the interpretation is made more objective and public. He uses the term *interpretive community* to describe this idea.

1. Do you agree or disagree with the following reactions to reader response criticism? Give reasons for your responses.
   a. To me, it makes sense to say that a reader "reconstructs" a text.
   b. In my view, reader response criticism exaggerates the role of the reader.
   c. In spite of what reader response critics argue, I think the author is more important than the reader.

Whether or not you agree with the idea that a text does not have meaning in and of itself, it is interesting to consider how a reader completes a text, just as you helped to complete "A Clean, Well-Lighted Place" when you did activities 6.5a–6.7c. Answer the following questions to determine how you "created" or "produced" the readings in this chapter.

2. How did you determine which speaker was saying a line?
3. Hemingway alludes to the Lord's Prayer but doesn't mention it directly. How does your knowledge of the prayer affect the way you read the story?
4. As a reader, how did you help to "create" or to "produce" Camus's essay on Sisyphus?

Activity 6.9

To learn more about existentialism, read the following imaginary discussion among three well-known existentialists: Søren Kierkegaard (1813–55), Friedrich Nietzsche (1844–1900), and Jean-Paul Sartre (1905–80). Imagine that they have gathered together for a panel discussion on existentialism. First read the passage silently and then discuss any new vocabulary terms with a classmate. Your instructor may ask you to read the conversation aloud in groups with one person taking the role of the announcer and others taking the roles of three philosophers.

> *Announcer:* Have you ever felt as if life had no meaning? Have you ever thought death was unfair and absurd? Have you ever felt that reason couldn't answer all your questions about life? Well, then, you have had an existential experience. Existentialism is a philosophy or belief system that focuses on the importance of an individual's freedom of choice in a world that—to an existentialist—appears to be otherwise meaningless and irrational, particularly since death is a part of life. Ultimately, existentialists reject the idea that **objective reason, systematic philosophy,** and science can an-

objective reason: thinking based on measurable effects and conclusions

systematic philosophy: an ordered way of understanding human thought processes

swer life's most difficult questions. Among the varieties of existentialism, the idea of individual freedom is a unifying idea.

We're happy to have three of the most famous existentialists gathered in our studio: the Danish philosopher Søren Kierkegaard, the German thinker Friedrich Nietzsche, and the French existentialist Jean-Paul Sartre. Kierkegaard, let's begin with you since you are the one who is commonly viewed has having developed existential themes into a philosophic system.

Kierkegaard: Thank you. Yes, it's true that I was the first philosopher to use the term *existential*. I chose this term to suggest that my philosophy focused on an understanding of an individual's existence and not on developing a philosophical system by which one could understand history or the nature of truth. To me, the philosophical question of whether something is objectively true or not is **irrelevant** because what matters is the individual's relationship to a given question. For example, a philosopher may question the **validity** of a particular faith because it lacks an objective or rational basis, but regardless of the philosopher's position, the individual must decide on how he or she will live on the basis of faith.

Announcer: So, you mean that, unlike the philosophers before you, such as Plato and Aurelius, who believed that a moral life was based on an objective standard of reason, you believe that it is up to the individual to decide how he or she will live based on his or her own **subjective** experience. In other words, people shouldn't simply follow societal codes.

Kierkegaard: I'd agree that my view is much more subjective, but this does not mean that anything is permitted. On the contrary, in my view, a person can choose to live an **aesthetic** life based on pleasure or an **ethical** life based on a committed choice to actively participate in life. But only the latter choice can enable a person to achieve individuality. Otherwise, people live only for themselves. I've written about these two ways of living in my book *Either/Or*.

Nietzsche: I'd have to question your views, Kierkegaard. I'll admit that during my lifetime, I never read your works or even heard of you, but now I know that you believed the ethical way of life could only have a religious character. In fact, I know that in your later book *Fear and Trembling* you argue that the Christian life represented the highest ethical commitment. Like you, I think a person has to make a choice about how to live life, but I reject Christianity and other religions because I believe that they have caused people to become weak willed and conformist. Besides that, church doctrines focus on an afterlife, not this life, and perpetuate too many **dualities** such as good versus evil and passion versus reason: all these are false divisions that the individual must rise above.

---

irrelevant: not related to; unimportant to something

validity: value; purposefulness

subjective: one's own personal feelings or thoughts on a subject

aesthetic: having to do with things that are beautiful and pleasing

ethical: having to do with human values and morals

dualities: pairs of opposites, e.g., north and south

Kierkegaard: First, let me say that I, too, have said that people must not simply live a **conventional** form of Christianity, one that has become "cheap" and "easy" by being institutionalized. Rather, I call people to a radical Christian or ethical way of life. The decision to live a moral life requires what I have called a *leap of faith* because a person must have faith in his or her subjective relationship to truth and not just in rational thought. In the face of **absurdity** and death, the individual must choose a life of faith even though it appears unreasonable. A person must ask, "Who am I?" and I believe that the answer—seen in the light of a religious faith put into practice—represents the one true freedom that a human being can experience.

Announcer: All right, now let's get in a word from Sartre. What's your view on the subject?

Sartre: Although I also believe that to live demands not reason alone but also the emotional power of a willful existence—the strength to choose how one will live in an unreasonable universe—I'm with Nietzsche in thinking that the answer can't be found in religious faith. Remember, I was a **partisan** in World War II, and I saw how much evil people are capable of. For me, the question is how to say "no" to the tyranny of evil and how to say "yes" to life. People can't fall back on preconceived ideas of what "**human nature**" is; instead, they must make an independent decision about how to act, how to exist. It's **imperative** to remember that existence comes before **essence**.

Announcer: That sounds interesting, but what exactly does it mean to say "no" to evil? Is it like the ad campaign against drugs in the United States that tells young people to "Just say 'no' to drugs?" And what do you mean by "existence comes before essence"?

Sartre: Let me respond to each question in turn. I'm not familiar with modern U.S. antidrug campaigns. I spent my life thinking of an answer to the nature of true freedom and wrote about it extensively in my books, particularly *Being and Nothingness.* For now I'll say it means that no matter how much the philosophers argue about the nature of human beings, the fact is that we exist so we have to find a way to exist meaningfully—that's why I argue that existence comes before essence. However, if you say "no" to evil and death, then the question is how to say "yes" to life. It appears to me that the Americans left that part out of their slogan.

Nietzsche: That's why I put forth my idea of the *Ubermensch,* or, in English, the *overman* or *superman.* In my view, the *Ubermensch* creates his own subjective values that enable him to live a life of freedom and creativity. Essentially, he rises over the herd mentality or slave morality of society and creates a master morality. I call

conventional: commonly accepted as normal behavior

absurdity: something having no logical reason

partisan: a resistance fighter in a small army

human nature: the way human beings think and act

imperative: having the nature of a command or an order to do something

essence: The basic qualities of something; its ultimate nature. Sartre argues that people focus too much on the accepted modes of behavior for human beings instead of developing their own personalities based on their subjective attitude toward the fact of their existence.

the individual's freedom to choose his or her own way in life the *will to power*. By this, I don't mean to imply that a person should rule others. No, I mean a person should exert self-mastery and self-discipline in order to fully develop as an individual. An overman would put his energies into creating his own worldview rather than into a belief in God. No man has achieved the status of an overman although I would say that some, like Julius Caesar and Leonardo da Vinci, have come close. You can read more about my ideas on the *Ubermensch* in my book *Thus Spake Zarathustra*.

Announcer: In your view, could a woman be an *Ubermensch*?

Nietzsche: In many ways, I believe that I was fifty years ahead of my time, but, as regards women, I was a man of the 1900s. I didn't consider the possibility that a woman could be an *Ubermensch,* but nowadays I understand many people disagree with me and call me sexist for the way I portrayed women.

Announcer: Didn't you make the claim that "God is dead"? I've heard it said that, upon hearing that, God turned around and said, "Nietzsche is dead."

Nietzsche: That just shows that people have misunderstood my point. I did not deny the existence of God; rather, I claimed that science and philosophy had "murdered" the idea of God, and, like Kierkegaard and Sartre, I did not want people to simply accept the worldview that was given to them in place of religion. First I wanted to shock people into realizing that they had accepted a "dead" religion, and then I wanted them to think about how to create a society of supermen. My God-is-dead statement was thus one of despair and hope.

Kierkegaard: But both Nietzsche and Sartre must recognize the paradoxical nature of their insights; for, if God is dead, and a person **negates** all meaning, then there is nothing left that is meaningful. In my *Christian Discourses,* I wrote, "To murder God is the most horrible form of suicide." I regret that Nietzsche never had the chance to read that.

Nietzsche: Well, I was also concerned about this very point. I warned that people, as yet unaware that they lived in a world without God, were in danger of becoming nihilists—those who **devalue** everything in life and find life itself to be useless. But, at the same time, I hoped that from this devaluation of traditional beliefs, the overman would have the freedom to rise up like a **phoenix** from the ashes of a self-destructive society. The *Ubermensch* would be able **to reconcile** all opposites within his personality, including the oppositions between reason and passion as well as good and evil. He would not be afraid to ask, "What is the meaning of life?" and he would not be afraid to create his own answer. At the same time, I

---

negates: says or shows that something isn't true

to devalue: to take away the value of something; to remove its importance

phoenix: a mythological bird said to have lived five hundred years, to have been burned to death, and then to have risen from the ashes

to reconcile: to bring into agreement or harmony

never claimed that the overman does not bear moral responsibility for his actions. Even so, I knew my beliefs in the overman would be used to justify tyrannical behavior. But, the important thing is for a person to act. In my journals, I have written, "Life must be lived forward, but understood backward."

Announcer: An intriguing statement. And Sartre, how would you respond to Kierkegaard's claim, that without the concept of God, human values are in danger of becoming irrelevant?

Sartre: In my own life and writings, I struggled with the idea of how to judge the nature of good and evil without **an objective standard** of truth. There's no question that the **atrocities** of World War II were evil. You could see how the Nazis' misapplied understanding of Nietzschean philosophy led to their belief in racial superiority and how this belief produced the tyranny that Nietzsche had feared. But I never did work out a satisfactory explanation of how a person could judge good and evil in a world without an objective standard of truth.

    I observed that **a finite point** has no meaning unless it is set in relation to the infinite; in other words, without an infinite reference point (if such a thing could exist), the particulars of existence and even human life become meaningless. So it follows that life is absurd. Because there is no infinite reference point, a person must create his or her own **infinitude** through action. No matter how absurd life appears, the fact remains that one exists, and so one must be willing to make difficult moral choices. Eventually one has to decide between good and evil. It's not enough to accept the French expression *C'est la vie*—one must act.

Announcer: So you mean that a person must accept that life is essentially without meaning or purpose and yet choose to live?

Sartre: Yes. Not that it's easy. I used the term **nausea** to describe the feeling that one would like to die but cannot. I believe that Kierkegaard called the same feeling "the sickness unto death."

Kierkegaard: That's correct, but I would like to add that I saw such despair as a positive step because it meant that a person would then ask existential questions about life; that is, "Who am I?" and "How shall I live?" By seeking the answers to such questions, he or she could find purpose and meaning. In this sense, despair is a necessary part of an individual's development because such a feeling forces the individual to question and to **transcend** a conventional, unexamined life. Thus, a person can escape despair and the "prison" of a pointless life.

Nietzsche: I think Sartre and I would agree with that. Clearly, even though we don't agree on some points, we do agree that modern society is characterized by **alienation** and a feeling of **dread**.

an objective standard: a logical way to determine what is true

atrocities: terrible acts against people

a finite point: A point that has measurable limits as opposed to the infinite, which has no limits. For example, a human being is finite because he or she has limited knowledge and must eventually die.

infinitude: The quality of having no limitations; of immorality. In a sense, Sartre argues that a person should do things that are remembered even after he or she has died.

C'est la vie: That's life.

nausea: the feeling that one will vomit

transcend: move beyond

alienation: separation from others

dread: the feeling that something terrible is going to happen without knowing what or when

People are separated from a true knowledge of themselves, other people, and nature . . .

Kierkegaard: And God.

Announcer: I don't want to simplify your views, but it appears that whether you take an **atheistic** or **theistic** view, all three of you want people **to affirm** their individuality but that you don't agree on how this affirmation should be realized in life: Kierkegaard suggests a committed action based on religious principles; Nietzsche uses the principle of self-mastery as a guide for the *Ubermensch;* and Sartre argues for decisive action based on a rejection of evil. No matter which view members of the audience take, it's important to remember that existentialist themes can be found in much modern literature and art, so it is helpful to be able to recognize the characteristics of existential thought.

I'd like to thank our guests for participating in our panel discussion. We will take questions from the audience now. Take a moment to write down a few questions that you may have regarding existentialism. You can discuss these with other members of the audience. Some people may be asked to answer the questions by taking on the identity of one of our panel members.

atheistic: not having a belief in God

theistic: having a belief in God

to affirm: to say that something is true or right

© 2000 University of Michigan

1. Without referring to the panel discussion, what can you recall about the following terms? Discuss the meaning of each term with a partner.

existential	an ethical life	a nihilist
a leap of faith	overman	nausea
will to power	"cheap" Christianity	theistic

2. How do the ideas presented in this debate relate to the experiences of the old man and the old waiter in "A Clean, Well-Lighted Place"?
3. How does a knowledge of existential philosophy change the way you read and respond to Hemingway's short story?

Activity 6.10a ⇨

When you examine a text from the point of view of reader response criticism, then you make the assumption that the author does not have full **authorial** control over his or her work. Another critical approach, called *deconstructionism,* also argues that the author has no control over the effects a work produces in a reader. In fact, one French critic, Roland Barthes (1915–80), wrote an essay on this topic called "The Death of the Author." Since deconstructionism has its roots in structuralism and

authorial: related to an author

Nietzschean philosophy, it is not surprising that the title of Barthes's essay alludes to Nietzsche's famous line: "God is dead."

Deconstructionist critics are interested in an act of reading that frees a text from an assigned meaning by refusing to give it an **ultimate** meaning. A deconstructionist critic would not be interested in a given "theme" of a work. In fact, he or she would argue that such a theme does not actually exist within the story but has been imposed on it by society. Like Nietzsche, deconstructionist critics argue that there is no objective or absolute truth, only subjective truth, and they seek to expose society's attempt to create "truths" for itself.

ultimate: final; complete; the best

Like the structuralists who were discussed in activities 3.5a–d, deconstructionists look for binary opposites found in texts such as *reason:madness, man:woman, wealth:poverty.* They point out that, in these sets of opposites, the first item in each set is privileged, whereas the second object is subverted. However, deconstructionists argue that the differences between the items in a set are arbitrary and imposed by society and/or by those who hold power in a society—just as the words used to designate objects in reality are **arbitrarily** chosen. For this reason, deconstructionists are not interested in asking, "What does this story mean?" but rather "What are the **assumptions** that underlie a given story?" and "What power relationships are established through the use of language?"

arbitrarily: by chance

assumptions: unspoken or unconscious beliefs about something

In essence, a deconstructionist critic acts like a formalist critic, but, rather than trying to construct a statement of meaning or a theme, a deconstructionist tries to "undo" or expose the differences and power relationships operating within a text. Also, a deconstructionist uses terminology that differs from the terms used by a formalist critic, so a symbol becomes *a signifier,* the plot is similar to what is called *the signifying structure,* and the dramatic conflict could be identified as *the difference between binary opposites.* Although it is simplistic to suggest a one-to-one correspondence between these two forms of terminology, it is nevertheless helpful to think in such terms.

At the same time, it is important to keep in mind the assumptions that underlie each approach. In general, traditional formalists believe that a text has a particular, unchanging meaning that is expressed by means of authorial control over the text. In contrast, deconstructionist critics argue the following: (1) meaning is unstable and multiple; (2) an author cannot control the meaning of a text; (3) a critic's job is to expose the hidden assumptions that operate within a text. In a sense, deconstruction devalues traditional approaches to literature so that the literature can be freed from conventional analyses. These generalized tenets of deconstructionism originated in the writings of Jacques Derrida (b. 1930), an Algerian-born and French-educated philosopher who was influenced by Nietzsche's brand of existentialism and by structuralism.

To better understand a deconstructionist view, consider one of the binary opposites that is assumed in the characterization of the two waiters in "A Clean, Well-Lighted Place"—*youth:old age*. In Western society, youth is privileged over old age. (A formalist critic might say that the dramatic conflict in the story is between youth and old age and that the story's theme is that old age is characterized by a feeling of "nothingness" whereas youth is full of confidence in the future.) This assumption causes the story to develop as it does. Another opposition or dichotomy found in the story is *meaning:nothingness*. A deconstructionist critic would be interested in analyzing how meaning is understood and privileged in society and how the feeling of nothingness is subverted. In "A Clean, Well-Lighted Place," when the old waiter says his version of the Lord's Prayer, he reverses the normal order of this opposition by placing nothingness first so that the opposites are ordered thusly, *nothingness:meaning*. Even though the old waiter has switched the order of the binary opposites, he is, ironically, still left with "nothing."

Like existentialists, deconstructionists emphasize the alienation that characterizes language—since people must use an arbitrary linguistic system to communicate their intended meaning, they can never say exactly what they mean, nor can they be fully understood. But, for the deconstructionist, words themselves are also a means of constructing reality. Because of this, a deconstructionist analyzes how words are used and interpreted to create power relationships in society. For example, a deconstructionist criticism of "A Clean, Well-Lighted Place" might consider how the word *nothing* takes on different meanings in the story. For instance, a critic might ask how the word *nothing* is meant when the older waiter says that the old man killed himself for "nothing." How is the word *nothing* contrasted with the word *everything* as when the older waiter tells the young waiter that he has "everything"? Finally, how are the words *nada* and *nothing* meant in the revision of the Lord's Prayer?

A deconstructionist critic would also be interested in instances wherein the communication between two people breaks down. In the story, this occurs when the bartender in the bodega fails to understand what the older waiter really wants and treats him in a **patronizing** way. A deconstructionist critic would analyze the language in "A Clean, Well-Lighted Place" to show that the story's meaning is not fixed but fluid and that just as there are many layers of meaning associated with language, so a story can be interpreted in many ways. Ironically, however, a deconstructionist must **resort to** using language to express his or her ideas.

You may have noticed that deconstructionist critics are in an ironic position for other reasons as well: (1) they must argue that there is no objective truth even as they provide an analysis that they claim is "true;" (2) simply to switch the order of the oppositions results in another set of oppositions that privileges one idea to the subversion of another. In fact, it

patronizing: in a manner that shows that one thinks little of something or someone

to resort to: to finally end up having to use something

is not uncommon for critics to "deconstruct" one another's analyses. In spite of the ironies associated with deconstructionism, the approach is useful in challenging oppositions and assumptions that are accepted without question by society. Once such imbalances have been revealed, people can then work to create a balance between the dichotomies found in the modern world.

1. Prepare a set of questions to ask a partner about deconstructionism. Use the following prompts to help you write your questions. Then ask a partner your questions and respond to theirs.

    a. According to the text . . . ?
    b. Why is it . . . ?
    c. What is meant by . . . ?
    d. What is the reason . . . ?
    e. Why do . . . ?
    f. Why can't . . . ?
    g. What do you think about . . . ?
    h. How does a . . . ?
    i. Do you agree with . . . ?

2. Based on the deconstructionist view of polar opposites, in what ways is the old waiter's revision of the Lord's Prayer a deconstructionist act?

Activity 6.10b ⇨

A deconstructionist critic would look at advertisements as well as literary texts to analyze the oppositions that they suggest. Think about the ways advertising privileges youth over old age. Write down a list of these examples or, if possible, bring in ads from magazines that **perpetuate** this opposition. The opposition may be implied and not directly stated or **imaged** in a photograph.

Hemingway wrote "A Clean, Well-Lighted Place" in 1933. How have ideas about old age changed in Western society since then?

to perpetuate: to cause something to last or to continue

imaged: presented as an image

Activity 6.10c ⇨

Activity 6.2 referred to the Mahabharata, a holy book of the Hindu tradition. This book contains what is known as the Bhagavad Gita, seven hundred verses about the nature of the divine, that are thought to have been written in the first or second century A.D. The title of the Bhagavad Gita is often translated as "The Lord's Song." The song is narrated by Krishna, the supreme Hindu God. Read what the Gita has to say about "pairs of opposites" such as those that are analyzed in deconstructionism. This quotation appears in the chapter entitled "Religion by Discernment," that is, by a vision into the nature of things.

bewildered: confused

quit with sin: no longer sinning or doing things that are wrong

to cleave to something: to hold something closely/tightly

> By passion for the "pairs of opposites,"
> By those two traps of Like and Dislike,
> All creatures lived **bewildered,** except for a few
> Who, **quit with sin,** holy in act, informed,
> Freed from the "opposites," and sure in faith,
> **Cleave to** me.

1. In your own words, explain the problem that "pairs of opposites" cause for people.
2. How do these ideas about "pairs of opposites" relate to deconstructionism?
3. How does Krishna say that a person can overcome the confusion caused by "pairs of opposites"?

Activity 6.10d

How might a deconstructionist critic deconstruct the language used in Richard Wright's *The Ethics of Living Jim Crow* and Barbara Mellix's "From Outside, In" found in activities 4.5 and 4.6? Give one or two examples from each text.

Activity 6.10e

Albert Camus's analysis of the myth of Sisyphus shares some of the characteristics of deconstructionist criticism. What binary opposites does Sisyphus challenge? What are the results?

Activity 6.11

If the waiters in "A Clean, Well-Lighted Place" knew that they were going to die at midnight, how might they feel, what might they do? Use details from the story to support your ideas. Try to use ideas taken from existentialism in your response.

Chapter 7

"Gimpel the Fool," by Isaac Bashevis Singer

Photograph courtesy of Rafael Kapelinski

"'Where are you going?' they said. I answered, 'Into the world.' And so I departed from Frampol."—Isaac Bashevis Singer, "Gimpel the Fool"

Activity 7.1 ⇨

This chapter focuses on the short story "Gimpel the Fool," by Isaac Bashevis Singer (1904–91). Singer was born in Warsaw, Poland, where his father was a **rabbi.** He grew up in a Jewish **ghetto,** and, at the age of thirty-one, he immigrated to the States—four years before the **Nazis** invaded Poland. In the United States, he worked as a journalist, a scriptwriter, and an author. In 1978, he was awarded the Nobel Prize in literature. Your analyses of Singer's short story will include the critical approaches introduced in the previous six chapters.

In "Gimpel the Fool," Singer portrays the life of Gimpel, a Jewish man who lives in an east European Jewish community before World War II (1939–45). Such communities, called *shtetls,* were destroyed by the Nazis during World War II. The Nazi effort to exterminate the Jewish people is now called an act of genocide. The term *genocide* is a combination of the Greek prefix *geno,* meaning tribe, and the Latin suffix *-cide,* meaning murder. The term did not exist until 1943 when it was coined by a Polish lawyer, Rafal Lemkin, to express the systematic killing of a people belonging to a racial or cultural group. In 1945, the United Nations passed the Genocide Convention which made acts of genocide crimes against humanity.

Singer's re-creation of the shtetl life, though fictionalized, helps readers to better understand what was lost with the destruction of the east European shtetls during World War II. To more fully appreciate "Gimpel the Fool," it is important to understand the European context of World War II. For a perspective on the loss of life caused by World War II, consider the following statistics based on the war in Europe.

rabbi: a Jewish religious teacher

ghetto: the part of a city where Jews were required by law to live

Nazis: Also called *National Socialism;* the political party that controlled Germany from 1933 to 1945 under Hitler. Nazism is associated with *fascism,* a political movement that places race and nation above the individual and is characterized by dictatorial rule and violence.

25 million	Total number of civilian deaths. (The total number of civilian deaths in World War I was 8 million.)
6 million	The number of Jews killed.
11 million	The Nazis estimated that there were approximately 11 million Jews living in Europe, including the Ukraine and Russia, at the war's onset.
19 million	The number of military deaths, (In World War I, the estimated number of military deaths was approximately 8.5 million.)

1. Based on these statistics, what conclusions can you make about World War II in Europe?
2. What do you know about the Nazi effort to exterminate the Jewish people?

3. Other examples of genocide include the following: the killing of 1.8 million Armenians in Turkey by nationalists during World War I (1914–18); the killing of 1.7 million Cambodians by the Khmer Rouge from 1975 to 1979; the murder of nearly half a million Tutsi in 1994 by the Hutu in Rwanda; the murder and forced expulsion of Albanians from Kosovo by the Serb military (1999). Why do you think these and other acts of genocide occur?
4. Given the statistics related to the war in Europe, how would you interpret the following quote, which is attributed to Stalin (1879–1953), the Secretary General of the Soviet Union from 1922 to 1953: "One death is a tragedy. A million deaths is a statistic"?
5. How might "The Tell-Tale Heart" by Edgar Allen Poe help to explain why acts of madness such as genocide take place?

Activity 7.2

The genocide of the Jewish people during World War II is called the *Holocaust*. The word *holocaust* means *a sacrifice consumed by fire,* and it can be used to describe a situation in which many innocent people die. However, when it is spelled with an uppercase *H* or preceded by the article *the,* it refers specifically to the attempt to exterminate the Jews in World War II. Below is a list of words that took on a particular meaning during World War II. Look up any new expressions in your dictionary or in an encyclopedia. How do they relate to World War II in Europe?

1. anti-Semitism
2. Gestapo
3. blitzkrieg
4. Aryan
5. concentration camp
6. liquidation
7. bath
8. Zyklon-B

Activity 7.3a

The nation of Poland (1939 boundaries) lost 17 percent of its civilian population during World War II. While Poland was under Nazi rule, the Germans set up many concentration camps there, primarily because a large Jewish population lived in central and eastern Europe. Of the 6 million civilians who were killed in Poland during the war, 2.9 million were Jewish.

The Nazis systematically killed the Jews in the death camps. In Poland, near the town of Auschwitz (Oswiecim), the Nazis built a series of camps that was collectively known as *Auschwitz.* At Auschwitz, 2.5 million people are believed to have been gassed, starved, beaten, or worked to death; or to have died of disease. Up to one-third of the Jews who died during the war were killed in Auschwitz. Along with the Jews, a large number of Poles, Roms, Soviet prisoners of war, and homosexuals were also killed.

The first camp, Auschwitz, was built in 1940 thirty miles outside the city of **Krakow** in what had been military **barracks**. In 1941, another camp, called *Birkenau* or *Auschwitz II,* was built not far from the initial camp. The entire complex is also called *Auschwitz-Birkenau.* In the four large "disinfecting chambers" and **crematoriums** found built at Birkenau, up to 20,000 people could be gassed in a day. The Nazis carefully documented their work and referred to the people as *stuke,* the German word for *pieces.* The slogan *Arbeit macht Frei* (Work Makes One Free) hung over the entrance to the camps because the Nazi wanted to make the death camps appear to be work camps.

Although the Nazis tried to destroy all evidence of the camps before the advance of the Soviet and U.S. troops, they were not able to do so. Barracks and **remnants** of the crematoriums used in Auschwitz remain, and a museum on the site memorializes those who died in the camp and those who survived. Survivors such as Viktor Frankl (1905–97), a Viennese professor of psychology and neurobiology, have written of their experiences in the Nazi camps.

In his book *Man's Search for Meaning: An Introduction to* **Logotherapy***,* Frankl writes of his personal experiences in Auschwitz. The following excerpt describes Frankl's arrival in the camp and personalizes an experience that is generally seen as statistical data.

From Man's Search for Meaning

Fifteen hundred persons had been traveling by train for several days and nights: there were eighty people in each coach. All had to lie on top of their luggage, the few remnants of their personal possessions. The carriages were so full that only the top parts of the windows were free to let in the grey of dawn. Everyone expected the train to head for some **munitions** factory, in which we would be employed as forced labor. We did not know whether we were still in **Silesia** or already in Poland. The engine's whistle had an **uncanny** sound, like a cry for help sent out in **commiseration** for the unhappy load which it was destined to lead into perdition. Then the train **shunted**, obviously nearing a main station. Suddenly a cry broke from the ranks of the anxious passengers, "There is a sign, Auschwitz!" Everyone's heart missed a beat at that moment. Auschwitz—the very name stood for all that was horrible: gas chambers, crematoriums, massacres. Slowly, almost hesitatingly, the train moved on as if it wanted to spare its passengers the dreadful realization as long as possible: Auschwitz!

With the progressive dawn, the outlines of an immense camp be-

---

Krakow: a town in southern Poland

barracks: large buildings in which soldiers or prisoners live

crematoriums: ovens where bodies of the dead are burned

remnants: the last pieces of something

logotherapy: a psychological therapy based on the belief that a human being must satisfy his or her need to determine what makes life meaningful

munitions: guns and ammunition used in war

Silesia: a part of Germany before World War II; now a part of southern Poland

uncanny: mysterious; having a supernatural character

commiseration: expression of sympathy

shunted: moved from one track to another

Photograph courtesy of Rafael Kapelinski

Auschwitz-Birkenau

"Those who were sent to the left were marched straight from the station to the crematorium."—Viktor Frankl

came visible: long stretches of several rows of barbed wire fences; watch towers; search lights; and long columns of ragged human figures, grey in the greyness of dawn, **trekking** along the straight **desolate** roads, to what destination we did not know. There were isolated shouts and whistles of command. We did not know their meaning. My imagination led me to see **gallows** with people dangling on them. I was horrified, but this was just as well, because step by step we had to become **accustomed** to a terrible and immense horror.

Eventually we moved into the station. The initial silence was interrupted by shouted commands. We were to hear those rough, shrill tones from then on, over and over again in all the camps. Their sound was almost like the last cry of a victim, and yet there was a difference. It had a rasping **hoarseness,** as if it came from the throat of a man who had to keep shouting like that, a man who was being murdered again and again. The carriage doors were flung open and a small **detachment** of prisoners stormed inside. They wore striped uniforms, their heads were shaved, but they looked well fed. They spoke in every possible European tongue, and all with a certain amount of humor, which sounded **grotesque** under the circumstances. **Like a drowning man clutching a straw,** my inborn optimism (which has often controlled my feelings even in the most desperate situations) clung to

trekking: making a difficult journey

desolate: miserable; wretched; without signs of life

gallows: Frames from which people are hung by a rope until dead. The noun is plural even if one person is hung.

accustomed: used to something

hoarseness: roughness

detachment: a small group

grotesque: very unnatural

like a drowning man clutching a straw: like a man reaching for something that can not save him

this thought: These prisoners look quite well, they seem to be in good spirits and even laugh. Who knows? I might manage to share their favorable position.

In psychiatry there is a certain condition known as "**delusion of reprieve**." The condemned man, immediately before his execution, gets the illusion that he might be reprieved at the very last minute. We, too, clung to shreds of hope and believed to the last moment that it would not be so bad. Just the sight of the red cheeks and round faces of those prisoners was a great encouragement. Little did we know then that they formed a specially chosen **elite**, who for years had been the receiving **squad** for new transports as they rolled into the station day after day. They took charge of the new arrivals and their luggage, including scarce items and **smuggled** jewelry. Auschwitz must have been a strange spot in this Europe of the last years of the war. There must have been unique treasures of gold and silver, platinum and diamonds, not only in the huge storehouses but also in the hands of the **SS**.

Fifteen hundred captives were **cooped up** in a shed built to accommodate probably two hundred at the most. We were cold and hungry and there was not enough room for everyone to squat on the bare ground, let alone to lie down. One **five-ounce** piece of bread was our only food in four days. Yet I heard the senior prisoners in charge of the shed bargain with one member of the receiving party about a tie-pin made of platinum and diamonds. Most of the profits would eventually be traded for liquor—**schnapps**. I do not remember any more just how many thousands of marks were needed to purchase the quantity of schnapps required for a "**gay evening**," but I do know that those long-term prisoners needed schnapps. Under such conditions, who could blame them for trying to dope themselves? There was another group of prisoners who got liquor supplied in almost unlimited quantities by the SS: these were the men who were employed in the gas chambers and crematoriums, and who knew very well that one day they would be relieved by a new shift of men, and that they would have to leave their enforced role of executioner and become victims themselves.

Nearly everyone in our transport lived under the illusion that he would be reprieved, that everything would yet be well. We did not realize the meaning behind the scene that was to follow presently. We were told to leave our luggage in the train and to fall into two lines—women on one side, men on the other—in order to file past a senior SS officer. Surprisingly enough, I had the courage to hide my **haversack** under my coat. My line filed past the officer, man by man. I realized that it would be dangerous if the officer spotted my bag.

He would at least knock me down; I knew that from previous experience. Instinctively, I straightened on approaching the officer, so

---

delusion: a false belief

reprieve: The act of removing someone's criminal sentence and giving that person freedom. In this case, the people in the concentration camp—who had been imprisoned unjustly—had the false belief that they would be shown mercy and given their freedom or would somehow be saved from the gas chambers.

elite: high level; of special importance

squad: a group of people trained to act as a unit

smuggled: brought into someplace secretly

SS: semimilitary part of the Nazi party called the *Schutzstaffeln*, the Elite Guard

cooped up: made to fit in a small place

five-ounce: 142.85 grams

schnapps: a sweet, alcoholic drink

gay evening: A happy evening. Singer has used quotation marks to suggest that he's being ironic.

haversack: a small bag carried over one shoulder

that he would not notice my heavy load. Then I was face to face with him. He was a tall man who looked slim and fit in his spotless uniform. What a contrast to us, who were untidy and **grimy** after our journey! He had assumed an attitude of careless ease, supporting his right elbow with his left hand. His right hand was lifted, and with the forefinger of that hand he pointed very leisurely to the right or to the left. None of us had the slightest idea of the **sinister** meaning behind that little movement of a man's finger, pointing now to the right and now to the left, but far more frequently to the left. It was my turn. Somebody whispered to me that to be sent to the right side would mean work, the way to the left being for the sick and those incapable of work, who would be sent to a special camp. I just waited for things to take their course, the first of many such times to come. My haversack weighed me down a bit to the left, but I made an effort to walk upright. The SS man looked me over, appeared to hesitate, then put both his hands on my shoulders. I tried very hard to look smart, and he turned my shoulders very slowly until I faced right, and I moved over to that side. The significance of the finger game was explained to us in the evening. It was the first selection, the first verdict made on our existence or non-existence. For the great majority of our transport, about 90 per cent, it meant death. Their sentence was carried out within the next few hours. Those who were sent to the left were marched from the station straight to the crematorium. This building, as I was told by someone who worked there, had the word "bath" written over its doors in several European languages. On entering, each prisoner was handed a piece of soap, and then—but mercifully I do not need to describe the events which followed. Many accounts have been written about this horror.

grimy: dirty

sinister: having an evil or dangerous appearance or atmosphere

We who were saved, the minority of our transport, found out the truth in the evening. I inquired from prisoners who had been there for some time where my colleague and friend P⎯⎯ had been sent. "Was he sent to the left side?"

"Yes," I replied.

"Then you can see him there," I was told.

"Where?" A hand pointed to the chimney a few hundred yards off, which was sending a column of flame up into the grey sky of Poland. It dissolved into a sinister cloud of smoke. "That's where your friend is, floating up to Heaven," was the answer. But I still did not understand until the truth was explained to me in plain words.

But I am telling things out of their turn. From a psychological point of view, we had a long, long way in front of us from the break of that dawn at the station until our first night's rest at the camp. Escorted by SS guards with loaded guns, we were made to run from the station, past electrically charged barbed wire, through the camp, to the cleansing station; for those of us who had passed the first selection, this was a real bath. Again our illusion of reprieve found confirmation. The SS men seemed almost charming. Soon we found out their reason. They were nice to us as long as they saw watches on our wrists and could persuade us in well-meaning tones to hand them over. Would we not have to hand over all our possessions anyway, and why should not that relatively nice person have the watch? Maybe one day he would do one a good turn. We waited in a shed which seemed to be the anteroom to the disinfecting chamber. SS men appeared and spread out blankets into which we had to throw all our possessions, all our watches and jewelry. There were still **naive** prisoners among us who asked, to the amusement of the more **seasoned** ones who were there as helpers, if they could not keep a wedding ring, a medal or a good-luck piece. No one could yet grasp the fact that everything would be taken away.

I tried to take one of the old prisoners into my confidence. Approaching him **furtively**, I pointed to the roll of paper in the inner pocket of my coat and said, "Look, this is the manuscript of a scientific book. I know what you will say; that I should be grateful to escape with my life, that that should be all I can expect of fate. But I cannot help myself. I must keep this manuscript at all costs; it contains my life's work. Do you understand that?"

Yes, he was beginning to understand. A grin spread slowly over his face, first piteous, then more amused, **mocking**, insulting, until he **bellowed** one word at me in answer to my question, a word that was ever present in the vocabulary of the camp inmates: "Shit!" At that moment I saw the plain truth and did what marked the **culminating point** of the first phase of my psychological reaction: I struck out my whole former life.

naive: innocent
seasoned: experienced

furtively: secretively

mocking: in a tone that makes fun of someone or something
bellowed: shouted something in a rude way
culminating point: the end; the crisis point

From *Man's Search for Meaning* by Viktor E. Frankl. © 1959, 1962, 1984, 1992 by Viktor E. Frankl. Reprinted by permission of Beacon Press, Boston, and by Hodder and Stoughton Limited, London.

1. In this excerpt, Frankl describes the process whereby he loses his "delusion of reprieve." In your own words, explain what Frankl means by this expression. What made him finally give up this delusion?
2. Why does Frankl say that "for those of us who had passed the first selection, this was a real bath"?
3. For Frankl, his scientific work represented the last part of his former identity that he tried to hold onto upon his arrival in the camp. What object might you try to hold onto in a similar situation? Why?
4. Frankl makes an effort to describe how he tried to "read" the situation in the camp according to the world he had known in everyday life. However, as he describes it, such an attempt to read the activities in the

Photograph courtesy of Rafael Kapelinski

From inside Auschwitz-Birkenau

camp failed. Why? How does Frankl's inability to "read" his situation reflect ideas found in reader response criticism? (See activity 6.8.)

5. In his description of camp life, Frankl tells how he found a small piece of paper in his camp uniform pocket. On this paper was written a verse called the *Schma Israel*. The verse comes from the Jewish Bible and is said as a prayer by the Jewish people: *Hear O Israel, the Lord thy God is one God.* Frankl found encouragement in this verse and in his faith. If you were in a situation full of so much unreason and horror, what might you think of to encourage yourself?

6. How does Frankl's description of the camp contradict any idea that the millions who died in the death camps were just statistics?

Activity 7.3b

In the development of his psychological theories, Frankl used the **microcosmic** world of the camps to analyze human nature under the most extreme conditions. In his book *The Doctor and the Soul*, he observes that even in the camp setting, people rose above their circumstances. He writes, "Even in this socially limiting environment, in spite of this societal restriction upon his personal freedom, the ultimate freedom still remains his: the freedom even in the camp to give some shape to his existence."

microcosmic: like a small replica of the larger world, or *macrocosm*

In *Man's Search for Meaning,* he argues, "That which was ultimately responsible for the state of the prisoner's inner self . . . was the result of a free decision. Psychological observations of the prisoners have shown that only the men who allowed their inner hold on their moral and spiritual selves **to subside** eventually fell victim to the camp's **degenerating** influences."

to subside: to sink or fall to the bottom of something; to become weaker

degenerating: lowering; to cause a decline in the quality of something

1. Using your own words, briefly summarize this short description of how people acted in the camps.
2. How are Frankl's views similar to those of existentialists?
3. How does Frankl's vision of the human personality differ from Freud's?

Activity 7.4 ⇨

In a death camp, societal norms are turned upside down. Instead of reason there is unreason; instead of purposefulness, purposelessness; instead of life, death. Do you think it is possible to look at the death camp from the point of view of a deconstructionist? Why or why not? Be prepared to discuss your answer.

Activity 7.5 ⇨

The philosopher Paul Feyerabend (1924–94) viewed death camps such as Auschwitz as an extreme example of behaviors that occur in society on a daily basis. Read the following excerpt from his book *Farewell to Reason* (1987).

manifestation: the process of making something evident

humanitarian: concerned for the well-being of other people

patriots: people with strong feelings of pride and respect for their nation

colossal: huge

conceit: great pride

relentless: without giving up; persistent

infantile: like an infant; childish

megalomania: the feeling or need to feel that one is all powerful and all important

blackmail: to trick someone into doing something

to mutilate: to tear or cut apart

I say that Auschwitz is an extreme **manifestation** of an attitude that still thrives in our midst. It shows itself in the treatment of minorities in industrial democracies; in education, education to a **humanitarian** point of view included, which most of the time consists of turning wonderful young people into colorless and self-righteous copies of their teachers; it becomes manifest in the nuclear threat, the constant increase in the number and power of deadly weapons and the readiness of some so-called **patriots** to start a war compared with which the [H]olocaust will shrink into insignificance. It shows itself in the killing of nature and of "primitive" cultures with never a thought spent on those thus deprived of meaning for their lives; in the **colossal conceit** of our intellectuals' belief that they know precisely what humanity needs and their **relentless** efforts to recreate people in their own sorry image; in the **infantile megalomania** of some of our physicians who **blackmail** their patients with fear, **mutilate** them and then persecute them with large bills; in the lack of feeling of many so-called searchers for truth who systematically torture animals, study their discomfort and receive prizes for their cruelty. As far as I am concerned there exists no difference between the **henchmen** of Auschwitz and these "**benefactors** of mankind."

henchmen: political followers whose support is mainly for personal advantage

benefactors: those who give benefits or good things to other people

Farewell to Reason, by Paul Feyerabend. Verso, 1987.

1. Why is *benefactors of mankind* in quotation marks? Why is the term *primitive* in quotation marks?
2. In this excerpt, Feyerabend "deconstructs" many examples of societal norms that he considers wrong. He exposes a number of binary opposites, such as *majority:minority* and *teacher:student.* List at least three other binary opposites that he refers to. Then, in your own words, summarize why you think Feyerabend feels that these polarities are wrong.
3. Do you agree with Feyerabend's argument? Why or why not?
4. Whether or not you agree with Feyerabend's point of view, are there other polarities that are accepted in society that you feel are unjust? Explain your answer.
5. Feyerabend does not give any solutions to the problems to which he refers in this excerpt. How might the opposites that Feyerabend lists be **reconciled**?

reconciled: brought into agreement or harmony

Activity 7.6 ⇨

To help characterize shtetl life in "Gimpel the Fool," Singer uses expressions common to the Yiddish language. Yiddish developed when Jews of the ninth century who lived in Germany began to adapt the German language to their own Hebrew language. In more recent times, Yiddish has been associated primarily with Jews from central and eastern Europe. Although it is written in Hebrew characters, it differs from the Hebrew language, and many Yiddish words derive from the German, Slavic, and Romanian languages as well as from Hebrew.

Since Yiddish is the language associated with the village life of the shtetl, the vocabulary and expressions found in the language relate to community life. Although Singer writes in English, he preserves the character of Yiddish by using idiomatic expressions and by **mimicking** the syntax of Yiddish.

mimicking: imitating or copying someone or something

As a result of Jewish immigration to the United States, many colorful Yiddish expressions are used commonly in American English. The following excerpt from *The Story of English,* by William Cram, Robert MacNeil, and Robert McCrum, describes the impact that Jewish immigrants to the United States have had on the English language, particularly as a result of the 1880–1919 immigration of over three million European Jews to the United States. They came through Ellis Island, "the isle of tears," where many of them would have their names changed or shortened by

U.S. immigration officials, so that, for example, *Ouspenska* would become *Spensky* and *Frankelstein, Stein.*

From The Story of English

garment: A piece of clothing. The *garment trade* has to do with the clothing industry.

preponderance: majority

brazen: bold; unafraid in an unpleasant way

intrepid: fearless and determined

skulking: moving in a secretive way as if to hide something

foothold: a position that can be used as the starting point for advancement

onomatopoeic: This describes words whose sound suggests their meaning, such as *tick-tock* or *drip-drop.*

unadulterated: Pure. The term *to adulterate* means to make impure or corrupt.

nonentity: someone without personality or importance

Oedipus-schmoedipus: A term used to show that something is not respected or believed; in this case, Freud's account of the Oedipus complex (see activity 2.13c). The prefix *schm-* is common in Yiddish.

Many of the East and Central European Jews ended up on the Lower East Side of New York City, working in the **garment** trade. Like the Germans, theirs was a strong subculture within American society. In the 1890s, the Yiddish newspaper the *Jewish Daily Forward* (which survives to this day) had a circulation of a quarter of a million. Excluded from the more established avenues of advancement, many American Jews moved into the entertainment business—newspapers, magazines, vaudeville, and later radio, films, and television. The spread of *Yinglish* (Yiddish and English) into the mainstream of the language is partly the result of the **preponderance** of Jewish Americans in the media of the United States, performers as well as executives. Thanks to stars like Woody Allen and Joan Rivers, the English-speaking world has learned about **brazen** *chutzpah,* the **intrepid** *kibitzer,* and the **skulking** *gonef,* all of which are now in the dictionary. As Leo Rosten, the champion of "Yinglish," remarks, "The **foothold** established on the hospitable shore of English may be glimpsed if you scan the entries beginning with *ch, k, sch, sh, y.*" In recent years, they have been joined by a richly **onomatopoeic** family: *shlep* ("to drag, pull, lag behind"); *shtik* ("business"); *kosher* ("authentic, **unadulterated,** the 'real McCoy'"); *mensch* ("someone of consequence"); *momzer* ("a bastard, a mischievous, amusing person"); *nebbish* ("a **nonentity**"); *shlemiel* ("a simpleton"); *schmooz* ("friendly, aimless talk"); *schmuck* ("a fool, a jerk"). . . .

The collision of English and Yiddish has also given America such expressions as *Get lost, Give a look, He knows from nothing, If you'll excuse the expression, I'm telling you, I need it like a hole in the head, Enjoy! Smart he isn't* and *I should worry . . .* and the sarcastic prefix: **Oedipus-schmoedipus** or *actor-schmactor.*

The Story of English, by William Cram, Robert MacNeil, and Robert McCrum. Viking Penguin, 1986.

1. Look up *chutzpah, kibitzer,* and *gonef* (or *ganef*) in a dictionary.

Activity 7.7a ⇨

Here is a partial list of the idioms that you will find in "Gimpel the Fool." Try to match up the idiom on the left with the correct definition on the right. The first one has been done for you. What themes do you notice among the idioms that follow?

1. to put one over on someone
2. to start up with someone or something
3. to come down on someone
4. to be a "no go"
5. to take stock in something
6. to have a screw loose
7. to get water on the ear
8. to make someone the butt of a joke
9. You can kiss my you-know-what
10. to rack your brains about something
11. to be rooked
12. to have your ship go and sink
13. to stick to your guns
14. to be a marked man
15. to give someone a going over

___ a. to not be able to listen to someone talking anymore
___ b. to believe in something or someone
___ c. to be slightly crazy
___ d. to have bad luck
___ e. to tell someone (impolitely) you don't care what they think
___ f. to think about something intently to find an answer
___ g. to be tricked or cheated of something
_1_ h. to successfully trick someone
___ i. to do what you intend to do no matter what happens
___ j. to criticize or punish someone severely
___ k. to be marked for punishment or to be killed
___ l. to "beat up" someone physically or with words for something you are angry about
___ m. to begin an argument
___ n. to make a person the subject of a joke
___ o. to be of no importance or to be lacking in skills or knowledge

Activity 7.7b ⇨

In addition to containing idiomatic expressions, Yiddish uses proverbs related to Jewish folk and **rabbinical** wisdom. For example, the Jewish Bible

rabbinical: having to do with the spiritual leaders of Judaism, the rabbis

contains a book entitled Proverbs that consists of wise sayings such as "A cheerful heart is good medicine, but a crushed spirit dries up the bones" (Proverbs 17:22) and "Of what use is money in the hand of a fool, since he has no desire to get wisdom?" (Proverbs 17:16).

A. In your own words, give your interpretation of these two proverbs.
B. Read the following examples of proverbial statements that are found in "Gimpel the Fool" and, using your own words, write a brief definition of how you think these proverbs relate to everyday life. The first one has been done for you.

1. No bread will ever be baked from this dough.

    Nothing will happen as a result of a person's efforts to do something.

2. Today isn't yesterday, and yesterday's not today.
3. Prayer never made any woman pregnant.
4. There isn't a woman in the world who is not the granddaughter of **Eve**.
5. Shoulders are from God, and burdens too.
6. You can't live without errors.
7. Today it's your wife you don't believe; tomorrow it's God Himself you won't take stock in.
8. The truth is out, like the oil upon the water.

Eve: In the Jewish creation story, Eve is the name of the first woman.

Activity 7.7c

Based on the idioms and proverbs used in "Gimpel the Fool," what do you think the story might be about? (*Note:* Gimpel is a man who works as a baker. Also, Gimpel says numbers 1, 5, 6, 7, and 8.)

Activity 7.8

Singer has divided "Gimpel the Fool" into four sections. After each section, write four questions that you think would help a reader to analyze the story. Relate your questions to the ideas that you have been introduced to in previous chapters. Be prepared to share your questions (and their answers) with your classmates. Your instructor may ask you to focus on one section of the story and to provide a summary of it.

Gimpel the Fool

I

I am Gimpel the fool. I don't think myself a fool. On the contrary. But that's what folks call me. They gave me the name while I was still in school. I had seven names in all: **imbecile,** donkey, **flax-head,** dope,

imbecile: someone who acts thoughtlessly or stupidly

flax-head: blond; here used as a derogatory term meaning "stupid"

glump, **ninny**, and fool. The last name stuck. What did my foolishness consist of? I was easy to take in. They said, "Gimpel, you know the rabbi's wife has been brought to **childbed**?" So I skipped school. Well, it turned out to be a lie. How was I supposed to know? She hadn't had a big belly. But I never looked at her belly. Was that really so foolish? The gang laughed and **heehawed**, stomped and danced and chanted a good-night prayer. And instead of the raisins they give when a woman is **lying in**, they stuffed my hands full of goat **turds**. I was no weakling. If I slapped someone he'd see all the way to Cracow. But I'm really not a **slugger** by nature. I think to myself, Let it pass. So they take advantage of me.

I was coming home from school and heard a dog barking. I'm not afraid of dogs, but of course I never want to start up with them. One of them may be mad, and if he bites there's not a **Tartar** in the world who can help you. So I **made tracks**. Then I looked around and saw the whole marketplace wild with laughter. It was no dog at all but Wolf-Leib the thief. How was I supposed to know it was he? It sounded like a howling **bitch**.

When the **pranksters** and **leg-pullers** found that I was easy to fool every one of them tried his luck with me. "Gimpel, the **Czar** is coming to Frampol; Gimpel, the moon fell down in **Turbeen**; Gimpel, little **Hodel Furpiece** found a treasure behind the bathhouse." And I like a **golem** believed everyone. In the first place, everything is possible, as it is written in the **Wisdom of the Fathers**, I've forgotten how. Second, I had to believe when the whole town came down on me. If I ever dared to say, "Ah, you're kidding!" there was trouble. People got angry. "What do you mean! You want to call everyone a liar?" What was I to do? I believed them, and I hope at least that did them some good.

I was an orphan. My grandfather who brought me up was already bent toward the grave. So they turned me over to a baker and what a time they gave me there! Every woman or girl who came to bake a pan of cookies or dry a batch of noodles had to fool me at least once. "Gimpel, there's a fair in heaven; Gimpel, the rabbi gave birth to a calf in the seventh month; Gimpel, a cow flew over the roof and laid brass eggs." A student from the **yeshiva** came once to buy a roll, and he said, "You, Gimpel, while you stand here scraping with your baker's shovel the **Messiah** has come. The dead have arisen." "What do you mean?" I said. "I heard no one blowing the **ram's horn**!" He said, "Are you deaf?" And all began to cry, "We heard it, we heard." Then in came Reitze the candle dipper and called out in her hoarse voice, "Gimpel, your father and mother have stood up from the grave. They're looking for you."

To tell the truth, I knew very well that nothing of the sort had happened, but all the same, as folks were talking, I threw on my wool vest

---

ninny: someone who is not very smart; a simpleton; a fool

childbed: to be in the process of giving birth

heehawed: laughed loudly like a horse or donkey (donkeys *heehaw* in English!)

lying in: lying in bed to give birth

turds: a slang term for animal droppings or dung, considered offensive

slugger: slang for a person who likes to hit, or "slug," people

Tartar: a person from the region of Tatary; someone who is violent

to make tracks: to move fast to avoid a situation

bitch: female dog

pranksters: people who like to play tricks or pranks on others

leg-pullers: slang for people who play tricks on others, as in "You're pulling my leg"

Czar: the leader of Russia before the 1917 revolution

Turbeen: the name of a village

Hodel Furpiece: the name of a woman in the village

golem: a simple person made from clay

Wisdom of the Fathers: the teachings of the religious leaders

yeshiva: Jewish school of theology

Messiah: The term used to describe the savior of the Jewish people. The Jews believe that their Messiah has not yet come. Christians believe that Jesus Christ, who was a Jew, was also the Messiah.

ram's horn: The blowing on a ram's horn was to signify the arrival of the Messiah and the raising of the dead to life.

and went out. Maybe something had happened. What did I stand to lose by looking? Well, what **a cat music** went up! And then I took a vow to believe nothing more. But that was no go either. They confused me so that I didn't know the big end from the small.

I went to the rabbi to get some advice. He said, "It is written better to be all your days a fool than for one hour to be evil. You are not a fool. They are the fools. For he who causes his neighbor to feel shame loses Paradise himself." Nevertheless, the rabbi's daughter **took me in.** As I left the rabbinical court, she said, "Have you kissed the wall yet?" I said, "No; what for?" She answered, "It's a law, you've got to do it after every visit." Well there didn't seem to be any harm in it. And she burst out laughing. It was a fine trick. She put one over on me, all right.

I wanted to go off to another town, but then everyone got busy **matchmaking,** and they were after me so they nearly tore my coat tails off. They talked at me and talked until I got water on the ear. She was no **chaste** maiden, but they told me she was virgin pure. She had a limp, and they said it was deliberate, from **coyness.** She had a **bastard,** and they told me the child was her little brother. I cried, "You're wasting your time. I'll never marry that **whore.**" But they said **indignantly,** "What a way to talk! Aren't you ashamed of yourself? We can take you to the rabbi and have you fined for **giving her a bad name.**" I saw then that I wouldn't escape them so easily and I thought, They're set on making me their butt. But when you're married the husband's the master, and if that's all right with her it's agreeable to me too. Besides, you can't pass through life **unscathed,** nor expect to.

I went to her clay house, which was built on the sand, and the whole gang, hollering and chorusing, came after me. They acted like **bearbaiters.** When we came to the well they stopped all the same. They were afraid to start anything with Elka. Her mouth would open as if it were on a hinge, and she had a fierce tongue. I entered the house. Lines were strung from wall to wall and clothes were drying. Barefoot she stood by the tub, doing the wash. She was dressed in a worn **hand-me-down** gown of **plush.** She had her hair put up in braids and pinned across her head. It took my breath away, almost, the **reek** of it all.

Evidently she knew who I was. She took a look at me and said, "Look who's here! He's come, the **drip.** Grab a seat."

I told her all; I denied nothing. "Tell me the truth," I said, "are you really a virgin, and is that mischievous Yechiel actually your little brother? Don't be **deceitful** with me, for I'm an orphan."

"I'm an orphan myself," she answered, "and whoever tries **to twist you up,** may the end of his nose take a twist. But don't let them think they can take advantage of me. I want **a dowry** of fifty guilders, and let

---

a cat music: the sound cats make when they are ready to mate

to take someone in: to fool someone

matchmaking: arranging for two people to meet and to marry; to "make a match" or a pair

chaste: pure; still a virgin

coyness: behavior that is overly cute or flirtatious

bastard: a derogatory term used to refer to a child without a legal father; a swear word

whore: a slang word for a prostitute, considered offensive

indignantly: done angrily as a result of something unjust or unworthy

to give someone a bad name: to hurt a person's reputation

unscathed: unharmed; untouched

bearbaiters: people who let dogs attack a chained bear

hand-me-down: something that is used; handed down from one person to the next

plush: a thick, luxurious material

reek: terrible smell

drip: slang for a weak-willed person

deceitful: untrue; full of lies

to twist someone up: to confuse or trick someone

dowry: a gift of money that a man traditionally gave for a bride

them take up a collection besides. Otherwise they can kiss my you-know-what." She was very plain-spoken. I said, "Don't bargain with me. Either a flat 'yes' or a flat 'no—go back where you came from.'" I thought, No bread will ever be baked from *this* dough. But ours is not a poor town. They **consented** to everything and proceeded with the wedding. It so happened that there was a **dysentery epidemic** at the time. The ceremony was held at the cemetery gates, near the little corpse-washing hut. The fellows got drunk. While the marriage contract was being drawn up I heard the most pious high rabbi ask, "Is the bride a widow or a divorced woman?" And the **sexton's** wife answered for her, "Both a widow and divorced." It was a black moment for me. But what was I to do, run away from under the **marriage canopy**?

There was singing and dancing. An old granny danced opposite me, hugging a braided white **chalah**. The master of **revels** made a "**God 'a mercy**" in memory of the bride's parents. The schoolboys threw burrs, as on **Tishe b' Av** fast day. There were a lot of gifts after the sermon: a noodle board, a kneading trough, a bucket, brooms, ladles, household articles galore. Then I took a look and saw two young men carrying a **crib**. "What do we need this for?" I asked. "Don't rack your brains about it. It's all right, it'll come in handy." I realized I was going to be rooked. Take it another way though, what did I stand to lose? I reflected, I'll see what comes of it. A whole town can't go altogether crazy.

II

At night I came where my wife lay, but she wouldn't let me in. "Say, look here, is this what they married us for?" I said. And she said, "My **monthly** has come." "But yesterday they took you to the **ritual bath**, and that's afterward, isn't it supposed to be?" "Today isn't yesterday," said she, "and yesterday's not today. You can **beat it** if you don't like it." In short, I waited.

Not four months later she was in childbed. The townsfolk hid their laughter with their knuckles. But what could I do? She suffered **intolerable** pains and wails. "Gimpel," she cried, "I'm going. Forgive me!" The house filled with women. They were boiling pans of water. The screams rose to the **welkin**.

The thing to do was to go to the House of Prayer to repeat **Psalms**, and that was what I did.

The townsfolk liked that, all right. I stood in a corner saying Psalms and prayers, and they shook their heads at me. "Pray, pray!" they told me. "Prayer never made any woman pregnant." One of the congregation put a straw to my mouth and said, "Hay for the cows." There was something to that too, by God!

---

consented: agreed
dysentery: disease in which a person has severe diarrhea
epidemic: a situation in which a disease spreads quickly among a population
sexton: a person who takes care of the grounds around a house of worship
marriage canopy: the cover under which the Jewish wedding ceremony takes place
chalah: a special bread eaten on the Jewish Sabbath and holidays
revels: wild celebrations
God 'a mercy: God have mercy
Tishe b'Av: a day set aside to remember the sufferings of the Jewish people
crib: a bed for a baby
monthly: a woman's menstrual period
ritual bath: a bath the Jews took to purify themselves symbolically
beat it: go away
intolerable: unacceptable; unbearable
welkin: the sky or the heavens
Psalms: a book of the Jewish Old Testament

synagogue: the name for the place where Jewish people worship

Ark: a special place in a synagogue where the Jewish Torah—the first five books of the Jewish Bible—is kept

circumcision: the act of cutting off a skin covering on the penis; a Jewish rite performed on male babies that symbolizes that the child is part of the Jewish community

She gave birth to a boy. Friday at the **synagogue** the sexton stood up before the **Ark,** pounded on the reading table, and announced, "The wealthy Reb Gimpel invites the congregation to a feast in honor of the birth of a son." The whole of the House of Prayer rang with laughter. My face was flaming. But there was nothing I could do. After all, I was the one responsible for the **circumcision** honors and rituals.

Half the town came running. You couldn't wedge another soul in. Women brought peppered chick-peas, and there was a keg of beer from the tavern. I ate and drank as much as anyone, and they all congratulated me. Then there was a circumcision, and I named the boy after my father, may he rest in peace. When all were gone and I was left with my wife alone, she thrust her head through the door and called me to her.

"Gimpel," said she, "why are you silent? Has your ship gone and sunk?"

"What shall I say?" I answered. "A fine thing you've done to me! If my mother had known of it she'd have died a second time."

She said, "Are you crazy, or what?"

"How can you make such a fool," I said, "of one who should be the lord and master?"

"What's the matter with you?" she said. "What have you taken it into your head to imagine?"

I saw that I must speak bluntly and openly. "Do you think this is the way to use an orphan?" I said. "You have borne a bastard."

She answered, "Drive this foolishness out of your head. The child is yours."

"How can he be mine?" I argued. "He was born seventeen weeks after the wedding."

She told me then that he was premature. I said, "Isn't he a little too premature?" She said she had had a grandmother who carried just as short a time and she resembled this grandmother of hers as one drop of water does another. She swore to it with such oaths that you would have believed a peasant at the fair if he had used them. To tell the plain truth, I didn't believe her; but when I talked it over the next day with the schoolmaster he told me that the very same thing had happened to Adam and Eve. Two they went up to bed, and four they descended.

"There isn't a woman in the world who is not the granddaughter of Eve," he said.

That was how it was—they argued me dumb. But then, who really knows how such things happen?

I began to forget my sorrow. I loved the child madly, and he loved me too. As soon as he saw me he'd wave his little hands and want me to pick him up, and when he was **colicky** I was the only one who could

colicky: suffering from colic, a stomach illness that babies often have

pacify him. I bought him a little bone teething ring and a little **gilded** cap. He was forever catching the **evil eye** from someone, and then I had to run to get one of those **abracadabras** for him that would get him out of it. I worked like an ox. You know how expenses go up when there's an infant in the house. I don't want to lie about it; I didn't dislike Elka either, for that matter. She swore at me and cursed, and I couldn't get enough of her. What strength she had! One of her looks could rob you of the power of speech. And her **orations! Pitch** and **sulphur,** that's what they were full of, and yet somehow also full of charm. I adored her every word. She gave me bloody wounds though.

In the evening I brought her a white loaf as well as a dark one, and also poppyseed rolls I baked myself. I thieved because of her and swiped everything I could lay hands on, macaroons, raisins, almonds, cakes. I hope I may be forgiven for stealing from the Saturday pots the women left to warm in the baker's oven. I would take out scraps of meat, a chunk of pudding, a chicken leg or head, a piece of tripe, whatever I could nip quickly. She ate and became fat and handsome.

I had to sleep away from home all during the week, at the bakery. On Friday nights when I got home she always made an excuse of some sort. Either she had heartburn, or a stitch in the side, or hiccups, or headaches. You know what women's excuses are. I had a bitter time of it. It was rough. To add to it, this little brother of hers, the bastard, was growing bigger. He'd put lumps on me, and when I wanted to hit back she'd open her mouth and curse so powerfully I saw a green haze floating before my eyes. Ten times a day she threatened to divorce me. Another man in my place would have taken **French leave** and disappeared. But I'm the type that bears it and says nothing. What's one to do? Shoulders are from God, and burdens too.

One night there was a **calamity** in the bakery; the oven burst, and we almost had a fire. There was nothing to do but go home, so I went home. Let me, I thought, also taste the joy of sleeping in bed in midweek. I didn't want to wake the sleeping **mite** and tiptoed into the house. Coming in, it seemed to me that I heard not the snoring of one but, as it were, a double snore, one a thin enough snore and the other like the snoring of a slaughtered ox. Oh, I didn't like that! I didn't like it at all. I went up to the bed, and things suddenly turned black. Next to Elka lay a man's form. Another in my place would have made an uproar, and noise to rouse the whole town, but the thought occurred to me that I might wake the child. A little thing like that—why frighten a little swallow like that, I thought. All right then, I went back to the bakery and stretched out on a sack of flour, and till morning I never shut an eye. I shivered as if I had had **malaria.** "Enough of being a donkey," I said to myself. "Gimpel isn't going **to be a sucker** all his life. There's a limit even to the foolishness of a fool like Gimpel."

---

to pacify: to quiet someone down who is angry or upset

gilded: edged with gold or a fine material

evil eye: *To give someone the evil eye* is to put an evil curse on that person by looking at him or her

abracadabras: *Abracadabra,* a term used in magic spells. The term has been made into a noun by adding *s.*

orations: speeches

pitch: a dark, sticky substance found in tar

sulphur (sulfur): a yellow, acidic chemical

French leave: To get leave from the army—a day off or a holiday—a solider had to have permission. To *take French leave* means to leave a situation without permission or to deal with a situation irresponsibly.

calamity: a terrible event that causes much suffering and loss

mite: Slang term meaning *small one.* A mite is a small insect.

malaria: a mosquito-borne illness that causes a person to have a high fever and chills

to be a sucker: to be a person who is easily fooled

commotion: sudden excitement and noisy confusion

beadle: a minor religious official

divinations: predictions of the future or revelations of hidden knowledge through supernatural powers

soiled: made itself dirty by having a bowel movement in its clothes

Ark of the Covenant: the holy place where the Jews kept their most important laws, the Ten Commandments

harlot: a word used to describe a prostitute

brood: the young of an animal

abscess: Infected skin swollen with pus. When the abscess bursts the infection can heal.

lad: young man

led her on: a slang expression meaning to trick someone by making that person think something is true

hallucinations: strange visions caused by a high fever or drugs

mannequin: a copy of a human figure that is often used to model clothes

quill: a feather used for writing

In the morning I went to the rabbi to get advice, and it made a great **commotion** in the town. They sent the **beadle** for Elka right away. She came, carrying the child. And what do you think she did? She denied it, denied everything, bone and stone! "He's out of his head," she said. "I know nothing of dreams or **divinations**." They yelled at her, warned her, hammered on the table, but she stuck to her guns: it was a false accusation, she said.

The butchers and the horse-traders took her part. One of the lads from the slaughterhouse came by and said to me, "We've got our eye on you, you're a marked man." Meanwhile the child started to bear down and **soiled** itself. In the rabbinical court there was an **Ark of the Covenant,** and they couldn't allow that, so they sent Elka away.

I said to the rabbi, "What shall I do?"

"You must divorce her at once," said he.

"And what if she refuses?" I asked.

"You must serve the divorce, that's all you'll have to do."

I said, "Well, all right, Rabbi. Let me think about it."

"There's nothing to think about," said he. "You mustn't remain under the same roof with her."

"And if I want to see the child?" I asked.

"Let her go, the **harlot**," said he, "and her **brood** of bastards with her."

The verdict he gave was that I mustn't even cross her threshold—never again, as long as I should live.

During the day it didn't bother me so much. I thought, it was bound to happen. The **abscess** had to burst. But at night when I stretched out upon the sacks I felt it all very bitterly. A longing took me, for her and for the child. I wanted to be angry, but that's my misfortune exactly, I don't have it in me to be really angry. In the first place—this was how my thoughts went—there's bound to be a slip sometimes. You can't live without errors. Probably that **lad** who was with her **led her on** and gave her presents and what not, and women are often long on hair and short on sense, and so he got around her. And then since she denies it so, maybe I was only seeing things? **Hallucinations** do happen. You see a figure or a **mannequin** or something, but when you come up closer it's nothing, there's not a thing there. And if that's so, I'm doing her an injustice. And when I got so far in my thoughts I started to weep. I sobbed so that I wet the flour where I lay. In the morning I went to the rabbi and told him that I had made a mistake. The rabbi wrote on with his **quill,** and he said that if that were so he would have to reconsider the whole case. Until he had finished I wasn't to go near my wife, but I might send her bread and money by messenger.

III

Nine months passed before all the rabbis could come to an agreement. Letters went back and forth. I hadn't realized that there could be so much **erudition** about a matter like this.

Meantime Elka gave birth to still another child, a girl this time. On the Sabbath I went to the synagogue and invoked a blessing on her. They called me up to the Torah, and I named the child for my mother-in-law, may she rest in peace. The **louts** and loudmouths of the town who came into the bakery gave me a going over. All Frampol refreshed its spirits because of my trouble and grief. However, I resolved that I would always believe what I was told. What's the good of *not* believing? Today it's your wife you don't believe; tomorrow it's God Himself you won't take stock in.

By an **apprentice** who was her neighbor I sent her daily a corn or a wheat loaf, or a piece of pastry, rolls or bagels, or, when I got the chance, a slab of pudding, a slice of honeycake, or wedding strudel—whatever came my way. The apprentice was a goodhearted lad, and more than once he added something on his own. He had formerly annoyed me a lot, plucking my nose and digging me in the ribs, but when he started to be a visitor to my house he became kind and friendly. "Hey, you, Gimpel," he said to me, "You have a very decent little wife and two fine kids. You don't deserve them."

"But the things people say about her," I said.

"Well, they have long tongues," he said, "and nothing to do with them but babble. Ignore it as you ignore the cold of last winter."

One day the rabbi sent for me and said, "Are you certain, Gimpel, that you were wrong about your wife?"

I said, "I'm certain."

"Why, but look here! You yourself saw it."

"It must have been a shadow," I said.

"The shadow of what?"

"Just of one of the beams, I think."

"You can go home then. You owe thanks to the Yanover rabbi. He found an obscure reference in **Maimonides** that favored you." I seized the rabbi's hand and kissed it.

I wanted to run home immediately. It's no small thing to be separated for so long a time from wife and child. Then I reflected, I'd better go back to work now, and go home in the evening. I said nothing to anyone, although as far as my heart was concerned it was like one of the **Holy Days**. The women teased and **twitted** me as they did every day, but my thought was, Go on, with your **loose talk**, the truth is out, like the oil upon the water. Maimonides says it's right, and therefore it is right!

---

erudition: high learning

louts: awkward, foolish people

apprentice: a person who is learning a trade by working with skilled workers

Maimonides: a Jewish philosopher (1135–1204 A.D.)

Holy Days: days set aside for religious reasons

twitted: made fun of

loose talk: careless talk; talk about a person's sexuality

At night, when I had covered the dough to let it rise, I took my share of a little sack of flour and started homeward. The moon was full and the stars were glistening, something to terrify the soul. I hurried onward, and before me a long shadow. It was winter, and a fresh snow had fallen. I had a mind to sing, but it was growing late and I didn't want to wake the householders. Then I felt like whistling, but remembered that you don't whistle at night because it brings the demons out. So I was silent and walked as fast as I could.

Dogs in the Christian yards barked at me when I passed, but I thought, Bark your teeth out! What are you but mere dogs? Whereas I am a man, the husband of a wife, the father of promising children.

As I approached the house my heart started to pound as though it were the heart of a criminal. I felt no fear, but my heart went thump! thump! Well, **no drawing back**. I quietly lifted the latch and went in. Elka was asleep. I looked at the infant's cradle. The shutter was closed, but the moon forced its way through the cracks. I saw the newborn child's face and loved it as soon as I saw it—immediately—each tiny bone.

Then I came nearer to the bed. And what did I see but the apprentice lying there beside Elka. The moon went out all at once. It was utterly black, and I trembled. My teeth chattered. The bread fell from my hands and my wife waked and said, "Who is that, ah?"

I muttered, "It's me."

"Gimpel?" she asked. "How come you're here? I thought it was forbidden."

"The rabbi said," I answered and shook as with a fever.

"Listen to me, Gimpel," she said, "go out to the shed and see if the goat's all right. It seems she's been sick." I have forgotten to say that we had a goat. When I heard she was unwell I went into the yard. The nannygoat was a good little creature. I had a nearly human feeling for her.

With hesitant steps I went up to the shed and opened the door. The goat stood there on her four feet. I felt her everywhere, drew her by the arms, examined her udders, and found nothing wrong. She had probably eaten too much bark. "Good night, little goat," I said. "Keep well." And the little beast answered with a "Maa" as though to thank me. I went back. The apprentice had vanished. "Where," I asked, "is the lad?"

"What lad?" my wife answered.

"What do you mean?" I said. "The apprentice. You were sleeping with him." "The things I have dreamed this night and the night before," she said, "may they come true and lay you low, body and soul! An evil spirit has taken root in you and dazzles your sight." She

---

no drawing back: no possibility to change one's mind or to start something over

screamed out, "You hateful creature! You moon calf. You **spook**! You **uncouth** man! Get out, or I'll scream all Frampol out of bed!"

Before I could move, her brother sprang out from behind the oven and struck me a blow on the back of the head. I thought he had broken my neck. I felt that something about me was deeply wrong, and I said, "Don't make a **scandal**. All that's needed now is that people should accuse me of raising spooks and **dybbuks**." For that was what she had meant. "No one will touch bread of my baking." In short, I somehow calmed her.

"Well," she said, "that's enough. Lie down, and **be shattered by wheels**."

Next morning I called the apprentice aside. "Listen here, brother!" I said. And so on and so forth. "What do you say?" He stared at me as though I had dropped from the roof or something.

"I swear," he said, "You'd better go to an herb doctor or some healer. I'm afraid you have a screw loose, but I'll hush it up for you." And that's how the thing stood.

To make a long story short, I lived twenty years with my wife. She bore me six children, four daughters and two sons. All kinds of things happened, but I neither saw nor heard. I believed, and that's all. The rabbi recently said to me, "Belief itself is beneficial. It is written that a good man lives by his faith."

Suddenly my wife took sick. It began with a **trifle**, a little growth upon the breast. But she evidently was not destined to live long; she had no years. I spent a fortune on her. I have forgotten to say that by this time I had a bakery of my own and in Frampol was considered to be something of a rich man. Daily the healer came, and every witch doctor in the neighborhood was brought. They decided to use **leeches**, and after that to try **cupping**. They even called a doctor from Lublin, but it was too late. Before she died she called me to her bed and said, "Forgive me, Gimpel."

I said, "What is there to forgive? You have been a good and faithful wife."

"Woe, Gimpel!" she said. "It was ugly how I deceived you all these years. I want to go clean to my Maker, and so I have to tell you that the children are not yours."

If I had been **clouted** on the head with a piece of wood it couldn't have **bewildered** me more.

"Whose are they?" I asked.

"I don't know," she said, "there were a lot.... but they're not yours." And as she spoke she tossed her head to the side, her eyes turned glassy, and **it was all up with** Elka. On her whitened lips there remained a smile.

---

spook: a ghost or spirit

uncouth: impolite; uneducated

scandal: a situation that would violate a society's standard's of behavior

dybbuks: souls of the dead that could take over the body of a living person

to be shattered by wheels: to have the feeling that one has been run over by something; to accept one's fate

a trifle: a small matter; something that is not so important

leeches: Blood-sucking worms that live in freshwater. People believed that they could draw out an illness by drawing blood using leeches.

cupping: placing hot cups on the back to create a vacuum that is believed to suck out an illness

clouted: hit hard with some object, usually over the head

bewildered: confused

to be all up with something or someone: to be finished; to be approaching death

I imagined that, dead as she was, she was saying, "I deceived Gimpel. That was the meaning of my brief life."

IV

One night, when the period of mourning was done, as I lay dreaming on the flour sacks, there came the Spirit of Evil himself and said to me, "Gimpel, why do you sleep?"

I said, "What should I be doing? Eating **kreplach?**"

"The whole world deceives you," he said, "and you ought to deceive the world in your turn."

"How can I deceive all the world?" I asked him.

He answered, "You might accumulate a bucket of urine every day and at night pour it into the dough. Let the **sages** of Frampol eat filth."

"What about judgment in the world to come?" I said.

"There is no world to come," he said. "They've sold you a bill of goods and talked you into believing you carried a cat in your belly. What nonsense!"

"Well then," I said, "and is there a God?"

He answered, "There is no God either."

"What," I said "*is* there, then?"

"A thick **mire.**"

He stood before my eyes with a goatish beard and horns, long-toothed, and with a tail. Hearing such words, I wanted to snatch him by the tail, but I tumbled from the flour sacks and nearly broke a rib. Then it happened that I had to answer the call of nature, and, passing, I saw the risen bread, which seemed to say to me, "Do it!" In brief, I let myself be persuaded.

At dawn the apprentice came. We kneaded the dough, scattered caraway seeds on it, and set it to bake. Then the apprentice went away, and I was left sitting in the little trench by the oven, on a pile of rags. Well, Gimpel, I thought, you've revenged yourself on them for all the shame they've put on you. Outside the frost glittered, but it was warm beside the oven. The flames heated my face. I bent my head and fell into **a doze.**

I saw in a dream, at once, Elka in her **shroud.** She called to me, "What have you done, Gimpel?"

I said to her, "It's all your fault," and started to cry.

"You fool!" she said. "You fool! Because I was false is everything false too? I never deceived anyone but myself. I'm paying for it all, Gimpel. They spare you nothing here."

I looked at her face. It was black. I was startled and waked, and remained sitting **dumb.** I sensed that everything hung in the balance. **A false step** now and I'd lose Eternal life. But God gave me His help.

---

kreplach: a type of dumpling filled with meat, cheese, or jam and heated in hot liquid

sages: wise people

mire: Thick mud. *To be mired in something* is to be stuck in something.

a doze: a light sleep

shroud: cloth covering that is wrapped around the dead

dumb: speechless

a false step: a mistake

I seized the long shovel and took out the loaves, carried them into the yard, and started to dig a hole in the frozen earth. My apprentice came back as I was doing it. "What are you doing, boss?" he said, and grew pale as a corpse.

"I know what I'm doing," I said, and I buried it all before his very eyes.

Then I went home, took my **hoard** from its hiding place, and divided it among the children. "I saw your mother tonight," I said. "She's turning black, poor thing."

They were so **astounded** they couldn't speak a word.

"Be well," I said, "and forget that such a one as Gimpel ever existed." I put on my short coat, a pair of boots, took the bag that held my prayer shawl in one hand, my stick in the other, and kissed the **mezzuzah.**

When people saw me in the street they were greatly surprised.

"Where are you going?" they said.

I answered, "Into the world." And so I departed from Frampol.

I wandered over the land, and good people did not neglect me. After many years I became old and white; I heard a great deal, many lies and falsehoods, but the longer I lived the more I understood that there were really no lies. Whatever doesn't really happen is dreamed at night. It happens to one if it doesn't happen to another, tomorrow if not today, or a century **hence** if not next year. What difference can it make? Often I heard tales of which I said, "Now this is a thing that cannot happen." But before a year had elapsed I heard that it actually had come to pass somewhere.

Going from place to place, eating at strange tables, it often happens that I **spin yarns**—improbable things that could never have happened—about devils, magicians, windmills, and the like. The children run after me, calling, "Grandfather, tell us a story." Sometimes they ask for particular stories, and I try to please them. A fat young boy once said to me, "Grandfather, it's the same story you told us before." The little **rogue,** he was right.

So it is with dreams too. It is many years since I left Frampol, but as soon as I shut my eyes I am there again. And whom do you think I see? Elka. She is standing by the washtub, as at our first encounter, but her face is shining and her eyes as radiant as the eyes of a saint, and she speaks outlandish words to me, strange things. When I wake I have forgotten it all. But while the dream lasts I am comforted. She answers all my queries, and what comes out is that all is right. I weep and **implore,** "Let me be with you." And she consoles me and tells me to be patient. The time is nearer than it is far. Sometimes she strokes and kisses me and weeps upon my face. When I awaken I feel her lips and taste the salt of her tears.

hoard: a hidden supply of something; in this case, money

astounded: surprised; amazed

mezzuzah: a container that held Bible verses written on small pieces of paper

hence: from now

to spin yarns: to tell long, magical stories

rogue: a mischievous person

implore: to ask for something in a deeply emotional way

hovel: a small, dirty house

shnorrer: a Yiddish word for a homeless person who begs for a living

No doubt the world is entirely an imaginary world, but it is only once removed from the true world. At the door of the **hovel** where I lie, there stands the plank on which the dead are taken away. The gravedigger has his spade ready. The grave waits and the worms are hungry; the shrouds are prepared—I carry them in my beggar's sack. Another **shnorrer** is waiting to inherit my bed of straw. When the time comes I will go joyfully. Whatever may be there, it will be real, without complication, without ridicule, without deception. God be praised: there even Gimpel cannot be deceived.

"Gimpel the Fool" by Isaac Bashevis Singer, translated by Saul Bellow, copyright 1953, 1954 by the Viking Press, Inc., renewed © 1981, 1982 by Viking Penguin, Inc., from *A Treasury of Yiddish Stories* by Irving Howe and Eliezer Greenberg. Used by permission of Viking Penguin, a division of Penguin Putnam Inc.

Photograph courtesy of Rafael Kapelinski

"When the time comes, I will go joyfully. Whatever may be there, it will be real, without complication, without ridicule, without deception."—Isaac Bashevis Singer, "Gimpel the Fool"

Activity 7.9

Although Gimpel does things that may seem unbelievable, he does seem real as a character. Use details from the story to answer the following questions.

1. What makes Gimpel seem "real" to you?
2. The townspeople characterize Gimpel as being foolish. How would you characterize him?
3. How does Gimpel characterize himself?
4. In what ways do the townspeople appear foolish in this story?
5. What do you find ironic about Gimpel's character?

Activity 7.10a

The characters in "Gimpel the Fool" are influenced by the community in which they live. For this reason, the setting takes on an important role in the story. Just as a writer uses details, actions, dialogue, and narration to create a character, so he or she may choose to give a detailed characterization of a setting by localizing it in a particular time and place. Although Frampol is an imaginary place, it nonetheless reflects the atmosphere of community life found in shtetls in particular and in village life in general. Frampol serves as a microcosm—a small world with its own laws and relationships—in which the character develops.

Village life is often characterized by a close community and traditions. List at least four of the shtetl traditions that are followed in Frampol. Make a note of how these experiences may differ from urban life in big cities or describe how these experiences differ from or relate to your own experience. (Keep in mind that the shtetls existed prior to the 1940s.) The first one has been done for you.

1. The villagers found a places for Gimpel to live after he was orphaned. Where I live, the government places orphans in special homes called orphanages.

Activity 7.10b

A formalist critic would be interested in answering the following questions related to a story's setting.

a. What kind of world does the character live in?
b. What laws govern this world?
c. How do this universe and its laws affect the main character?

How would you answer questions a–c based on the microcosmic world of Frampol and Gimpel's character?

Activity 7.10c ⇨

Consider Elka's character from a feminist viewpoint. How does her role in the community differ from Gimpel's? Why is this the case? How does Elka express her independence?

Activity 7.11 ⇨

How might a Freudian critic analyze Gimpel and his relations with Elka and the townspeople?

Activity 7.12 ⇨

How might a deconstructionist critic explain the various meanings of the word *fool* as it is used in relation to Gimpel?

Activity 7.13 ⇨

In what ways is Gimpel an existential hero?

Activity 7.14 ⇨

Third World: A term used to refer to countries whose economies are not industrialized. Generally, the term refers to countries in Africa, Asia, and Latin America and suggests that a country has a low standard of living. However, this term is often seen as being negative and limiting because it is a generalization about large groups of people.

mimicry: the act of copying behavior

Singer describes a village way of life that was destroyed by war and genocide; however, today many village communities are slowly being destroyed by a process called *globalization*—a process whereby global developments in trade and technology create a more uniform cultural system throughout the world.

The writer Paul Harrison has called globalization *a process of Westernization* because the values and lifestyle of Western culture are spread through the West's dominance in trade and technology. In his book *Inside the Third World* (1981), Harrison writes:

> Go to almost any village in the Third World and you will find youths who scorn traditional dress and sport denims and T-shirt.... Every capital city in the world is getting to look like every other.... And it is not just in consumer fashions: the **mimicry** extends to architecture, industrial technology, approaches to health care, education, and housing.

Harrison argues that the people of the world should not simply abandon their traditional ways to blindly accept Western ways. He calls Westernization a "virus" because he views the process of Westernization as being a kind of infectious disease that no society can escape. He points out that people in the Western world are ethnocentric—they assume that their cultural ways are best and should be adopted by everyone.

In essence, Harrison views Westernization as a slow process of cultural genocide. In response to Harrison's ideas, answer the following questions.

1. How might a community be negatively influenced by Westernization? If possible, use examples with which you are familiar. Explain what happened and why.
2. Are you aware of communities that have been positively influenced by Westernization? If so, describe what happened and why.
3. When a village community such as a shtetl is destroyed, what is lost?
4. How might a deconstructionist critic understand the conflict between village life and urbanization? How might he or she suggest a balance between these two lifestyles?

Activity 7.15 ⇨

Take another look at the statistics presented in activity 7.1.

1. After having read the materials in this chapter, why do you think it is important that people attempt to personalize such statistics? What happens when statistics are viewed **impersonally?**
2. How has your reading of "Gimpel the Fool" changed your understanding of those statistics?
3. How has your reading of "Gimpel the Fool" been similar to the way a sociological critic would read the story?

impersonally: without personal involvement

Photograph courtesy of Rafael Kapelinski

Old Jewish cemetery in Prague, the Czech Repubic
"One death is a tragedy. A million deaths is a statistic." —Joseph Stalin

Activity 7.16a

In some ways, "Gimpel the Fool" is like a fable and a tale because it focuses on everyday life, yet it includes strange events. The story also has a moral: "No doubt the world is entirely an imaginary world, but it is only once removed from the true world."

1. How would you explain this moral in your own words?
2. How is Gimpel's moral similar to Plato's concept of ideal forms?

Activity 7.16b

If you applied Gimpel's moral to literature so that it read "No doubt literature is entirely an imaginary world, but it is only once removed from the true world," how would you interpret this statement?

Activity 7.16c

If you applied Gimpel's moral to literary criticism so that it read "No doubt literary criticism is entirely an imaginary world, but it is only once removed from the true world," how would you interpret this statement?

Chapter 8

Using Source Materials and Critical Approaches to Write about Literature

Photograph courtesy of Marco Fenaroli

"So, the world happens twice—
once what we see it as,
second it legends itself
deep, the way it is."
—William Stafford, "Bi-focal"

Introduction

As you read and respond to the stories in *Literary Odysseys,* your instructor may ask you to write an essay or a research paper in which you analyze a given story based on one of the critical approaches to literature. When writing your paper, it is important to support your ideas with quotations from the original story—your primary source—and/or from other writings found in the textbook or in additional sources from the library—secondary sources. In a research paper, whenever you make a direct quotation of another person's ideas, whether the question is lengthy or only a short phrase, you will need to give that person credit for his or her work. Using such a format will also help you avoid being accused of plagiarizing—simply copying—someone else's ideas. The first part of this chapter provides you with some guidelines for integrating source materials into your writing. The second part includes two sample essays.

Integrating Source Materials into Writing

citation: a quotation whose original source is noted

Quotations from your primary and secondary sources should follow a consistent format. The **citation** format that is often used in writing about literature is called the *MLA format* after the Modern Language Association, the United States–based academic association that developed it. Although the MLA style changes slightly every year, the general principles of the format remain the same. The following explication provides a general overview of the method, but you can refer to the most recent edition of the *MLA Handbook for Writers of Research Papers* (published by the MLA in New York) and the Internet for a more detailed and current explanation of the MLA citation format and a sample Works Cited list.

Essentially, the MLA format allows you to integrate source materials into your own writing in a clear and uncomplicated way. The format relies on parenthetical information that follows each citation so that the reader can refer to a Works Cited list at the end of your paper. In this list, a reader can find all the bibliographic information about the texts that you cite in your paper—the author, the title, the publisher, and the date of publication—so that he or she knows where the information originally appeared and can look it up if necessary. Since a reader can refer to the Works Cited list, your job is to give him or her just enough information to help connect a quotation with a given source on the list.

The following examples are based on texts taken from chapter 1. As you read through the examples, note the variety of ways that source materials can be integrated. When you write your papers, you will want to vary the format of your citations so that your style does not become predictable and monotonous. Since your source will often be the textbook *Literary Odysseys,* simply use the page number on which a quotation appears in the textbook.

1. Generally, the first time you quote or paraphrase an author's work, cite the full name of the author and of the text. You may also want to give a brief explanation of the person's background. Because you're introducing the author to your readers, it's as if you are making a formal introduction and explaining to your reader why this author is important to your research.

   Since the author's name was in your main text, you need only include the page number of the original source. The following example includes a paraphrase of the last line from Marcus Aurelius's *Meditations* followed by explanatory notes.

   Example

   a. In his *Meditations* Marcus Aurelius, a Roman emperor, points out that reason is a gift nature gives to humankind (34).

   Explanatory Notes

   A. The parentheses come after the last word of the sentence.
   B. The page number goes within the parentheses.
   C. The period goes after the closing parenthesis.

2. Once you have introduced an author to your readers, you can just use the author's last name. If you cite the author's name, you do not need to mention the name of the text again. However, you may choose to do so for stylistic reasons.

   Examples

   a. Aurelius declares: "A man's true delight is to do the things he was made for" (33).
   b. "A man's true delight," as Aurelius declares, "is to do the things he was made for" (33).

3. Once you've introduced an author, you can also make a citation in which you include the title of a text but not the author's name. In this case, you only need to include the page number within the parentheses since your reader can refer to your Works Cited list to find the author's name. The following example contains paraphrased information.

   Example

   a. The *Meditations* make it clear that pain can be overcome through the power of reason (34).

4. After having introduced an author and his or her work, you may find that you want to use a quote to make a point but that you do not want to include the author's name or the name of the source in your main text. In this case, you will need to include the author's last name—along with a page number—within parentheses. In this way, a reader can easily refer to your Works Cited list to find the name of the original text. In this case, the example is a paraphrase.

Example

   a. If a person wants to be happy that person should do what he or she was made to do (Aurelius 33).

Explanatory Notes

   A. There is no comma between the last name and the page number.
   B. If you are quoting an author that has written two or more of your sources, then include a shortened version of the title along with the author's name, i.e., (Aurelius, *Meditations* 33).

5. If you cite the same author and the same work in two sentences that follow one another in your paper, you only need to include the page numbers of the different quotes.

Example

   a. According to Aurelius, "Pain must be an evil either to the body or the soul" (33).
   b. Because of this, he believes that a person must refuse to consider pain an evil in order to keep "the soul's skies calm and unclouded" (33).

6. If you use a quotation that is more than four lines long, you should set it off from the main text by indenting from the left margin ten spaces. Avoid using more than one long quote per every two to three pages. Generally, longer quotes are double-spaced, but your instructor may prefer that you use single spacing with long citations. When using long citations, it is helpful to introduce a long quote with a sentence that prepares the reader for the information that follows.

Example

The Buddha believes that people should make more of an effort to control their senses because the five senses can mislead a person:

> For the five senses are rather like arrows which have been smeared with the poison of fancies, have cares for their feathers and happiness for their points, and fly about in the space provided by the range of the sense-objects; shot off by Kama, the God of Love, they hit people in their very hearts as a hunter hits a deer, and if men do not know how to ward off

these arrows, they will be their undoing; when they come near us we should stand firm in self-control, be agile and steadfast, and ward them off with the armor of mindfulness. (26)

For this reason, the Buddha advises people to practice the "restraint of the senses."

Explanatory Notes

A. Use a colon at the end of the introductory sentence.
B. In quotations over four lines, the period comes before the parentheses.
C. Avoid ending a paragraph with a long quotation. At the end of the quote, be sure to include a sentence in your own words that summarizes why the quote is important.

In the preceding examples, the literature is written about in the present tense even though the source material was written at an earlier date. When writing about literature, you use the present tense because you are writing about the author's views *as if* they were a general truth.

As previously mentioned, the examples from the MLA format present general guidelines to help you integrate source materials into your own writing. As you write your paper, you will no doubt find that you are not always sure how to cite a source correctly. The best advice in such an instance would be to refer to the most recent edition of the *MLA Handbook,* to check the Internet, or to ask your instructor. Remember that there is a wide range of possibilities that you can use to vary the way you use sources but, just like anything else, it takes time and practice to become comfortable using different techniques.

Here is a list of words that can help you to vary the way you introduce your source materials. Be sure that the word you choose fits the way you are using a citation.

The author—observes, declares, explains, points out, illustrates, notes, emphasizes, determines, asserts, summarizes, expands on a view, elaborates, believes, argues, **concedes,** concludes.

concedes: acknowledges that another opinion is correct

The point is to try to vary the way in which you integrate source materials so that it does not become predictable and monotonous.

Essays: "The Heart Tells All" and "The Eye of the Id"

As you become more familiar with the techniques used to analyze literature, you will find it easier to write about a literary work because the content of your essay will be organized around a given approach. For example, if you write a paper about the formalistic devices used in a short story, you could choose to focus on the setting, the narrator's point of view, or the characterization methods, etc. In this case you could devote a few paragraphs to each technique or you could choose to focus on one aspect such as the narrative techniques used in Edgar Allen Poe's "The Tell-Tale Heart." Your main job would be to provide evidence from the readings to support your ideas.

To illustrate this point, consider the following short essay based on the materials in chapter 2. The first essay focuses on the narrative techniques used in "The Tell-Tale Heart." The second essay analyzes the narrator's character from a Freudian point of view. The underlined sentence is the author's **thesis** statement. Answer the questions that follow each piece.

thesis: The main point that an author wants to analyze. Often the thesis statement of a paper is found in the first paragraph but not always.

The Heart Tells All

In his "The Tale and Its Effect," Edgar Allen Poe argues that a writer of a tale should have in mind "[a] single effect to be wrought out" (37). <u>In "The Tell-Tale Heart," Poe successfully follows his own advice by using the narrator's voice and the events in the story to create the effect of madness.</u> His narrative demonstrates how madness uses the powers of reason for destructive purposes. In the end, the reader gains insight into the very "heart" of the narrator's madness.

The first sentence in the tale causes the reader to suspect that the narrator is unreliable. The narrator's emphatic "but *why will* you say that I am mad?" immediately causes the reader to question the narrator's sanity. Although the narrator admits that he is nervous, he argues that he is simply overly sensitive. However, his claim that he "heard all things in the heaven and in the earth" suggests that he has a **distorted** perception of reality (42). Perhaps sensing that his claim is exaggerated, the narrator then goes on to prove his sanity by demonstrating how calmly he can tell his story. In spite of this claim, his speech is highly excited, and Poe uses dashes, exclamation points, and italicized words to show that the narrator's speech is **emotionally charged**. Additionally, when he tries to think of why he killed the old man, he seems to be unsure of his motive until he suddenly remembers the eye that had so obsessed him. By his manner of speaking, the narrator **unintentionally** convinces the reader of his madness.

As if sensing his audience's doubt, the narrator determines to prove his sanity by another means: he will convince his audience of his wisdom and reasoning powers. As the narrator retells the events in the rising action that leads to the old man's murder, he unwittingly gives more evidence of his insanity. For example, he takes an entire hour to place his head in the old man's room. He always opens the door at midnight; and, he has to wait for the old man's eye to be open

distorted: twisted beyond a normal shape or meaning

emotionally charged: Very emotional. *To charge something up* means to give it energy from an electric current.

unintentionally: doing something without meaning or intending to do so

before he can kill the old man, for it is the "Evil Eye" and not the old man who bothers him (42). Also, even though the narrator, is proud of the way in which he tries to hide the old man's corpse, the **dismemberment** of the old man's body seems irrational and excessively violent. Curiously, the narrator, who has such an acute sense of hearing, does not seem concerned by the smell that will eventually come from the old man's **decomposing** body beneath the floorboards. The irrationality of the narrator's acts testifies to his perverse powers of reason.

dismemberment: tearing or cutting off the limbs of a body

decomposing: rotting

Ironically, each event the narrator describes in defense of his sanity and cunning only serves to deepen the reader's suspicions that he is mad. Throughout the story, Poe uses dramatic irony to emphasize the gap between the narrator's opinion of himself and the reader's view of him. The final scene of the story clearly demonstrates Poe's technique. In this scene the narrator believes that the officers are pretending not to hear the beating of the old man's heart, whereas the audience knows that, in fact, the policemen cannot hear the heart at all since the old man is dead. But, the narrator declares:

> Oh God! what *could* I do? I foamed—I raved—swore! I swung the chair upon which I had been sitting, and grated it on the floorboards, but the noise arose over all and continually increased. It grew louder—louder—*louder*! And still the men chatted pleasantly, and smiled. Was it possible they heard not? Almighty God!—no, no! They heard!—they suspected!—they *knew!*—they were making a mockery of my terror!—this I thought, and this I think. (45)

Perhaps he hears the beating of his own, fearful heart, but, at this point, the narrator, who has taken such pride in his cleverness, can not bear to be made a fool of by the police. To show that he is clever enough to recognize their "trick," he points it out to them, thus revealing his crime and his madness.

In the end, the narrator's madness and the murder can not be hidden. Poe's ironic point of view suggests that the narrator may **delude** himself but he can not succeed in deluding his audience: the narrator's "clever" reasoning has been used for destructive ends. What the narrator perceives as evidence of sanity is understood as evidence of insanity by his audience. Even so, the title "The Tell-Tale Heart" leaves one wondering if Poe has not caused his readers to participate in the narrator's madness and to thereby feel the "heart" of their own madness. The narrative forces the reader to think about why apparently sane people commit murder and then try to hide it. Why, for example, is the narrator's reason for killing the old man any more or less insane than the "normal" or "understandable" reasons society accepts for murder, such as war? If the narrator had managed to get away with

to delude: to trick, mislead, or deceive

his crime would his audience have thought him sane? These are the questions that "The Tell-Tale Heart" asks indirectly and leaves to the reader to answer. Poe's ironic point of view questions not only the narrator's sanity but also the sanity of those who judge him.

© 2000 University of Michigan

Questions for "The Heart Tells All" ⇨

1. About how many citations are there in each paragraph? How many citations are made up of at least one complete sentence? How many are made up of phrases? How many citations are over four lines long?
2. In paragraph 2, the author argues that the narrator's way of speaking convinces the reader of his madness. What evidence from "The Tell-Tale Heart" does she use to prove her point.
3. In paragraph 3, the author suggests that the narrator fails to prove his sanity by convincing his audience of his reasoning powers. What details from the story does she use to support her idea?
4. In paragraph 4, the author claims that Poe uses dramatic irony to emphasize the gap between the narrator's opinion of himself and the reader's view of him. What scene from the story does the author use to illustrate her claim?

The Eye of the Id

As Edgar Allen Poe argues in his "The Tale and Its Effect," a writer of a tale should have in mind "[a] single effect to be wrought out" (37). In "The Tell-Tale Heart," Poe successfully follows his own advice by using the narrator's voice and the events in the story to create the effect of madness. His narrative demonstrates how madness uses the powers of reason for destructive purposes. In the end, the reader gains insight into the very "heart" of the narrator's madness. <u>A Freudian analysis of the narrator can provide further insights into the character's possible motivations and madness.</u>

Although it is clear from the story's initial sentence that the narrator is unreliable, if not mad, his **articulateness** and his desire to appear wise may momentarily persuade his audience **to suspend their judgment.** From the beginning, the narrator tries to appeal to the superegos of his audience by assuming that they share his cleverness. He flatters their egos, thus encouraging his audience to continue listening to him. He explains: "Now, this is the point. You fancy me mad. Madmen know nothing. . . . You should have seen how wisely I proceeded . . . to kill the old man" (42). Although he claims to possess the superego's voice of calmness and reason, his manner of speaking—punctuated with dashes, italicized words, and exclamation

articulateness: the ability to use words effectively; eloquence

to suspend judgment: to wait for all the evidence before forming an opinion

points—**undermines** his claim. In fact, his overly developed superego apparently contributes to his insanity: he thinks it admirable that he "heard all things in the heaven and in the earth" (42); and he thinks his reaction to the old man's eye is completely rational. As if sensing that the reader doubts the claims of his superego, the narrator determines to prove his sanity by convincing the reader of his wisdom and reasoning powers. He proceeds to describe in careful detail the events leading up to the old man's murder, but this account causes the reader to further question the narrator's sanity. It seems irrational that the narrator took an hour to put his head inside the old man's door and even more irrational that he did this for seven nights in a row, exactly at midnight. Also, the narrator's overdeveloped superego causes him to reveal his deed primarily because he felt that the police mocked him by pretending not to hear the beating of the old man's heart.

<small>undermines: weakens</small>

But there is a reason to the narrator's madness: he can not kill the old man unless he sees the open eye because it is the eye, and not the old man himself, that disturbs the narrator. Ironically, the narrator himself suggests the nature of his psychological ailment: he has projected the evil of his own id onto the **deformity** of the old man's eye. The narrator obsessively describes the eye in detail; it resembles "that of a vulture—a pale blue eye, with a film over it" (42). Subconsciously, the narrator links the eye with the vulture, a bird that symbolizes death. Since the narrator is unaware of his own evil, he can not explain why he is so obsessed with the old man's eye. Because he lacks a conscious understanding of his motivations, his own unconscious fears cause him to kill the old man. He destroys the eye rather than facing the evil within his id.

<small>deformity: an unnatural shape</small>

The narrator's decision to dismember the corpse with a knife, a phallic symbol, suggests that he had repressed aspects of his own sexuality. His relationship to the old man is unclear, but he does say that he "loved the old man" (42), and he may have subconsciously resented the old man as a father figure. Also, his instinctive decision to dismember the old man in order to hide the body suggests that his sexual nature had been repressed and perverted. Clearly, the narrator takes a certain perverse pleasure in describing the details of the dismemberment:

> First of all I dismembered the corpse. I cut off the head and the arms and the legs.
>
> I then took up three planks from the flooring of the chamber, and deposited all between the scantlings. I then replaced the boards so cleverly, so cunningly, that no human eye—not even *his*—could have detected anything wrong. There was nothing to wash out—no stain of any kind—

> no bloodspot whatever. I had been too wary for that. A tub had caught it all—ha! ha! (44)

His laughter is the pleasure the id takes in its release.

In an analysis of the narrator's character, it is up to the reader to provide the balancing powers of the ego in order to mediate between the extremes of the narrator's superego and id. Since the reader supposedly has a healthy ego, he or she can recognize the gap between the narrator's opinion of himself and the opinion his audience must have of him. Poe's ironic point of view forces the reader to recognize that the narrator has violated accepted societal norms. But, however much readers may try to suppress their ids while reading "The Tell-Tale Heart," they cannot help wondering what might drive them to murder another human being and whether or not that murder would be judged sane or insane by society. Poe's narrative forces his readers to consider their own subconscious desires and fears. As a result, such unconscious feelings can then be dealt with by the ego and superego. The reader becomes aware that the tell-tale heart is not only the heart of the narrator or of the old man but also his or her own.

© 2000 University of Michigan

Questions for "The Eye of the Id" ⇨

1. About how many citations are there in this essay? How many are there per paragraph? How many citations are made up of at least one complete sentence? How many are made up of phrases? How many citations are over four lines long?
2. In paragraph 2, the author points out that the narrator tries to appeal to the superegos of his audience but fails. What examples from "The Tell-Tale Heart" does the author give to suport her point?
3. In paragraph 3, the author observes that the narrator himself suggests the nature of his psychological problems. What details from the story does she provide to give weight to this observation?
4. In paragraph 4, the author focuses on the scene in which the narrator describes how he dismembered the corpse. How does the author relate the narrator's actions in this scene to Freudian psychology?
5. In what ways do the two essays differ? How are they similar?

Chapter 9
Biographies

Photograph courtesy of Rafael Kapelinski

"I am learning both sides
of the window, and standing between, turning to glass."
—William Stafford, "Tracks in the Sand"

Aurelius, Marcus (121–80 A.D.)

The Roman emperor Marcus Aurelius believed that a moral life could be lived through the power of reason. He also stressed the **Stoic** belief that self-control and public service were the **hallmarks** of the good life. He gathered ideas about how to live a moral life into twelve books called the *Meditations*. Aurelius used a collection of aphorisms—short, insightful statements—to emphasize his point. Aurelius compiled his notes while governing and while leading defensive campaigns to protect the northern borders of Rome from Germanic tribes. Although he is known as a protector of the poor and for having established progressive tax and criminal laws, he also persecuted Christians because he felt Christianity **undermined** the rule of the Roman state.

As emperor, Aurelius recognized the need for Roman society to exert self-discipline to retain its power. He warned against living a life based solely on pleasure and encouraged people to live a morally **upright** life. In spite of Aurelius's efforts to protect Rome's borders from "**barbaric**" tribes and to motivate Romans to act selflessly for the state, the Roman Empire broke up within two hundred fifty years of his death.

> **Stoic:** one who follows the Stoic idea that wise people should be controlled by reason, not emotions
> **hallmarks:** the main characteristics of something
> **undermined:** weakened
> **upright:** marked by correct behavior; just
> **barbaric:** unnaturally cruel; wild; lacking the qualities of civilization

Baldwin, James (1924–87)

The title of Baldwin's collection of essays *The Fire Next Time* (1963) testifies to the more radical approach he took toward the subject of race in the United States. In his essays and in his novels, stories, and plays, Baldwin gives creative expression to the rage and anguish felt by those who are oppressed because of their race and/or sexual orientation—as an African American and a homosexual, Baldwin had firsthand experience of both. He saw himself as a writer and as a revolutionary whose works would cause people to **grapple** with social injustices.

Baldwin spent ten years writing his first novel, *Go Tell It on the Mountain!* (1953), a work of autobiographical fiction that gained him recognition as a spokesperson on race relations in the United States. He began writing the novel in Greenwich Village, an artist community in New York. While in New York, Baldwin met Richard Wright, who was already established as a writer. Wright helped Baldwin to find work as a reviewer and encouraged his writing. The publication of Baldwin's first short story, "Previous Condition," enabled him to receive a writing **fellowship** in 1948. The fellowship funded his move to Paris, where much of *Go Tell It on the Mountain!* was written. He returned to the States in 1957 and was an activist in the Civil Rights movement of the 1960s. In 1987, Baldwin died in Paris, far from his birthplace in Harlem, New York, where he was raised with his eight brothers and sisters.

As a fourteen year old, Baldwin experienced a religious **conversion** and became a **Pentecostal** preacher, but, after graduating from high

> **to grapple:** to struggle with something
> **fellowship:** a financial award that allows a person to study
> **conversion:** the experience of deciding to believe in a particular faith
> **Pentecostal:** a Christian religion that focuses on the work of the Holy Spirit

school, he turned from preaching to writing—a tool he saw as a more effective means of bringing about social change. In Baldwin's "Fifth Avenue, Uptown: A Letter from Harlem" (1960) he writes, "One cannot deny the humanity of another without **diminishing** his own: in the face of one's victim, one sees himself." This idea was later echoed by Martin Luther King in his "Letter from Birmingham Jail" in 1963.

diminishing: making less; decreasing

BARTHES, ROLAND (1915–80)

In **postwar** France, Roland Barthes was one of the central **proponents** of structuralism and poststructuralism. He drew heavily from the theories advanced by the anthropologist Lévi-Strauss in order to analyze not only works of literature but also the "language" of popular culture found in "texts" such as advertisements and wrestling matches. His first major work was *Le Degre Zero de l'Ecriture* (Writing Degree Zero, 1953, trans. 1968), which he wrote in response to Jean-Paul Sartre's *What Is Literature?*

postwar: after the war
proponents: those who put forward and support an idea

During his years as a professor at the Ecole Pratique des Hautes Études in Paris and at the College of France, he published numerous critical works, including an essay entitled "The Structuralist Activity" (in *Critical Essays*, 1964, trans. 1972) wherein he lays out the central principles of structuralism. He identifies the structuralist or the "structural man" as one who has "the power to speak the old languages of the world in a new way." Because of this, structuralism is an "activity," not just a critical method by which one reconstructs "an 'object' in such a way as to manifest thereby the rules of the functioning ('the functions') of this object." In other words, the structuralist makes visible a structure that had previously remained hidden or unseen in the object itself. In this sense, the structuralist creates what Barthes calls a *simulacrum* of the original object: a **representation** of the original object but one that differs from the original version because it *consciously* exposes the object's structure. Thus, the structuralist creates something new: that is, an understanding of how meaning is **fabricated** in a work of art or in a society. By so reconstructing a work, a structuralist adds to it. Barthes points out that the structural approach would change as society changed because "structuralism, too, is a certain form of the world, which will change with the world."

representation: an image; copy

fabricated: made

BROOKS, CLEANTH (1906–94)

Brooks is viewed as a founder of the New Criticism movement that took shape during his years as a student of literature at Vanderbilt University. There, along with other students from the South, such as Robert Penn Warren and Allen Tate, and his professor John Crowe Ransom, Brooks formed a group known first as the Southern **Agrarians** and then as the

agrarians: those who work the land

> fugitives: runaways from the law
>
> tenets: beliefs; principles

Fugitives. From this group's discussion about literature and literary criticism, New Criticism developed. In 1947, Brooks published a collection of essays entitled *The Well-Wrought Urn* that set forth the **tenets** of New Criticism and applied New Criticism to the analysis of poetry. The title of the collection comes from a poem by John Keats (1795–1821) to which Brooks applies the New Criticism. After his years as a student in the States and in Oxford, Brooks taught at Louisiana State University and then at Yale.

CAMUS, ALBERT (1913–60)

Camus's first novel, *The Stranger,* was published when he was twenty-eight. His second, *The Plague,* appeared in 1947 and was written during Camus's service in the **French Resistance.** While Camus's writings reflect existential themes, Camus did not **align** himself with any philosophical or ideological system. He was, however, actively involved in social reform. Having been born into a poor Algerian family, Camus was familiar with the struggles of the poor and working-class families. In grade school, Camus received encouragement from his teacher Louis Germain, who served as his **mentor** throughout his life.

> French Resistance: those who fought against the Nazis in France during World War II
>
> to align: to associate oneself with something
>
> mentor: a teacher who gives special guidance

In addition to his novels, Camus wrote philosophical works such as *The Myth of Sisyphus* (1942, trans. 1955), dramas, and essays. He traveled extensively, worked as a journalist, and was involved in both amateur and professional theater. During World War II, he worked as a coeditor with Jean-Paul Sartre on a **left-wing** newspaper, but, in 1948, he left the newspaper when he disassociated himself from political writing. In 1957, he received the Nobel Prize in literature. Only three years later, at the age of forty-six, Camus was killed in a car accident. Because of this, his autobiographical novel *The First Man* and his *Notebooks* were published posthumously by his family.

> left-wing: holding more liberal political views as opposed to right-wing or conservative views

DERRIDA, JACQUES (b. 1930)

Derrida, an Albanian-born and French-educated philosopher, has gained worldwide attention for his "deconstruction" of Western philosophy. His **seminal** ideas can be found in his first three published works: *Speech and Phenomena* (1967, trans. 1973), *Writing and Difference* (1967, trans. 1973), and *Of Grammatology* (1967, trans. 1974). Even as Derrida's theories on language and the reading of a text have reshaped approaches taken by disciplines such as literature and linguistics, his work remains **controversial** and has been criticized for having undermined traditional notions of reality and personality as well as language and literature. Derrida, however, has argued that the word *deconstruction* has nothing to do with the act of destruction but that "it is simply a question of . . . being alert to the implications, to the historical **sedimentation** of the language which we use—and that is not destruction."

> seminal: original; creative
>
> controversial: problematic; causing disagreement
>
> sedimentation: multiple layers, usually of soil, but, in this case, of language and meaning

Derrida, who has taught alternately at the Sorbonne in Paris and at universities in the United States, has a strong following among his peers and those who apply his philosophical theories to their respective disciplines. Terms and ideas common to his approach, such as *underlying assumptions, hierarchies of power,* and *authority,* have made their way from intellectual circles into a wider public **discourse** that includes even movie titles such as that of the film *Deconstructing Henry* (1997), directed by Woody Allen.

discourse: oral or written communication

Edwards, Jonathan (1703–58)

From 1729 until 1750, Edwards served as the minister of a church in Northampton, Massachusetts, where he gave nearly one thousand sermons that have been preserved. His most famous sermon is called "Sinners in the Hands of an Angry God." In this sermon, he says that God holds sinners over "the pit of hell" as if they were a spider dangling from a thread, and thus he urges his listeners to acknowledge their sin so that they can become "holy and happy children of the King of kings."

Although Edwards believed in God's love, his writings reflect the Puritan's belief in the **depravity** of humankind and the fear that one could never live a fully holy life. In his *Personal Narrative,* Edwards gives a description of his own conversion experience in which he became sure of his calling to become a minister. In 1751, Edwards accepted a position as a minister in an isolated part of Massachusetts. Eventually, he was appointed as the president of Princeton University. Edwards's writings and life reflect his determination to live out the Puritan code.

depravity: evil

Feyerabend, Paul (1924–94)

Although Paul Feyerabend is considered to be a philosopher, he would probably rather be known as an antiphilosopher. In books such as *Against Method* (1975) and *Farewell to Reason* (1987), he questions the belief that scientific method is truly objective and **disinterested.** He argues that the scientific view of the world can also be subjective and can serve the self-interest of scientists and the state, and he expresses his concern that a scientific approach to life leads to conformity and **dehumanizes** the individual.

disinterested: not interested in gain

dehumanizes: takes away a person's humanity or dignity

Feyerabend was born and raised in Vienna, Austria, where he ended up studying physics at the university, although he also was interested in the opera and had studied acting and singing as a youth. In 1938, when Germany occupied Austria, Feyerabend hoped to avoid combat by enrolling in an officer's school. But, in 1945, he found himself on the Russian front. While retreating from the Soviet army, Feyerabend was shot in the back. After a long rehabilitation, he regained his ability to walk and returned to the university, where he switched from the study of physics to philosophy. In the 1950s, he went on to study at the London School of Economics and then to the University of Bristol in England, where he was a professor. In 1959, he became a professor at the University of Berkeley in California. In his retirement, he moved to Switzerland, where he died of a brain tumor in Geneva. His autobiography, *Killing Time*, was published posthumously in 1995.

FISH, STANLEY (b. 1938)

Stanley Fish's reputation as a reader response critic followed the publication of his 1967 work *Surprised by Sin: The Reader in "Paradise Lost."* In this work, Fish, whose academic background is in seventeenth-century literature, focuses on the reader's response to the poem "Paradise Lost" (1667), by John Milton (1608–74). Rather than focusing on the form of the poem, Fish focuses on ways in which the reader's experience of the poem gives it meaning. During the course of his academic career as a professor at the University of California at Berkeley and at Johns Hopkins University, Fish expanded his views in works such as *Self-Consuming Artifacts: The Experience of Seventeenth Century Literature.* In this work, he argues that a "real reader" will make every effort to be an informed and educated reader of a text. And, in his 1980 essay "Interpreting the *Variorum*" (the *Variorum* is another work by Milton) Fish puts forth his idea of "interpretive communities." He reasserts his belief that the meaning of a text is not within the text itself but within the mind of the reader, a reader who, rightly or wrongly, comes to a text with preconceived strategies for creating meaning. In many ways, Fish, having moved beyond formalism and structuralism, approached a deconstructionist view of a text

FRANKL, VIKTOR (1905–97)

Viktor Frankl was born and raised in Austria, where he studied at the University of Vienna. After graduation, he became a professor there and taught in the fields of neurology and psychiatry. In 1942, the Nazis imprisoned Frankl, and he managed to survive two and a half years in four different concentration camps. His personal account of his experiences in the death camps can be read in his *Death Camp to Existentialism* (1959) as well as in *Man's Search for Meaning: An Introduction to Logotherapy* (1962). Frankl's concept of Logotherapy is based on the belief that a human being must satisfy his or her need to determine what makes life meaningful. After the war, Frankl taught at Harvard University and the Southern Methodist University in the United States.

FREUD, SIGMUND (1856–1939)

Freud is generally associated with the **Viennese** school of psychiatry. He studied at the University of Vienna (1873–83), worked for three years at

Viennese: having to do with Vienna

the General Hospital of Vienna in the field of psychology and nervous diseases, and went on to establish a private practice in Vienna that specialized in nervous disorders. In 1902, he became a professor at the University of Vienna. Most of Freud's most influential ideas developed from the late 1880s through the turn of the century. In the years that followed, he developed his method of depth psychology, or psychoanalysis. As a student, Freud had been interested in the relationship between **neurology** and mental illness, but, during his work at the General Hospital of Vienna, he studied **hysteria** and became interested in the link between psychology and mental and physical disorders. At this time, he began to shape his theories of the unconscious and human sexuality.

Freud's ideas initially provoked disapproval from those who were shocked by his **conceptualization** of the human psyche and particularly by his belief that sexuality shaped human behavior—in children as well as adults. Nonetheless, his views eventually gained acceptance, and he is now considered by many to be the founder of modern psychology. In 1938, when the Nazis invaded Austria, Freud was placed under **house arrest** because of his Jewish ancestry. When the Germans released Freud, his family escaped to London, England, where he died in 1939. His escape to England sadly echoed his family's escape from his town of birth, Freiberg (now Pribor in the Czech Republic), when Freud was three years old—at that time, his family moved to Vienna in order to avoid **anti-Semitic** riots.

neurology: the study of the nervous system

hysteria: a state of unnatural emotional excitement

conceptualization: the way a person thinks of an idea or concept

house arrest: the state of being kept under guard in one's own home

anti-Semitic: against Jewish people

GAUTAMA, SIDDHĀRTHA (563–483 B.C.)

The name *Buddha* means *enlightened one.* In the Buddhist tradition, a person who is enlightened has found the path out of human suffering. This path leads to Nirvana, in which a person escapes from the cycle of **reincarnation** and is at peace. To achieve enlightenment, the Buddha developed the Eight-Fold Path, a way of life that includes rules of behavior such as meditation, correct living, and self-control—the Eight-Fold Path is described in the Buddhist Scriptures. Since Siddhārtha Gautama is believed to have reached a stage of enlightenment, he is called the *Buddha.*

Because the Buddha did not write down an account of his own life or of his teachings, accounts of his life are based on historical texts. According to tradition, the Buddha led a **sheltered** youth as a Nepalese prince, and it was not until he was twenty-nine that he first witnessed human suffering. He then determined to leave his family, wife, and wealth behind in order to seek the path to enlightenment so that he could teach people how to escape suffering. After years of meditation and **ascetic** living as a wanderer, he achieved enlightenment while gazing upon the morning star. The Buddha's teaching spread from India to Asia and resulted in the formation of different schools of Buddhist thought.

reincarnation: rebirth on this earth after one's death

sheltered: protected

ascetic: marked by self-denial and spiritual discipline

Harrison, Paul

As a French lecturer at the University of Ife in Nigeria, Harrison developed an interest in Third World countries. From 1975 to 1980, Harrison traveled throughout the Third World, spending time in ten countries in Africa to South America and India. His book *Inside the Third World* (1981) came out of his firsthand experiences in these places. Harrison, a London-based freelance writer, has contributed to *Encyclopedia Britannica* and has also written for magazines as varied as the *Guardian* and *New Scientist* as well as for international organizations such as UNICEF and the World Health Organization.

Hawthorne, Nathaniel (1804–64)

> **to subscribe to:** to hold a belief in something
>
> **atonement:** payment made to cover a person's sin

Although much of Hawthorne's work focuses on the Puritan heritage of his ancestry, he himself did not **subscribe to** a particular religion. His works explore the Puritan psyche in particular and the human psyche in general, especially as issues of sin, pride, guilt, punishment, and **atonement** shape human behavior. After his graduation from college in 1825, he returned to Salem, where he lived with his mother and sisters. For twelve years, he lived in semiseclusion reading and writing. The short story "Young Goodman Brown" first appeared in a gift magazine. In 1837, a collection of his stories was published in his first book length work, entitled *Twice Told Tales*.

> **modest:** a small amount
>
> **the eve of:** immediately before the beginning of

During the summer and fall of 1849, Hawthorne took to writing full-time, up to nine hours a day, and wrote his first successful novel, *The Scarlet Letter*. The book's popularity provided Hawthorne with a **modest** income. In the next three years, he wrote two more novels and more short story collections. His work received critical acclaim and established him as an American author of importance. In 1857, his family moved to Italy and did not return to the States until 1860, upon **the eve of** the Civil War. He died in 1864 before the war's end.

Hemingway, Ernest (1899–1961)

> **correspondent:** A person who communicates with another by letter. A *war correspondent* sends news to a newspaper or to a broadcast network, frequently from a faraway location.

Hemingway's life and writings span the experiences of World Wars I and II. At the age of eighteen, Hemingway left the peaceful surroundings of his hometown, Oak Park, Illinois, for war-torn Italy during World War I. Since an eye defect kept him out of the army, he volunteered to be an ambulance driver. In Italy, he saw fighting as an infantryman with the Italian army. Between the world wars, he worked as a newspaper correspondent in Spain during the Spanish Civil War (1936–39). During World War II, he served as a war **correspondent** and was present at several key battles, including the invasion of Normandy. Hemingway's war experiences formed the basis for many of his most well-known novels, such as *A*

Farewell to Arms (1929) and *For Whom the Bell Tolls* (1940). The generation between the wars became known as the *lost generation,* and Hemingway's works are said to speak for the moral confusion of the generation that had experienced a loss of values and a growth of cynicism as a result of World War I. His novel *The Sun Also Rises* (1926) depicts the lifestyles of Americans and Britons living in Europe between the world wars.

In his writing, Hemingway **cultivated** a direct and clear style that he said a person with a high school education should be able to read and understand. He wanted his writing to convey a realistic experience using as little direct characterization as possible. In his personal life, Hemingway cultivated the image of athleticism and adventure. His interests in outdoor sports and bullfighting are evident in his works. In 1954, Hemingway received the Nobel Prize in literature. Seven years later, in ill health, Hemingway committed suicide by shooting himself in the forehead with a double-barreled shotgun.

cultivated: took care to make something grow; improved by labor

HITLER, ADOLF (1889–1945)

The dictator of Germany from 1939 to 1945, Adolf Hitler was raised in the Austrian countryside. As a young man, Hitler considered himself to be an artist. Twice he attempted to enter the Vienna Academy of Arts: the first time he failed the test and was advised to pursue a career in architecture, for which he apparently had talent; the second time he was not given the chance to sit for the exam. After his second rejection, in 1909, he lived in a home for men, living off a small pension and earning a bit of money selling paintings and drawings of scenes of Vienna. He lived in this way from 1909 until 1914. During this time he developed his **anti-Marxist** and anti-Semitic views.

Hitler, who had volunteered to fight during World War I (1914–18), viewed Germany's defeat as a great blow to German **nationalism** and German pride. Upon leaving the army in 1920, he joined a nationalistic organization that came to be known as the National Socialist German Workers Party, or the Nazi Party. In 1921, he was voted chairman of the party. He organized the development of an armed force called *storm troopers* who used violence to terrorize his political opponents, a pattern that he followed throughout his political career. In 1923, he attempted to overthrow the leadership of the Weimar Republic in order to establish a regime that would restore Germany as a national power. For his involvement in the failed **putsch,** Hitler was arrested and ordered to serve a five-year prison term, but he spent only nine months in jail and used the time to write his *Mein Kampf* (My Struggle), in which he described his life and his political beliefs. After his release, Hitler built up his party via legal means. He used this opportunity to put forward his anti-Marxist, anti-Semitic

anti-Marxist: against the beliefs of Karl Marx (1818–83), a German philosopher and the founder of communism

nationalism: a belief system that puts one's nation before all others; national pride

putsch: an attempt to overthrow a government

views and to attract many voters who were disillusioned with the government in power. In 1933, he was voted **chancellor** of Germany. As chancellor, he moved quickly to establish Nazi Party members in key government positions, banned all opposition parties, and put thousands of his opponents into concentration camps. Hitler set out to restore Germany's military, which had been destroyed by the Treaty of Versailles of 1919. By 1938, he felt confident enough to invade the western portion of the former Czechoslovakia. This marked the beginning of World War II. At the war's end, Hitler committed suicide.

chancellor: the chief executive officer of a state system

HUGHES, LANGSTON (1902–67)

Langston Hughes was one of the first African American writers to gain national and international standing. When he was still in high school, one of his poems appeared in a magazine published by the National Association for the Advancement of Colored People (NAACP). Although pressured by his father to study engineering, Hughes was determined to be a writer. This decision resulted in Hughes's **estrangement** from his father. To mark this estrangement, Hughes shortened his birth name, James Langston Hughes, by dropping his father's name, James, and taking his mother's maiden name, Langston, as his pen name.

estrangement: unfriendly separation

After his break with his father and from the university, he joined the **merchant marines** in 1923 as a chef's assistant. His job with the merchant marines took him to Africa. From there he made his way to Paris, France, working at odd jobs and experiencing the art world. After his return to the States he took a job as a waiter's assistant in a hotel. There he crossed paths with the poet Vachel Lindsay, who used his influence to publish Hughes's poetry in a newspaper. This publication led to a scholarship to Lincoln University and a book of poems entitled *The Weary Blues,* which won him national attention. After his graduation from college, Hughes traveled extensively through Cuba, Haiti, the United States, the Soviet Union, and Asia. His travels eventually led to the writing of the autobiographical work *I Wonder as I Wander* (1956).

merchant marines: individuals who are paid to work on ships that are associated with a naval force

Hughes is known for giving a voice to the African American experience by using themes related to the everyday life of the black community and by **incorporating** the rhythms of black music and speech patterns into his writing. His work served as an inspiration for the Harlem Renaissance, a period in the early twentieth century in which African American artists and intellectuals began to shape and promote black art. In addition to writing poetry, Hughes wrote plays, short stories, children's books, and four novels. He also founded three theaters for black artists. In his adult years he traveled in Russia and Asia and reported on the Spanish Civil War for a U.S. newspaper. His poetry and prose depict the injustices in society in a realistic and often humorous or satirical style.

incorporating: using; involving

Jacobs, Harriet Ann (1813–97)

Harriet Jacobs took the pen name Linda Brent to write of her experiences as a slave in North Carolina. Jacobs tells of her relatively happy childhood years until the death of her mother when Jacobs was six. Only after her mother's death did Jacobs realize that she was a slave. In her diary, she describes her years as a slave in the household of Dr. James Norcom (called Dr. Flint in her diary) and her decision to escape from slavery at the age of twenty-two. After her escape, she hid in her grandmother's attic for seven years before she was able to gain secret passage to the North to Philadelphia. Jacobs had to wait another six years before her children, who were fathered by a white man, would manage to escape to the North as well.

Even though Jacobs had escaped to the North, she still had **to evade** the efforts of slaveholders to have her captured. At the age of forty, she finally obtained legal freedom when her northern employer "purchased" her and then gave Jacobs her freedom. In the preface to her autobiography, Jacobs writes, "I do earnestly desire **to arouse** the women of the North to a realizing sense of the condition of two millions of women at the South, still in bondage, suffering what I suffered, and most of them far worse. I want to add my **testimony** to that of **abler** pens to convince the people of the Free States what Slavery really is. Only by experience can any one realize how deep, and dark, and foul is that pit of **abominations**." Her diary is a powerful testimony against slavery and racial prejudice.

to evade: to avoid; to escape from

to arouse: to cause; to awaken

testimony: evidence given by a witness

abler: more able; with more talent

abominations: unnatural, evil acts

Jung, Carl Gustav (1875–1961)

Born and raised in Switzerland, Jung graduated from college in 1902 with a degree in medicine. After his graduation, he married Emma Rauschenbach, with whom he had five children. In 1905 he became a lecturer on the medical faculty at the University of Zurich, and, by 1906, Jung was in **correspondence** with Freud, with whom he developed a professional and personal relationship. In 1912, Jung published a book entitled *Psychology of the Unconscious* in which he put forward his theory of the collective unconscious, a part of the psyche made up of archetypal images. Jung believed that the collective unconscious exists independently of the individual and is part of a person's psychic makeup. According to Jung, archetypes shape the human personality. Jung found evidence of the archetypes in the fact that symbols and myths from different cultures reflect the images found in the fantasies of **psychotic** patients. Jung also argued that the individual was primarily motivated by the creative energy of the **collective** unconscious rather than by sexual desires.

Freud refused to accept Jung's ideas, believing that Jung had rebelled against him. After the break, Jung went on to develop his own theory of

correspondence: communication by letters

psychotic: having a mental and/or emotional disorder

collective: marked by individuals in a group having shared characteristics or similarities

the psyche. He outlined the process of individuation whereby an individual can integrate his or her personal unconscious with the collective unconscious, thus achieving psychological wholeness. He also developed the concept of the female archetype, the *anima,* and the male archetype, the *animus,* which he understood as possessing **inherent** gender-based characteristics. According to Jung, the anima and animus are part of the psychic makeup of men and women. Jung believed that such archetypes are initially shaped by our parents and then by the collective force of the archetypes themselves.

inherent: a natural, inborn part of something

Many feminists regard his theory of the male and female aspects of the human personality as sexist and reductive. Nonetheless, Jung's efforts to develop a new psychological method of analysis, *analytical psychology,* broadened the picture of the human psyche. He also inspired many Jungian and mythic critics who would look for parallels between cultural myths and human experience, including literature in their investigations. Throughout his life, Jung traveled around the world gathering information about myths and symbols that he then related to his study of the psyche.

KIERKEGAARD, SØREN (1813–55)

Lutheran: one who follows the teachings of Martin Luther (1483–1546)

aesthetic: having to do with things that are beautiful and pleasing

Kierkegaard was raised in a strict, **Lutheran** household. At the age of seventeen, he began his studies at the University of Copenhagen. During his studies, he rejected the strict codes of his religious upbringing and lived a life of what he would later call **aesthetic** pleasures. At the university, he also developed an interest in philosophy and wrote his dissertation, which was entitled "On the Concept of Irony," an analysis of Socratic irony. Although he had studied theology intensely, he chose not to become a minister, and, in 1841, at the age of twenty-seven, he broke off his engagement to the seventeen-year-old Regine Olon. Rather than pursue the ministry or marriage, he chose to devote himself to writing and wrote twenty books from 1841 until his death. Nonetheless, the decision to break off his engagement to follow his calling as a philosopher caused him great anguish and doubt that are reflected in his writings.

KING, MARTIN LUTHER, JR. (1929–68)

Dr. King is the only American who was not a president to be honored with a federal legal holiday. That holiday is on the third Monday in January. Twenty-five years after his assassination, King received this honor for his work as the leader of the Civil Rights movement in the United States. Before his death King had been planning a "poor people's march" on Washington, a march that would have carried on the tradition of the Freedom March on Washington, DC, which he led in 1963. At the Freedom March, he led a crowd of nearly three hundred thousand people to the Lincoln Memorial and gave his "I Have a Dream" speech. As well as being the main spokesperson for the struggle of the African American community to obtain and to realize their civil rights as guaranteed by the U.S. Constitution, King also spoke out against the **Vietnam War**. In 1964, King was awarded the Nobel Peace Prize for his efforts to lead a campaign of nonviolent direct action against the racial discrimination and social injustices found in the United States.

> Vietnam War: a controversial war in which the United States fought to keep North Vietnamese communists out of South Vietnam, 1959–75

King became actively involved in the Civil Rights movement shortly after receiving his doctorate in theology from Boston University when he was asked to lead a bus boycott in Montgomery, Alabama. As a result of the boycott, which lasted more than a year, King was jailed—the first of many arrests. In 1956, the Supreme Court outlawed segregation, and the boycott ended. However, the Civil Rights movement had just begun in earnest. Over the years, King organized black voter registration, led marches and sit-ins, and gave speeches to protest racial discrimination and to campaign for the establishment of a civil rights bill, a bill that eventually passed in 1964. King's philosophy of nonviolent direct action had its roots in his faith, the writings of Thoreau, and the nonviolent political activism of Mohandas Gandhi. Tragically, King, a proponent of nonviolent civil disobedience, was killed by an assassin's bullet on April 3, 1968. He was buried in his hometown of Atlanta, Georgia.

Lévi-Strauss, Claude (b. 1908)

Lévi-Strauss puts forth his concept of the mytheme in his article "The Structural Study of Myth" (1963). Strauss's approach to anthropology and sociology has its roots in the structuralism of Ferdinand de Saussure, who had taught at the Sorbonne, where Strauss was later a student. Strauss developed his methodological approach to anthropology while conducting **field studies** of tribes in Brazil, where he was a professor at the University of Sao Paulo from 1934 to 1938. Strauss's work, in turn, has been used by literary critics as a tool for the analysis of narrative structure.

> field studies: research done in the natural environment, not in a lab

For Strauss, the idea of a "text" moves beyond an actual story to anything that has a narrative line, whether that line be in a musical score or a how-to manual. In his research, he looked for the commonalties underlying such narrative structures as a way to understand the "language" of human relationships. Titles of his books, such as *The Elementary Structures of Kinship* (1949, trans. 1962) and *Structural Anthropology* (1958, trans. 1963), suggest the bond between his own field of anthropology and that of linguistics. His willingness to incorporate linguistic structuralism into his own research opened other fields in the human sciences and literature to such theories as well. In addition to his academic work as a professor of social anthropology, Strauss has worked as the French cultural attaché in the United States and as an associate director of the Museum of Man in Paris.

Maugham, Somerset (1874–1965)

An English writer of novels, short stories, and plays, Maugham is known for his ironic point of view and clear narrative style. Born in Paris, raised in England, and educated in Germany and England, Maugham received an education in philosophy, literature, and medicine. Although he was a qualified surgeon, he left his medical practice after a year to focus on writing. He then published one of his most well-known novels, *Of Human Bondage* (1915), which contained material from his days as a student and as a doctor in the poorer districts of London. His experiences working for the Red Cross during World War I, traveling in the Far East, and spending time as a patient in a **tuberculosis sanitarium** also made their way into his fictional works. During the **onset** of World War II, he served as a British agent in France, where he had been living since 1928. In 1940, he left France for the States and remained there until 1946. There he wrote another of his successful novels, *The Razor's Edge* (1945). Maugham's work is characterized by its realism and directness—two qualities that can be observed in the short work "Appointment in Samarra."

tuberculosis: a lung infection
sanitarium: a place where people recuperate from illnesses
onset: the first part; the beginning

Mellix, Barbara (b. 1945)

The excerpted passages taken from "From Outside, In" give a glimpse into Mellix's childhood. Mellix, who has an M. F. A. in creative writing, has also taught courses in writing and literature.

Nietzsche, Friedrich (1844–1900)

Nietzsche was raised in what was then the country of Prussia. His father, a Lutheran minister, died when Nietzsche was four years old. His mother, along with her mother, two sisters, and her daughter, took care of Nietzsche until he left home to attend the University of Basel in Switzerland. At the university, where Nietzsche studied classical **philology**, his brilliant work resulted in his appointment as a professor at the age of twenty-four. Nietzsche taught at the university for eleven years, until his poor eyesight and violent headaches forced his early retirement in 1879. Until he suffered a complete mental breakdown in 1889, Nietzsche wrote **prolifically**. Much of his writing was done at his house in the Swiss village of Sils Maria. Among his many works *Beyond Good and Evil* (1886), *Thus Spake Zarathustra* (1883), *Ecce Homo* (1889), and *Will to Power* (1901, published posthumously from his notes) have been the most influential. Nietzsche claimed that he was fifty years ahead of his time and that people would realize the import of his teachings only as they began to see them **manifested** in the world. In his *Will to Power,* he predicted terrible ideological wars, a general loss of faith in oneself and others, and the de-

philology: the study of language as used in literature

prolifically: producing a great amount

manifested: made visible

velopment of a technologically based science that would end in undermining life by claiming it had no meaning or purpose.

OLSEN, TILLIE (b. 1913)

Olsen's "I Stand Here Ironing" appeared in her first and only collection of fictional writing, entitled Tell Me a Riddle, which was published in 1961. The stories in this book won Olsen the O. Henry Award for the short story form and brought her much acclaim as a writer, enabling her to receive many awards, fellowships, and grants. Although Olsen had published fiction in a magazine as early as 1930, it was not until 1955 that she received the creative-writing fellowship from Stanford University that provided her with the time and money to write additional publishable works. From her first marriage in 1936 until 1955, Olsen spent most of her time raising her four children and working full-time at temporary office jobs to help support her family. Only when her youngest daughter was five did she apply for the Stanford fellowship. In 1974, she finished the novel Yonnonido that she had begun at the age of nineteen but that she had set aside because of personal circumstances.

As do her short stories, the novel brings to life the relations between mothers and daughters of working-class families. Like the characters in her own works, Olsen was raised in a family of **blue-collar** workers with little money. She had to drop out of high school in order to earn money, but, as she herself has said, public libraries provided her with a good education, and she was able to stay in school longer than many other depression-era children. Her nonfictional work Silences, published in 1978, gives voice to Olsen's search for the relationship between social circumstances and the writing of literature, particularly as such circumstances relate to women writers.

blue-collar: related to factory jobs in which a person often wears a blue shirt

PIPHER, MARY

Mary Pipher is a doctor of clinical psychology. Her book Reviving Ophelia (1994) came out of her years of experience as a therapist for adolescent girls and her studies in cultural anthropology. In Reviving Ophelia, Pipher analyzes some of the broader social problems that limit the development of a young girl's selfhood. Rather than focusing on the family as the source of psychological ills, Pipher focuses on the cultural context in which adolescent girls find themselves and on the cultural **conditioning** they experience in the larger world through the arts, media, education, etc. Dr. Pipher also teaches at the University of Nebraska and Nebraska Wesleyan University. As a radio commentator for Nebraska Public Radio and as a writer, she has reached a wide audience.

conditioning: the development of predetermined behaviors via social pressures

Plato (ca. 428–348/47 b.c.)

Plato, a Greek philosopher, was born in Athens into an aristocratic family. As a young man, he planned to go into politics, but he gave up his political ambitions because he disapproved of the corrupt Athenian government and because the Greek philosopher Socrates, his teacher, was unfairly sentenced to death at the hands of the Athenian state.

The best known aspect of **Platonic** thought is Plato's concept of ideal forms. He thought that every object in the physical and **temporal** world is imperfect; however, he believed that each object also has a corresponding ideal form that exists in an eternal realm that is unchanging and that can be **accessed** through the power of reason. In other words, he would say that the different kinds of roses are reflections of the ideal rose that can be found in an eternal realm. In a way, he saw objects in the real world as shadows cast by the ideal forms. Plato argued that the world of the senses is inferior to the world of forms and the world of ideas. To Plato, mathematics **testifies** to the world of eternal ideas because abstract formulations such as $2 + 2 = 4$ and geometric **theorems** can be proven and are unchanging, whereas people might have differing opinions about how they perceive reality with their senses.

Plato stressed that people need to develop their reasoning powers in order to free their **immortal** souls from the bounds of everyday life. People can regain the knowledge of ideal forms through study and analytical thinking. To this end, Plato wrote his *Republic* as a series of dialogues in which a question is asked and then answered in a way that eventually leads to the truth. The dialogues follow the analytical method exemplified by his teacher, Socrates. Plato's search for knowledge and truth is reflected in the academy he started in Athens. The academy served as a center of learning for over one thousand years, and the word *academic* is still associated with the search for knowledge.

Platonic: having to do with the teachings of Plato
temporal: related to measurable time
accessed: entered; reached
testifies: gives evidence of something
theorems: mathematical formulas that can be proven
immortal: the quality of living forever

Poe, Edgar Allan (1809–49)

Although Poe considered himself to be a poet, he is best known for his short stories, which he began writing in the late 1930s as a means of financial support. In childhood, Poe was orphaned and raised by middle-class **foster parents** who sent him, at the age of six, to a private school in England. At the age of eleven, Poe returned to the States and eventually attended the University of Virginia. His heavy drinking and gambling in college resulted in large debts that his foster parent, John Allan, refused to pay. As a result, he had to leave college and work as a clerk, a job he disliked and soon quit, thus further angering his foster father. Poe then joined the army for two years, writing two volumes of verse on the side. Hoping that Poe would settle into a career, his foster father arranged for him to study at the military academy West Point. After only a few months,

foster parents: persons who give parental care even though they are not actual relatives

Poe was **expelled** from the academy. His expulsion led to a complete break with his foster family and to a job as a book reviewer and magazine contributor; it also led to his stay at his aunt's home, where he met and eventually married his cousin. She died from **tuberculosis** in 1847. In 1849, Poe was found dead on a Baltimore, Maryland, street, apparently from alcohol poisoning. He left behind him a series of short stories such as "The Bells" (1849) and "The Purloined Letter" (1844) that earned him a reputation as the **forerunner** of the detective and mystery genres.

expelled: sent out of

tuberculosis: a lung infection

forerunner: one who comes before; who sets one of the first examples

SARTRE, JEAN-PAUL (1905–80)

Sartre's life and work are interwoven with French existentialism. Born and raised in Paris, he studied at University of Fribourg in Switzerland and at the French Institute in Berlin. In 1929, he met Simone de Beauvoir, who at the time was studying philosophy. Beauvoir became a well-known French existentialist and feminist. Both Sartre and Beauvoir believed that existential choice required a creative effort and self-mastery. The two became lovers and established a lifelong relationship.

After his graduation from the university, Sartre taught philosophy in high schools until he was called into the French military, where he was taken as a prisoner of war by the Germans. He spent one year in a German prison camp. After his release in 1941, he continued teaching and writing. He also worked in **underground** activities with the French Resistance. He managed to publish *Being and Nothingness* in 1943 while the war was still going on. A few years after the war ended, Sartre openly supported **Marxism** even though he never actually joined the Communist Party. In addition to his philosophic writings, Sartre also wrote plays and novels. In 1964 he was chosen to receive the Nobel Prize for literature, but he rejected the award.

underground: illegal

Marxism: a belief in the teachings of Karl Marx (1818–83), a German philosopher and the founder of communism

SAUSSURE, FERDINAND DE (1857–1913)

Although Saussure is associated primarily with the field of linguistics, his structural theory of language has shaped the approaches used in diverse fields such as anthropology and literary criticism. While a university student, Saussure wrote his only book, a study on the vowel system of Indo-European languages. His most influential work, *Course in General Linguistics* (1859), was published posthumously by his students, who compiled his lecture notes into book form. In addition to teaching general linguistics, Saussure lectured on Sanskrit, the ancient source of Indo-European language, as well as on comparative grammar.

Born and raised in Geneva, Switzerland, Saussure originally studied science at the University of Geneva but **transferred** to the University of Leipzig in 1876 in order to pursue his interest in the history of languages. After his graduation, he taught at the Ecole des Hautes Études (The

transferred: moved over to

School of Higher Studies) in Paris for ten years and then returned to the University of Geneva.

Singer, Isaac Bashevis (1904–91)

Awarded the 1978 Nobel Prize in literature, Isaac Singer wrote novels, plays, twelve books of short stories, thirteen children's books, and four autobiographical works. One of his works was made into the film *Yentl,* directed by Barbra Streisand. His works reflect the traditions and folklore of east European Jews. With the publication of *The Family Moskat* in 1950, Singer first gained national standing as a writer outside of the Jewish community in New York where he had worked for years with a Yiddish-language newspaper, the *Jewish Daily Forward.*

The Family Moskat follows the experiences of a Jewish family in Warsaw, Poland, over three generations. To write the novel, Singer drew on his own experiences of growing up as a rabbi's son in the Warsaw ghetto and on his years as a student in rabbinical seminary. Singer left his homeland in 1935 to escape the Nazis and became a citizen of the United States in 1943.

Socrates (470?–399? b.c.)

Socrates, a Greek philosopher, was raised in Athens, where he received a basic education in the arts. In later life, Socrates taught himself about the rhetorical and philosophical systems that shaped Athenian culture. Socrates did not write his teachings down, nor did he develop a philosophic school. Instead, he is said to have spent time in the market squares of Athens, where he would involve people in philosophical arguments that caused them to examine their lives. According to Plato, who studied under Socrates and wrote down many of his ideas, Socrates believed that abstract moral concepts such as goodness, love, and justice had an objective nature that could be understood through the power of reason and self-knowledge. Socrates argued that evil is the result of ignorance and a lack of self-knowledge and is **reputed** to have said that the unexamined life is not worth living. During an argument, he would sometimes act as if he were **ignorant** so that his opponents would be forced to explain their positions more carefully—a behavior that came to be known as *Socratic irony.*

Although Socrates followed the laws of the Athenian state, some Athenians felt threatened by his teachings, particularly those against the death penalty. Finally, in 399 b.c., he was brought to trial and charged with having taught a corrupt morality to young people and with having introduced new gods. A jury of five condemned Socrates to death. Rather than escaping from Athens or pleading for mercy, Socrates accepted his sen-

reputed: having the reputation of

ignorant: uneducated; lacking knowledge

tence, and, after spending his last day in prison with his followers, he drank the poison **hemlock** and died.

hemlock: a type of pine that is poisonous

STALIN, JOSEPH (1879–1953)

Stalin, the leader of the Soviet Union from 1922 to 1953, was born into a peasant family in Georgia. His parents, who had been **serfs** until 1864, when they were liberated, named him Josif Djugashvili. His mother sent him to an Orthodox Church school so that he could fulfill her dream of becoming a priest. From there he went on to win a scholarship to attend seminary. During his studies, he began to read books that were **smuggled** into the school, including works by Karl Marx and **Charles Darwin.** He also became involved in an underground socialist group and began to consider himself a revolutionary agitator. In 1899, he was expelled from the seminary for failing to show up for his exams, and his revolutionary career began in earnest.

serfs: those who must take care of the land for a "master"

smuggled: brought in secretly

Charles Darwin: 1809–82, a scientist who put forth the idea of evolution

From 1899 to 1917, Stalin was involved in **anti-czarist agitation** and became a Russian **nationalist**, though he himself was Georgian and not of Russian descent. During this period, he was arrested and exiled numerous times for revolutionary activities such as distributing anti-czarist **propaganda** and robbing a bank to fund the revolution. He managed to escape from prison or exile eight times. In 1912, Lenin promoted Stalin to the **Bosheviks'** Central Committee, where he was close to the center of power. After the October Revolution took place, followed by civil war, Stalin worked primarily as an advisor to Lenin and as a commander.

anti-czarist agitation: actions taken against the czar, the leader of Russia before 1917

nationalist: one who promotes his or her nation

propaganda: information, true or false, that is spread to help one's position or cause

Bolsheviks: the communists who followed Lenin (1870–1924), leader of the communist revolution in Russia

In 1922, after establishing a power base within the Bolshevik administration, he became the head of the party as secretary-general. He used his position to consolidate his political power and exiled those who opposed him. As a leader of the Soviet Union, Stalin has been admired for the rapid educational reforms and industrialization that he set into motion. However, many of the large-scale industrial projects were done using a prison population that grew during the political purges in which millions of party officials, military leaders, and ordinary citizens disappeared into a system of prisons known as **the Gulag.** Stalin is also remembered for having led his people, at great sacrifice, in victory against Hitler, who invaded the Soviet Union in 1941.

the Gulag: the Russian name for a network of prisons and work camps for "class enemies" of the Soviet Union

consolidated: brought together

cold war: a period of tense diplomatic relations between the Soviet Union and the West from 1945 to 1990

to revere: to greatly admire and respect

despot: a cruel ruler; a tyrant

After World War II, Stalin again **consolidated** his power, but this time he extended his rule over countries liberated by the Soviet armies, creating a Soviet sphere of influence in eastern Europe and setting the stage for the **cold war** between the Soviet Union and Western powers. He died in 1953 shortly before he was to initiate yet another purge. In Russia, many people still **revere** Stalin as a great leader who strengthened and expanded the Soviet Empire, while others argue that he was a **despot** whose legacy was one of tyranny and terror.

Steinbeck, John (1902–68)

Steinbeck, the 1962 Nobel Prize winner in literature, is best known for his realistic fiction such as *Of Mice and Men* (1937), *The Grapes of Wrath* (1939), and *East of Eden* (1952). Born into a middle-class family in Salinas, California, Steinbeck determined to become a writer at the age of seventeen, when he went to Stanford University to study. Although he took classes over a period of years, he never received a degree.

It was during these years that he began to work at the many jobs that provided the themes and characters of his novels. To support himself, he worked variously as a farmhand and ranch hand, as a day laborer, a surveyor, a reporter, and a bricklayer and on a cattle boat. He became familiar with the lives of laborers and blue-collar workers, and he gained firsthand experience of poverty during the Great Depression. In 1935, with the publication of his fourth novel, *Tortilla Flats,* Steinbeck finally gained national recognition as a writer.

Thoreau, Henry David (1817–62)

Although Thoreau is now considered to be one of the United States' great literary figures, he was not well known during his lifetime. He was born in Concord, Massachusetts, and worked in his family's pencil-making factory, earning money to put himself through Harvard. Throughout his life, Thoreau worked as a teacher and lecturer. He also wrote **copiously**, but only two of his books were published before his death: *A Week on the Concord and Merrimack Rivers* (1849), about a weeklong canoeing trip he had taken, and *Walden: or, Life in the Woods* (1854), about the years from 1845 to 1847 when he lived in a small cabin on the shores of Walden Pond. (Thoreau wrote the former book while living in Walden.) After leaving Walden, he spent the next five years transforming his journals from that time into a collection of essays in which he dealt with the role of the individual in society and in shaping his or her own life in an imaginative way. His ideas were influenced by transcendental thought—the belief that human beings participate in an **intuitive** or spiritual world that transcends material existence. As a transcendentalist, he **espoused** a life of simplicity and closeness to nature and warned against the deadening effects of materialism and a comfortable lifestyle that can take away a person's individualism and conscience.

In his essay "Civil Disobedience," published in 1849, Thoreau explored the relation of the individual to social concerns and to the state. He developed the idea of nonviolent civil disobedience, an idea later applied on a massive scale by Martin Luther King, who credited Thoreau with having shaped his decision to use civil disobedience as a tool in the Civil Rights movement. Thoreau's ideas on civil disobedience were af-

---

copiously: producing something in great amounts

intuitive: knowing things without having direct knowledge of them

espoused: put forward an idea

fected by his personal experience: in 1845 he was arrested for refusing to pay a poll tax that was being levied to fund a war with Mexico, a war he felt was unjust. As a result of his refusal to pay the tax, Thoreau was put into jail. Because his aunt paid the tax for him, he was only required to stay one night in prison; nonetheless, his experience with active civil disobedience profoundly affected his thinking on the subject, and his action became symbolic of nonviolent resistance to civil government. Thoreau also opposed slavery, and he refused **to comply** with laws such as the **Fugitive** Slave Act (1850), which made it a criminal act to help escaped slaves or to refuse to help the authorities in catching them. To promote his ideas, Thoreau gave lectures. In fact, his essay "Civil Disobedience" was first given as a lecture entitled "Resistance to Civil Government." Although *Walden* was published in 1854, it was not until some seventy years after his death that his work received critical attention.

to comply: to follow the rules

fugitive: a runaway from the law

WALKER, ALICE (b. 1944)

Walker, a poet, essayist, and novelist, won the Pulitzer Prize for her most widely known work *The Color Purple* (1982), which was also made into a film by Steven Spielberg. The novel and the film bring to life Walker's social activism and feminism. In general, her fiction and essays reflect her effort to record the experiences of African American women. Born the daughter of a **sharecropper** and the youngest in a family of eight children, Walker grew up poor in material goods but rich in the stories passed down by her grandparents and, in turn, by her own parents. These narratives later made their way into her writing.

sharecropper: a person who is allowed to farm someone else's land and then must share the profits

After graduating from college in 1965, Walker taught black literature. Her first short story collection, *In Love and Trouble,* in which the story "Everyday Use" appears, was published in 1973. Her collection of essays, *In Search of Our Mothers' Gardens* (1984), honors the creative spirit of her mother and of her grandmothers, who were slaves. Both in her writing and in her life, Walker has been an active spokesperson for the Civil Rights movement and feminism. Walker has written five novels, two short story collections, and four books of poetry.

WOOLF, VIRGINIA (1882–1941)

Woolf is best known for her artistic contribution to the development of the novel, particularly works such as *Mrs. Dalloway* (1925) and *To the Lighthouse* (1927), in which she experiments with traditional **modes** of narration and theme. In addition to her work as a novelist, Woolf published numerous critical essays and several biographies. Her home in the Bloomsbury district of London became the meeting point for a group of writers and critics who met there to talk about literature. Because of this,

modes: ways

the group became known as the Bloomsbury Group or, more informally, as the Bloomsberries. In 1917, Woolf and her husband, Leonard Woolf, started their own publishing company, called Hogarth Press, as an **outlet** for upcoming writers.

outlet: an opening that something can get through; in this case, a means of becoming published

Woolf was one of the early feminists and argued in favor of women's rights in works such as *A Room of One's Own* (1929). As a girl, Wolf received an education from her father, who was a philosopher. As a young woman, she received an inheritance from an aunt that enabled her to have some financial independence. Woolf emphasized the need for women to receive an education and to have an independent source of income so that they would have the freedom to express themselves as they chose. In 1941, Woolf chose to take her own life rather than succumbing to a mental illness. After her death, in 1953, her husband published portions of her journal in *A Writer's Diary*.

WRIGHT, RICHARD (1908–60)

The excerpts included in this textbook from *The Ethics of Living Jim Crow* vividly portray the environment in which Wright lived and worked. Born to a sharecropper and a teacher in Mississippi, Wright grew up knowing firsthand the poverty caused by racially discriminatory codes and segregation. After his father left the family in 1913, Wright's mother soon became ill; as a result, Richard and his brother Leon were placed in an orphanage before being moved to their grandparents' home. Wright had to leave school at the age of ten to help support the family. In 1920, he returned to school, working as a newspaper boy and as an assistant to an insurance agent. He graduated from high school as the school **valedictorian**.

valedictorian: the person in a graduating class with the highest grades

After his graduation, Wright moved to Chicago, Illinois, where he worked in a post office, was active in the Communist Party, and wrote poetry, novels, and short stories. The novel *Native Son* (1940) won him national acclaim, and the book was made into a film. *Black Boy* followed in 1945 and was well received by critics and the U.S. public. Wright's visit to France in 1946, at the request of the French government, eventually led to his decision to settle in Paris, where he experienced less racism than in the United States. Paris remained his home until his death.

Answer Key

Photograph courtesy of Rafael Kapelinski

"Then death will drift upon me from seaward, mild as air, mild as your hand."—Homer, *Odyssey*

Chapter 1
Activity 1.2

1. 1480 A.D.
2. political leaders
3. entertainment
4. rhetoricians
5. moral
6. Buddha
7. animal
8. 50 A.D.
9. Reed
10. translated
11. English

Activity 1.3

1. The king recognized the importance of the small as well as the great, or in death he sees this is true.
2. Sample morals: Obscurity often brings safety. Flexibility gives great strength. The small may be stronger than the great.

Activity 1.4a

3 to thresh the wheat
6 to bake bread with flour
5 to grind the wheat
4 to take the wheat to the mill
2 to cut a stalk of wheat
1 to plant a grain of wheat

Activity 1.4b

The Little Red Hen

One day, when the little red hen was scratching around for food, she found a grain of wheat. Instead of eating it right then and there, she turned to the other animals in the barnyard and said, "Who will help me plant this wheat?"

"Not I," said the duck
"Not I," said the cat.
"Not I," said the pig.
"Then I shall plant it myself," said the little red hen. And she did.
The wheat grew into a tall stalk. "Who will help me cut the wheat?" she asked.
"Not I," said the duck.
"Not I," <u>said</u> the cat.
"<u>Not I</u>," said the pig.
"Then I <u>shall</u> cut it myself," said the little <u>red</u> hen."
And she did.

At the top of the wheat grew a large cluster of grain. "Who will <u>help</u> me thresh the wheat?" she asked.
"Not <u>I</u>," said the duck.
"Not I," said the cat.
"<u>Not</u> I," said the <u>pig.</u>
"Then I shall <u>thresh</u> it myself," said the <u>little</u> <u>red</u> hen. And she <u>did.</u>
Soon she had a sack of grain. " <u>Who</u> will help me take the wheat to the mill?"
"<u>Not</u> I," said the <u>duck.</u>
"<u>Not</u> I," said the <u>cat.</u>
"<u>Not</u> I," said the <u>pig.</u>
"Then I shall <u>take it</u> myself," said the <u>little red hen.</u>
And <u>she did.</u>

The mill ground the wheat into flour for baking bread. " <u>Who will help me</u> bake the bread?" said the little red hen.

"Not I," said the duck.
"Not I," said the cat.
"Not I," said the pig.
"Then I shall bake it myself," said the little red hen. And she did.

And she baked a big round loaf of bread. "Now, who will help me eat the bread?" she asked.

"I will!" said the duck.
"I will!" said the cat.
"I will!" said the pig.

"Oh no," said the little red hen. "You did not help me plant the wheat. You did not help me cut the wheat. You did not help me take the wheat to the mill to grind into flour for baking bread, and you did not help me bake it. So you will not help me eat the bread. I will eat it myself. And she did.

Activity 1.4d

Sample moral: If you don't share in the work, you don't share in the rewards.

Activity 1.4e

1. in a barnyard; on a farm
2. The hen finds a grain of wheat and asks for help to plant it.
3. a hen, a duck, a cat, and a pig
4. The other animals won't help her.
5. the duck, the cat, and the pig.
6. This sequence follows the order in activity 1.4a. Also, when the hen asks for help, no one helps her.
7. All the other animals want to help her.
8. She eats the bread.
9. disappointed; perhaps sorry that they never helped the hen

Activity 1.4f

Sample answer: The fable illustrates the cultural values of hard work and the necessity of working together in order to share the results.

Activity 1.5a

5 But the harder he blew, the more closely did the man hold his coat until the wind gave up trying to make him take off his coat.
3 The sun said, "Whichever of us can make that man take off his coat is the stronger."
1 The wind and the sun were arguing about who was the stronger.
4 The wind began to blow cold air on the man.
6 Then the sun came out and shone upon the man, who soon became very hot and took off his coat.
2 Suddenly they saw a man walking on the road, and the sun said, "I see a way to end our argument."

Activity 1.5b

1. If Plutarch is viewed as the man with the coat, then it seems that his wife had more influence over him when she was pleasant rather than ill-tempered. Or, the roles could have been reversed. Either way, people may have been afraid to comment on the relationship directly.
2. Sample moral: Kindness does more than unpleasantness.

Activity 1.6a (possible questions)

2. What is the Eight-Fold Path?
3. How old was he when he first witnessed human suffering?
4. When did the Buddha achieve enlightenment?

Activity 1.6b

A. the five senses: smell, touch, taste, sight, hearing; common sense; intuition
B. thoughtfulness; thinking carefully before taking action
1. <u>For the five senses are like arrows . . . like voracious dogs who can never have enough.</u>
2–3 open-ended answers

Activity 1.6c

1. The dog is looking for the piece of meat that he dropped.
2. Buddha might say that the dog did not control his senses.

Activity 1.7a (possible questions)

2. Why did Plato like mathematics?
3. How did Plato think the realm of ideal forms could be reached?
4. How is the *Republic* organized?

Activity 1.7b

1. A man and woman are casting these shadows. They are wearing winter clothes.
2. A shadow is made when light shines from behind an object.
3. The shadows are like reflections of the human form, but they are not real in the sense of being human. Because of this, the shadows are imperfect reflections of the ideal human form.

Activity 1.7c

1. Sketches should be based on the introduction to the passage.
2. The prisoners in the cave mistake the shadows for real people.
3. We are "prisoners" in this world of shadows.
4. He is confused because he thinks that the shadows are more real than the actual people around him. He doesn't realize that the people had cast the shadows on the wall.
5. He can not look at the light because it causes him pain after he has been in the darkness of the cave.
6. He realizes that the shadows are caused by the light.
7. He thinks that the game is silly because the prisoners do not realize that the shadows are not real people and things.
8. He has trouble playing the game because his eyes are not used to the darkness.
9. They think that the escaped prisoner has lost his mind.
10. The cave represents the world that we live in, the world of the senses, the visible world.
11. The fire represents the sun's light and the power of reason.
12. The journey out of the cave can represent the process of learning by which people come to understand the world.

13. The "idea of the good" means having an understanding of the truth. According to "The Allegory of the Cave," this can only be reached through study and intellectual effort.
14. Both Plato and the Buddha are concerned that people are fooled by their senses.
15. Sample morals: Do not mistake a lie for the truth; the truth can only be known through reason.

Activity 1.8a (possible questions)

2. What is an aphorism?
3. What did Aurelius encourage the Roman people to do?

Activity 1.8b

A–C open-ended answers
1. Aurelius would have liked the fable because it shows what happens when the power of reason isn't used.
2. Like the Buddha, Aurelius also advises people to "rise above [their] senses."
3. Both Aurelius and Plato share the belief that the power of reason can help a person overcome his or her senses.

Activity 1.9b

A. <u>The introduction or exposition:</u> The lion catches the mouse and decides to let it go because he finds it amusing to think that the mouse might one day save him.
B. <u>The dramatic conflict:</u> In this fable, there is a conflict between those who are weak and those who are strong. The mouse could be seen as the protagonist who is antagonized by the lion, but the lion, in turn, becomes a protagonist who needs to be rescued from those who hunt him.
C. <u>The rising action:</u> 1. The lion catches the mouse and lets him go. 2. The lion is caught in a trap. 3. The mouse saves the lion.
D. <u>The climax or crisis:</u> The mouse saves the lion even though it seems unlikely that he could do so.
E. <u>The resolution:</u> The mouse is shown to be as strong as the lion in his own way.

Activity 1.12

1. The Buddha might have said that the cat, the duck, and the pig lacked discipline and were greedy.
2. He might say that the cat, the duck, and the pig failed to analyze the situation correctly while the hen used her powers of reasoning successfully.
3. Aurelius would have liked this fable because it shows what happens when we do not do what we should. The hen used her reason but the other animals acted thoughtlessly.
4. It shows the cross-cultural influences at work in fables.

Chapter 2

Activity 2.1b

1. It is effective because it is unusual to have Death speaking.
2. open-ended answer

Activity 2.1c

1. Having Death as a narrator gets the reader's attention.
2. This isn't made clear, but Death is speaking to whoever is reading the text.

3. Death is intelligent but not all knowing. Death can be surprised. Death is personified as being female.
4. Sample morals: No one can escape death; death comes unexpectedly; you can't outwit death.

Activity 2.2a

a. Omniscient: all knowing
b. Objective: able to express facts without expressing emotions
c. Selective: choosing one or two from among many
d. Participatory: taking part, joining in
e. Editorial (omniscience): *Editorial* means that one makes judgmental comments about something as an editor would.

1. b
2. c
3. d
4. a
5. e

A. A participatory narrator. This is clear because the narrator uses the first-person pronoun *I* to tell the story. The story is told from the narrator's point of view.

Activity 2.2b

Example: The Little Red Hen. An objective narrator.

Activity 2.3

1. Every detail is necessary to make it clear why Death was surprised to see the merchant in Baghdad.
2. no
3. The tale is metaphorical and symbolic because it teaches the reader about the nature of death.

Activity 2.4

1. The narrator seems unreliable. He's nervous and he begins by talking about madness.
2. the first-person point of view
3. that he is not mad
4–5 open-ended answers

Activity 2.8 (sample list)

Events	Plot
2. plans to kill the old man because of his eye	dramatic conflict
3. takes an hour to put his head in the old man's door	rising action
4. could not kill the old man when his eye was shut	rising action
5. is pleased by his sense of power over the old man	rising action
6. says he can hear the beating of the old man's heart	rising action
7. kills the old man and smiles	rising action
8. dismembers the old man's body	rising action
9. places his own chair over the body	rising action
10. hears the dead man's heart beating and confesses	crisis/climax

Note: It could also be argued that the murder of the old man is the climax of the story and that what follows is the resolution. It is also interesting to note that, from the narrator's point of view, he is the protagonist and the eye the antagonist whereas the reader may feel that the old man is really the protagonist while the narrator is seen as the antagonist.

Activity 2.9

The narrator's speech is full of exclamations and pauses that suggest his nervousness and excitability. He also stresses many words. As a whole, his manner of speaking is highly emotional, making him seem unstable.

Activity 2.10a

1. Irony: Something is shown to be the opposite of what is meant or intended. Adjective— *ironic*; adverb— *ironically*
2. He welcomes the police even though he doesn't want them to come in. He asks the police to search well even though the reader knows that he doesn't want them to find the body. He says they knew that the heart was beating even though the reader knows it was not possible for them to hear it. He calls the police villains when he is the villain.
3. The policemen do not know that the old man's body is under the floorboards. Also, the narrator places his chair upon the spot where the man's body is hidden.
4. The old man must die because of his eye. The narrator is obsessed with the eye, and this obsession causes him to murder an innocent man.
5. The narrator is mad but he does not realize it.

Activity 2.10b

Maugham uses dramatic/situational irony. The servant thinks he can escape death but ends up going to where Death will be waiting for him. There is also irony of fate in that people try to outwit death but cannot.

Activity 2.11

Open-ended answer. It could be argued that, although the details of the story contribute to its total effect, the dismemberment of the old man may be considered unnecessary by some readers. Also, it could be argued that the "evil eye" is symbolic of the evil we project onto others.

Activity 2.12

1. Sample answer: The narrator is proud of the cleverness he showed in killing the old man and in hiding his body.
2. See responses to questions 2–4 that accompany "The Heart Tells All" in chapter 8.
3. Sample answer: Another theme could be: People project their own evil onto others. This is shown by how the narrator sees the old man's eye is evil even though the old man himself is good.

Activity 2.13b

1. unconscious: not aware; the part of the psyche that is not conscious
2. latent: hidden; unseen
3. repress: to put something down by force; to force feelings and thoughts into the unconscious
4. libido: emotional and sexual energy that is in the psyche
5. phallic: having to do with the male penis
6. therapy: treatment for a physical or emotional problem
7. associations: to make connections between different things
8. complex: a whole made up of many interrelated parts; an abnormal behavior that has its origins in the unconscious

9. neurosis: an illness caused by the mind
10. id: part of the psyche that is unconscious; the id contains great psychic energy
11. projection: the act of putting one's own feelings onto someone or something else
12. ego: the self; the part of the psyche that connects a person to reality
13. superego: the part of the psyche that tries to follow societal rules and morals

Activity 2.13c

1–2 open-ended answers
3. The sketch should show the three divisions of the psyche. Often, Freud's view of the psyche is portrayed as a triangle with the tip representing the superego, the middle portion the ego, and the lower portion the unconscious or id. Sometimes, an image of an iceberg is used, with the conscious part of the personality represented by the tip of the iceberg and the unconscious part represented by the section of the iceberg that is underwater.
4. Disagree. The narrator has projected his own evil onto the eye. He is not conscious of his reasons for killing the old man. Apparently, he has repressed his feelings, and they come out through the murder of the old man. The murderer is very careful to preserve his superego. He wants the reader to think he is intelligent and powerful.
5. It can be reductive to apply Freudian theories to a fictional character because a character in a work of fiction is not a real person with a past and a future.

Activity 2.14

The title "The Tell-Tale Heart" could be used because the imagined beating of the old man's heart causes the narrator to confess the murder.

Activity 2.15

1. Sample answer: The narrator could be dreaming about his experiences: his actions have the dreamlike quality of a nightmare.
2. If the story is a dream, then the apparently "mad" narrator does a reliable job of describing his "dream." The narrator could learn much about his feelings through the symbols and symbolic actions in the story.

Chapter 3
Activity 3.1

A. 1692
B. 1621
C. 1643
D. 1630
E. 1620

Activity 3.2

b. Privileged values: a belief that actions are judged; strict control over one's behavior
   Subverted values: feelings of guilt; repression of desires
c. Privileged values: self-discipline; control of one's desires
   Subverted values: sensuality; passion; extravagance
1. open-ended answer
2. Puritans maintained observance of such codes by exerting social pressure. People had to conform to the society's rules, or else they were excommunicated, that is, cast out of the community as exiles. Modern society also has established codes that people must follow or else face fines and imprisonment and, in some countries, death.

3. A Puritan would have approved of the fable "The Little Red Hen" because it promotes the value of hard work. Puritans were known for their strong work ethic.

Activity 3.3

1. The name suggests that he was basically a good person. He was young and "average," as the color brown could suggest.
2. Faith's name suggests that she was also basically good and one who believed in God and in other people.

Activity 3.4

1. A Puritan would say that goodness comes only from God. Goodness is marked by love and is patient, kind, faithful, forgiving, hopeful, etc.
2. Puritans believed that the devil was the source of evil. Evil is selfish, unkind, unloving, etc.
3. Puritans believed that people, without God, were basically evil.
4. Puritans believed that evil should be rejected. They followed strict moral codes to ensure that their behavior would be "good," and they attempted to resist the temptation of evil through prayer and study of the Bible.
5. open-ended answer

Activity 3.5a

1. Generally the sunset is associated with the unconscious, creativity, and death—concepts associated with the night and the moon; in contrast, the sunrise is associated with birth and consciousness. Taken together, the sunrise and sunset suggest the circular movement of the life cycle.
2. Pink is generally associated with innocence and purity. The ribbon can be associated with femininity.
3. The Puritan town was usually enclosed and was considered a place that was civilized and orderly.
4. For the Puritans, the forest was a wild and unsafe place. They were afraid of the wild animals in the forest. They also feared Native Americans who they referred to as "Indians." Because of their ignorance of Native American culture, the Puritans considered them to be savage and uncivilized.
5. In Western traditions, the snake is a symbol of evil and is associated with the devil, who is the personification of evil. In the Puritan faith, the devil is believed to have been an angel who rebelled against God and was thrown out of heaven into hell, where he lives with other fallen angels called *demons*.
6. In archetypal studies, the witch is associated with fear of the unknown spiritual world and death. In "Young Goodman Brown," Hawthorne uses imagery that is associated with witches: (1) broomsticks that people can fly upon, (2) the wild plants that are used to cast a spell—juice of smallage and cinquefoil and wolf's bane, (3) the ceremony of the Black Sabbath, in which new members are initiated into a community of witches in a special ceremony called a *communion*. A male witch is called a *wizard*. People believed to be witches or wizards were often drowned, hung, or burned alive.
7. The number four is generally associated with physical life and the cycle of life as in the four seasons—summer, winter, spring, and fall—and the four elements—earth, air, fire, and water. In contrast, the number three is associated with spirituality. For example, in Christianity, God is viewed as being one in the three aspects of the trinity: The Father, Son and the Holy Ghost. And, in Chinese thought, three is considered to be a perfect number representing the marriage of Heaven and Earth and the birth of humankind.

Activity 3.5b

Sunrise vs. sunset
Day vs. night (implied)
The pink ribbon vs. the witch
The pink ribbon vs. the snake
Witch vs. saint (implied)

Activity 3.5c

1. a pink ribbon: the privileged value of temperance
2. a witch or wizard: the subverted value of doing something wrong or evil

Activity 3.7

a. 11
b. 9
c. 13
d. 5
e. 3
f. 12
g. 4
h. 6
i. 16
j. 2
k. 1
l. 10
m. 14
n. 15
o. 8
p. 7

Activity 3.8

1. open-ended answer
2. The climax could be during the baptism ceremony when Brown calls out to Faith to resist the "wicked one."
3. The first time Brown tries to turn back the old man asks him to walk on a little further and to talk with him some more. The second time Brown says he will leave because he doesn't want Faith to get hurt, but then the old man points to Goody Cloyse and Brown tries to hide. The third time, the old man tells Brown to sit and rest awhile, and he leaves Brown his staff. When Brown picks up the staff, it leads him to the Black Sabbath ceremony.
4. Her name is used allegorically when Brown cries out, "My Faith is gone." He means both his own faith in God and his wife, Faith, who is with the witches. At the Black Sabbath ceremony Brown asks, "But where is Faith?" The question could be about his wife and about his lost faith.
5. "Young Goodman Brown" is similar to a tale in that it has strange events in it and in that it has a strong effect on the reader.
6. open-ended answer

Activity 3.9

1. Sample answer: A townsperson could be telling the story. He may have known Brown and outlived him because he knew what was written on Brown's tombstone. Also, the narrator uses Puritan expressions.
2. Hawthorne uses the third-person point of view. His narrator is selectively omniscient and makes a few editorial comments in the last paragraph of the story.
3. In the last paragraph, the narrator seems to feel sorry for Brown. The use of the expression *alas* suggests this feeling. Also, he seems sorry that Brown is no longer able to enjoy his family.

Activity 3.10

1. Sample answer: (1) When Brown refers to his wife Faith: "Faith kept me back awhile"; "My Faith is gone." (2) When the traveler Brown meets in the forest he says

that his relationships with political figures are "state-secrets." (3) When Goody Cloyse encounters the traveler in the forest she exclaims, "The devil!", an exclamation of surprise and also a reference to the man's true identity.

2. Sample answer: Brown plans to meet the devil in the forest and he takes part in the Black Sabbath ceremony, but he judges others and not himself as being evil. Also, at the ceremony, he sees that nearly everyone he thought of as being good was actually evil.

3. Sample answer: Brown's life is ruined by one night's experience. Also, his family suffers as a result.

Activity 3.11

1–2 open-ended answers

3. Many of Brown's experiences in the forest seem unreal; for instance, the moment the staff appears to turn into a serpent; the moment when Brown hears familiar voices coming from the clouds; and, at the end of the story, when everyone who was with Brown at the ceremony suddenly disappears.

Activity 3.13

b. a pink ribbon: the innocent ego
c. a town: the superego; its rules and regulations
d. the forest: the id; the wild, dark, unconscious part of the psyche
e. a snake: the id; unconscious, hidden knowledge; projection
f. a witch or wizard: the id; repressed desires; projection
g. the four burning pine trees: the id

Activity 3.15

Sample answers.

1. Hawthorne's view of human goodness and evil seems to be less clear than that of the Puritans. For example, Goodman Brown may be "good" but he treats his family and friends unkindly and is, in this way, "evil." It is unclear whether Brown imagined his experiences in the forest, but, assuming he did, it seems he has projected his own evil onto others. If his experiences were real, they suggest that those who appear good may actually be evil.

2. Freud would most likely view evil as an aspect of the id in conflict with the superego. In this case, the concept of whether a person is good or evil has more to do with the rules of a given society than with a person's character.

3. open-ended answer

Activity 3.16 (sample themes)

1. The theme of the story is that the lines between goodness and evil are not always clearly drawn.
2. The evil we imagine in others is in ourselves.

Activity 3.18

The images on the tombstone reflect the conflict between good and evil that the Puritans focused on. For example, the angels are agents of divine goodness, whereas the demons are agents of evil. The skeleton represents the death that comes as a result of evil. The sun could represent the conscious part of the personality, a person's reasoning powers, whereas the moon could represent the unconscious part of the personality, the creative and emotional powers.

Chapter 4
Activity 4.1

2. <u>The Fourth Amendment</u>

   Civil rights: A person has a right to protection under the law.
   Necessity: Sometimes governments violate laws to control citizens.

3. <u>The Sixth Amendment</u>

   Civil rights: A person has the right to defend him- or herself in court.
   Necessity: Sometimes governments arrest people without trial.

Activity 4.2

1. Harriet is viewed as a piece of property, not as a human being.
2. There was "no shadow of a law" to protect Jacobs because the Bill of Rights did not apply to black people at that time.
3. "[T]he maintenance of the right" refers to the fact that all people in the United States should have the same rights. She feels this can be achieved through the words and actions of noble men and women.

Activity 4.3

1. <u>(1868) The Fourteenth Amendment</u>

   Civil rights: Every citizen should be protected.
   Necessity: Sometimes, only those of a certain class or of certain groups receive protection from the state.

2. <u>(1870) The Fifteenth Amendment</u>

   Civil rights: Every citizen has the right to vote.
   Necessity: Sometimes governments make laws to keep part of the population from voting.

Activity 4.4

Part 1
a. Many people do not actually know how to take care of themselves.
b. Most people depend on technology and the service industry for their existence.
c. Americans believe that they live close to nature.

Part 2
1. open-ended answer, but, in general, the American dream is associated with the individual's right to own property and pursue his or her personal happiness
2. He thinks the dream might be possible to achieve because people have been able to imagine it as a reality.
3–4 open-ended answers

Activity 4.5

1. Blacks and whites lived in separate communities.
2. The white boss is in a position of great power over Richard. Richard must call him "sir," and the boss looks at Richard as if he were a trained dog.
3. The expression "working my way up" may be in quotes because it refers to the American dream of improving one's situation in life through hard work that is rewarded by promotions and financial gain. It could also be in quotes because the

possibility of working one's way up in white society was closed to most black people.
4. Pease and Morrie are in a position of power over Richard. Morrie uses the term *boy* to refer to Richard, and Pease doesn't bother to say anything at all.
5. The unspoken code is that skilled work is for whites. Richard asks to be shown how to do something. Pease accuses him of trying to "get smart" and not knowing his place.
6. Richard felt there was no point in telling the boss about his difficulties. Nothing would change because the boss was also a white man.
7. open-ended answer
8. It was an insult because it was believed to show a lack of respect and by putting oneself in a position of equality, which was something blacks were not allowed to do at that time.
9. He tries to make his explanation neutral by saying he doesn't remember not using "Mr."
10. open-ended answer
11. It's an ironic title because Jim Crow laws were unethical.

Activity 4.6

1. Possible rephrasing: That sure is a pretty dress you're wearing. If she doesn't stop bothering me, I'm going to tell her what I think. I was so mad I could have done something unexpected. He's always putting someone down. Isn't that the worst thing you've ever heard?
2. They differ in terms of vocabulary. BEV uses more colorful idioms. Many word forms are shortened, and the continuous- *ing* endings are dropped. The present perfect form is shortened as well and often not used. *Ain't* is used for *isn't*.
3. open-ended answer
4. Her father demanded that he be treated equally in terms of language. He expected to be called "sir" or "mister."
5. He was expected to get off the sidewalks to allow whites to pass and to use separate facilities for blacks.
6. I'm going to wash my feet.
7. Standard English was felt to be too formal and not as intimate.
8. She had two ways of speaking and thinking.
9. She had to prove that she was "educated," but Toby didn't.
10. open-ended answer

Activity 4.7

a. A church: A place of worship; a group of people who share a religious faith. The church is also supposed to be a place where those in need can go for help. Members of the Christian church are to follow the teachings "I am my brother's keeper" and "Do unto others as you would have others do unto you." These teachings are not followed in "On the Road."
b. A crucifix: According to the Christian tradition, two thousand years ago, Christ, the son of God, was crucified on a cross, died, was buried, and is believed by Christians to have risen again on the third day. After he returned to heaven, he is said to have sent his spirit and his powers to those who believed in him so that they could do good works.
c. Samson: When a literary work refers to an event, a place, or a character in another work of literature this is called an *allusion*. When the allusion refers to an event or a character in the Bible, a holy book from the Jewish and Christian traditions, it is called a biblical allusion. In the first section of the story, Hughes makes a biblical allusion to the story of Samson found in the Jewish Bible. Read the summary of Samson's story that follows.

The historical Book of Judges 16:1–31 recounts the story of Samson, a Jewish man whom God blessed with great strength so that one day he could free the Israelites from the power of their enemies, the Philistines. But the Philistines discovered the secret of his strength—his long hair. And while he was sleeping, his Philistine wife, Delilah, betrayed Samson by cutting his hair. The Philistines tied Samson up in chains, blinded him, and forced him to grind wheat in a prison mill. While Samson was in prison, his hair grew back. One day, when the Philistines had gathered in a temple to offer a sacrifice to their god Dagon and to celebrate, they called for Samson to entertain them with demonstrations of his strength. They wanted him to stand between two great pillars so that he would be on display for all to see. As he was being led to the pillars, he asked the boy leading him to guide him to the pillars that supported the building so that he could lean against them. Samson called out to his god, Yahweh, to give him strength to kill his enemies, the Philistines. Samson stood between the two pillars and braced himself against them, his left hand pushing against one, his right hand pushing against the other. He began to push with all his strength. Suddenly the temple began to crumble. The building and all who were in it, including Samson, were killed.

Answers to questions

1. The reverend has been in a warm place, so he notices the snow right away.
2. He emphasizes this because Sargeant didn't have a home and the reverend did.
3. "To draw the color line" means to say that blacks may not enter a certain place.
4. It is a "white folks' church" because only white people go there.
5. Sargeant has crossed the "color line" by trying to enter the church. He'll likely be punished.
6. It alludes to the collapse of the Philistines' temple in the story of Samson. It could also express the collapse of a society built on Jim Crow laws.
7. "The idea" is an expression of surprise to show that they think Sargeant has stepped out of his expected place in life.
8. He gets out from under the rubble unhurt and throws a pillar six blocks.
9. One possible meaning is that the narrator feels the values that Christ represents have not been lived out or experienced in the church.
10. The conditions in the camps were makeshift, and the people who lived there were homeless and hungry.
11. Sargeant says that he can sleep in the camp because the camp has no doors. The symbolic meaning of that statement is that Sargeant will be better off in the camp than in a "white folks" church.
12. Sargeant realizes that he's being hit on the knuckles with a club.
13. The cops have complete power over Sargeant. They have the keys to the door and the club that can be used to beat Sargeant.
14. Sargeant ends up in jail. He does not revenge himself as Samson does.
15. Christ is on the road. This could mean that there is some hope that the injustices in the society may be righted now that Christ is out of the church and on the road. It could also mean that, like Sargeant, Christ has no real home.

Activity 4.8

1. The First and Fifteenth Amendments have been violated.
2. One paradox is that a law may appear just but in practice is not. Another paradox is that a person must break an unjust law in the name of justice.
3. open-ended answer
4. Sample answer: The man is looking for scraps of food outside a restaurant where he cannot afford to eat. This suggests that not all people experience the good side of the American dream and that the dream may have aspects of injustice and inequality.

Activity 4.10

1. Both King and Thoreau feel that unjust laws should not be obeyed and that nonviolence should be used to overcome injustice.
2. In the United States, wealth and power should be gained through just and reasonable means, not through injustice.

Activity 4.11

1. They fear feeling inferior and having to look at themselves too closely.
2. Dorset is afraid of being black and powerless himself. He would need to be willing to be homeless and powerless to overcome his fear of Sargeant.
3. open-ended answer
4. People don't really want to be equal to others; they want to feel superior. One possible reason why Americans are afraid to examine the dream too closely is that they might have to acknowledge that it is not based entirely on justice.
5. He uses the Freudian concept of projection. In this case, whites have projected their own fears and evil onto blacks.
6. Baldwin argues that Negroes should "precipitate chaos" in order to gain power. His words suggest the use of violence. King also argues for civil disobedience, but he says such acts should be done "openly and lovingly."

Activity 4.12

1. The American dream (see Activity 4.4)
2–4 open-ended answers

Activity 4.13

1863—Emancipation Proclamation
1865—End of the Civil War
1868—The 14th Amendment is added to the Constitution.
1870—The 15th Amendment is added to the Constitution.
1896—The U.S. Supreme Court rules that "separate but equal" facilities are legal, thus legalizing segregation.
1952—Hughes writes "On the Road."
1954—The Supreme Court rules that public school segregation is illegal.
1955—Rosa Parks refuses to give up her seat on a bus; Martin Luther King organizes bus boycotts and is arrested for the first time.
1957—The courts move to desegregate schools.
1963—King is arrested for leading sit-ins; Freedom March on Washington on August 28; Baldwin writes *The Fire Next Time*. President John F. Kennedy is assassinated on November 22.
1964—Martin Luther King receives the Nobel Peace Prize; Civil Rights Act is passed.
1965—Voting Rights Act.
1968—Martin Luther King is assassinated.
1983—The third Monday in January is designated as Martin Luther King Day, a federal holiday.

1. Individual acts of nonviolent civil disobedience include Rosa Parks's refusal to give up her seat. Hughes's story may also be seen in this category. Collective efforts include sit-ins, marches, and boycotts. These resulted in civil rights legislation.

Chapter 5
Activity 5.1a

1. A quilt is made by stitching together pieces into squares that form a design. Two layers of cloth are then filled with cotton or wool and sewn together. Often, the quilt-maker uses scraps of material that have a special, personal meaning.
2. Sample answer: Quilts have traditionally been made by women. Feminist criticism is interested in the contributions women have made to art, so they would look at the creativity shown in quiltmaking.

Activity 5.1c

1. open-ended answer
2. The quotation marks suggest that people were mistaken when they said that such women were "crazy" or "sainted."
3. Answers may include Billie Holiday, Ella Fitzgerald, Whitney Houston, Macy Gray.

Activity 5.1d

1. Because the quilt is an exquisite work of art made by a black woman.
2. Sample answer: These women were both disadvantaged in society. They were poor and both most likely had to work hard to survive. The quiltmaker was forced to be a slave whereas Walker's mother was at a disadvantage because she was a black and a woman in a society with both racial and sexual prejudices.
3. open-ended answer

Activity 5.1e

1. Dee now recognizes that they are works of art.
2. She may give the quilts to Maggie because it is she who has kept the traditions of the women in her family alive.
3. Dee thinks the quilts should be displayed as art and not used.
4. open-ended answer
5. She could mean that they don't understand the value of the quilts. The *new day* most likely refers to the new role of women, particularly black women, in the modern world.
6. Open-ended. Sample answer: The story deals with the creativity of women and how it is expressed even in oppressive situations.

Activity 5.2

1, 2, and 5 are true.
3, 4, and 6 are false.
Note that women usually married in their early teens.
7. Sample answer: Women did not write literature because they were not educated and did not have independence.

Activity 5.3b

1. Shakespeare was educated and allowed to experience life.
2. Shakespeare went to London to seek his fortune. The woman would have been treated as an outcast if she had not married Shakespeare.
3. Judith wasn't educated and was expected to stay home doing household chores. Because of this, she couldn't get the experience a writer needs to have.

4. Judith didn't love the man she was to marry, and she wanted to act. She was also only seventeen.
5. open-ended answer
6. Judith is not allowed to work in the theater. She finds herself pregnant and unmarried and ends up killing herself. Because he is a man, Shakespeare is allowed to work in the theater and he has great success in London.

7–8 open-ended answers

Activity 5.4

Both Woolf and Walker understand that women, whether slaves or free, have experienced oppression because of their sex. They differ in that Walker focuses on the experience of black women, who are oppressed not only because of their sex but also because of their race.

Activity 5.5b

1. Survey: Disagree—Olsen points out that most never married. 2. Disagree—If married they had few or no children. 3. Agree—All the women she lists had help of some sort. 4. Disagree—She states that she is not "resaying" the theory that women have no need to create art. 5. Disagree—She argues that circumstances and upbringing can keep a person from realizing his or her creative capacities. 6. Agree—She argues that men are taught to have confidence in their own opinions. 7. Disagree—She argues that it was nearly impossible to find time to write between her work as a mother and as an office worker. 8. Agree—She says that women are taught as girls to please and support others and to be deferential.
2. She includes the quote to show that Woolf would have had to care for her father instead of writing if he had lived.
3. She means that young girls are taught to be more concerned with appearance than with character. The dolls reflect one ideal of feminine beauty that is nearly impossible to reach.
4. One could say that the statue is "silent." Also, the figure of a woman looks still, not active.
5. A possible response may be that a woman will be the narrator of the story since it is women who often end up ironing clothes. This assumption shows that women are often expected to fulfill certain domestic duties.
6. The short phrases are more emphatic because they are unexpected. As a woman and a writer, Olsen has tried to break through social rules. She has also developed her own style of writing that does not conform to all the rules of traditional writing.

Activity 5.5c

1. Both Jacobs and Olsen complain of not having time to write.
2. Jacobs manages to rise above her circumstances and to express herself creatively in spite of the oppression she has experienced.

Activity 5.6a

Sample answers: Lucille Ball, Carol Burnett, Whoopie Goldberg, Gilda Radner. In the United States, women did not gain full acceptance as comedians until the mid–1900s when women such as Lucille Ball achieved popular success on television. Before then, comedy was viewed as a "man's" profession and female comedians were rarely given opportunities.

Activity 5.6c

1. The narrator could be talking to a teacher, a school counselor, or a social worker.
2. Perhaps the narrator recalls her first moments of intimacy with the baby. She also remembers her guilt over having waited to feed her until the clock said she could instead of responding to her daughter's cries.
3. She's not the child of slaves, but she is in a disadvantaged position in society. She doesn't have much money or education and is a young, single mother who has to support herself and her child.
4. To the babysitter, Emily is just another baby, a way of making some money. The narrator gets a night job so she can spend days with her daughter. The stress of having to work full-time at night and being a full-time mother was too much for her.
5. The narrator talks about the many distractions in her life and the difficult time she had both being a mother and working outside of the home.
6. She wonders if Emily was pressured to be good instead of having the freedom to develop and express her personality. This echoes the point Olsen makes in *Silences* when she says that the desire to please others is instilled in little girls.
7. Emily was her first child, and she was nervous. Also, she was a single-mother trying to raise Emily on her own.
8. She was sent to a convalescent home to recuperate from measles. The social workers thought Emily would get more attention there since her mother had a new baby at home. The place was cold and impersonal.
9. Emily's work was never considered good enough to get a star. This detail shows that Emily was not considered special by others and suggests that her gifts weren't recognized.
10. Her physical appearance concerns her most. She wants to fit in. Also, she is considered to be a slow learner.
11.

Emily	Susan
thin, dark, foreign looking	chubby cheeked, blond
silent	talkative
sickly	healthy
introverted	extroverted
slow to mature	quick to mature

12. They are significant because Susan fits into the image of the ideal child of that time, like Shirley Temple, but Emily does not.
13. She isn't able to make up for the past. She can't protect Emily from the way people treat her outside of the home. She can't protect her from "youthful competition."
14. The mother has another baby to take care of, and her husband is away fighting in World War II, so she is alone with the children.
15. She may have been in despair because she did not fit in at school and because she felt lonely.
16. Her gift is recognized at a school amateur/talent show.
17. People treat her differently because of her talent.
18. open-ended answer

Activity 5.6d

1–3. open-ended answers
4. Sample answer: The picture suggests that life is like a maze a woman must go through to discover her true self.

Chapter 6

Activity 6.3

1. open-ended answer
2. Sisyphus is an "absurd hero" because, unlike most heroes, he doesn't seem to do anything that is heroic, yet, he is heroic because he does not fear the gods, not even

death. Also, he gives the purposeless activity of rolling the stone up the hill meaning because he relies on his own strength and willpower to complete his task. He does not give up, nor does he despair.
3. He imagines Sisyphus happy because he has found a way to give meaning to an absurd task.
4. He might say that a person should live every moment to its fullest.
5. The stone could represent the effort we make every day to give life meaning. It could also represent the burdens we try to bear with grace: our need to earn a living, difficult relationships, etc.
6. open-ended answer

Activity 6.4

A–B open-ended answers
1. O "Last week he tried to commit suicide," one waiter said.
   Y "Why?"
   O "He was in despair."
   Y "What about?"
   O "Nothing."
   Y "How do you know it was nothing?"
   O "He has plenty of money."
   . . .
   Y "The guard will pick him up," one waiter said.
   O "What does it matter if he gets what he's after?"
   Y "He had better get off the street now. The guard will get him. They went by five minutes ago."
2–3 open-ended answers
4. He's irritated with the old man for keeping him at the café and calls him a "nasty thing." He feels that the old man doesn't respect the fact that he wants to go home. He doesn't respect the old man.
5. He understands that the old man has no family to go home to and is lonely. He thinks that the old man is clean and trying to maintain his dignity even though he is drunk.
6. The old man sitting in the shadow rapped on his saucer with his glass. The younger waiter went over to him.
   Y "What do you want?"
   The old man looked at him. "Another brandy," he said.
   Y "You'll be drunk," the waiter said. The old man looked at him. The waiter went away.
   Y "He'll stay all night," he said to his colleague. "I'm sleepy now. I never get into bed before three o'clock. He should have killed himself last week."
   The waiter took the brandy bottle and another saucer from the counter inside the café and marched out to the old man's table. He put down the saucer and poured the glass full of brandy.
   Y "You should have killed yourself last week," he said to the deaf man. The old man motioned with his finger. "A little more," he said. The waiter poured on into the glass so that the brandy slopped over and ran down the stem to the top saucer of the pile. "Thank you," the old man said. The waiter took the bottle back inside the café. He sat down at the table with his colleague again.
   Y "He's drunk now," he said.
   O "He's drunk every night."
   Y "What did he want to kill himself for?"
   O "How should I know?"
   Y "How did he do it?"
   O "He hung himself with a rope."
   Y "Who cut him down?"
   O "His niece."
   Y "Why did they do it?"

O "Fear for his soul."
Y "How much money has he got?"
O "He's got plenty."
Y "He must be eighty years old."
O "Anyway I should say he was eighty."
Y "I wish he would go home. I never get to bed before three o'clock. What kind of hour is that to go to bed?"
O "He stays up because he likes it."
Y "He's lonely. I'm not lonely. I have a wife waiting in bed for me."
O "He had a wife once too."
Y "A wife would be no good to him now."
O "You can't tell. He might be better with a wife."
O "His niece looks after him."
Y "I know. You said she cut him down."
Y "I wouldn't want to be that old. An old man is a nasty thing."
O "Not always. This old man is clean. He drinks without spilling. Even now, drunk. Look at him."
Y "I don't want to look at him. I wish he would go home. He has no regard for those who must work."

7. The old man looked from his glass across the square, then over at the waiters.

"Another brandy," he said, pointing to his glass. The waiter who was in a hurry came over.

Y "Finished," he said, speaking with that omission of syntax stupid people employ when talking to drunken people or foreigners. "No more tonight. Close now."

"Another," said the old man.

Y "No. Finished." The waiter wiped the edge of the table with a towel and shook his head.

The old man stood up, slowly counted the saucers, took a leather coin purse from his pocket and paid for the drinks, leaving half a peseta tip. The waiter watched him go down the street, a very old man walking unsteadily but with dignity.

O "Why didn't you let him stay and drink?" the unhurried waiter asked. They were putting up the shutters. "It is not half-past two."
Y "I want to go home to bed."
O "What is an hour?"
Y "More to me than to him."
O "An hour is the same."
Y "You talk like an old man yourself. He can buy a bottle and drink at home."
O "It's not the same."
Y "No, it is not," agreed the waiter with a wife. He did not wish to be unjust. He was only in a hurry.
O "And you? You have no fear of going home before your usual hour?"
Y "Are you trying to insult me?"
O "No, hombre, only to make a joke."
Y "No," the waiter who was in a hurry said, rising from pulling down the metal shutters. "I have confidence. I am all confidence."
O "You have youth, confidence, and a job," the older waiter said. "You have everything."
Y "And what do you lack?"
O "Everything but work."
Y "You have everything I have."
O "No. I have never had confidence and I am not young."
Y "Come on. Stop talking nonsense and lock up."
O "I am of those who like to stay late at the café," the older waiter said. "With all those who do not want to go to bed. With all those who need a light for the night."

Y "I want to go home and into bed."
O "We are of two different kinds," the older waiter said. He was now dressed to go home. "It is not only a question of youth and confidence although those things are very beautiful. Each night I am reluctant to close up because there may be some one who needs the café."

8. *Older Waiter*   *Younger Waiter*
   a. not in a hurry   in a hurry
   b. had never had confidence   has confidence
   c. says it's not the same to drink   says the old man can drink at home
      alone at home   eager to close the café
   d. wants to leave the café open   thinks the old man is a "nasty thing"
   e. thinks the old man is clean;
      dignified

9. The younger waiter feels insulted because he thinks the older waiter is implying that he doesn't want to go home.
10. He thinks the older waiter is talking nonsense. Perhaps he does not think of the older waiter as being old even if the older waiter feels that way.
11. The bodega is a bar, not a café. The light is bright and pleasant, but the bodega is not clean; it is unpolished.
12. Such a place kept them from feeling lonely.
13. He thinks the older waiter is crazy. This is sadly ironic because he doesn't realize that the older waiter is just lonely. It is also situational irony because the reader realizes that the waiter is not crazy whereas the bartender does not.
14. This is ironic because it's not just insomnia that's bothering him; it's the feeling of meaninglessness. This is a form of verbal irony since the waiter says this to himself without realizing what his problem really is. Because the audience realizes this, it is also a form of situational irony, and perhaps also an ironic point of view if one believes Hemingway also realized this.
15. It could mean the feeling of nothingness as in the prayer.
16. He gets up every day and completes his seemingly meaningless job.

Activity 6.5a

The allusion to the Lord's Prayer makes the old waiter's prayer a kind of antiprayer. He may use Spanish because it makes the word and its meaning stand out. He may also prefer the sound of the word.

Activity 6.5b

1. The older waiter has lost his faith in God. The younger waiter has not.

   Younger Waiter   *Older Waiter*

   a. God is alive.   God is dead.
   b. God is everywhere.   God is nowhere.
   c. God should be praised.   There is no God to praise.
   d. God's kingdom is coming.   There is no kingdom of God.
      (There is a sense of purpose.)   There is no future purpose.
   e. God's will is done on earth.   God's will is not done on earth.
   f. God provides for our needs.   No one provides for our needs.
   g. God forgives.   There is no need for forgiveness.
                                              There is no forgiveness.
                                              There is no sin.
   h. There is eternal life.   There is no eternal life.

   Younger Waiter   *Older Waiter*

   Other: God is a loving God.   There is no love.

2. The younger waiter feels that it is possible to have relationships with others, to know and to be known. The older waiter does not.

Younger Waiter

a. People should forgive.
b. People do sin.
c. People follow God's will.
d. People can communicate with God and with other people.
Other: People can hope for the best.

Older Waiter

There is no forgiveness.
There is no temptation, no sin.
God's will is not at work in people's lives.
True communication with God and others is not possible.
There is no hope.

3. The younger waiter might say that life has meaning and purpose. The older waiter would not.
4. The prayer appears in the climax/crisis of the story. It is critical because it expresses the older waiter's feelings of loss.

Activity 6.7a

Younger waiter

a. in a hurry—the narrator says this
b. has confidence—says this about himself and the older waiter says this about him
c. says the old man can drink at home—says this himself
d. eager to close the café—implies this when he says he wants to go home
e. thinks the old man is a "nasty thing"—says this himself

Older Waiter: Action

1. wants to keep the café open
2. goes to the bodega instead of going home
3. says the *nada* prayer

Characterization

1. understands the old man
2. doesn't want to go home
3. feels life is meaningless

Younger Waiter: Action

1. tells the old man he should have killed himself
2. refuses to give the old man another brandy
3. closes the café

Characterization

1. He's impatient.
2. He is determined to go home.
3. can't understand the old man

Activity 6.7c

1. The adverbs would come too close together, and the -*ly* ending would be too repetitive.
2. The statements are short, and it is easy to imagine how they contrast with one another. The universalizing techniques that Hemingway uses make it easy for the reader to identify with each character and how that character might say something.

Activity 6.9

1. Discussion of terms. The answers can be checked in the text if necessary.
2. This question is open ended, but some of the main correspondences are as follows: (a) The older waiter feels the purposelessness of life and yet tries to give life some meaning. (b) The older waiter's "prayer" reflects his despair, but he blames his feelings on insomnia. (c) The old man gives into his despair and tries to commit suicide—not a valid response for an existentialist. (d) The old men in the story are alienated from others and lonely; this causes them to realize how absurd their situation is.

(e) Both men find a feeling of connectedness at the clean, well-lighted café. This gives them a sense of purpose.
3. open-ended answer

Activity 6.10a

1. open-ended answer
2. The revision of the prayer is a deconstructionist act because it puts forward, or privileges, the feeling of nothingness or meaninglessness that the prayer holds back, or subverts. It switches the order of the binary opposite *meaning: meaninglessness*.

Activity 6.10b

Sample answer: Most advertisements in Western culture feature young and beautiful people. Advertisements that target the elderly generally deal with health care. However, in the past few years, as the populations of urbanized countries have aged, ads have begun also to feature elderly people as models for a wider range of goods. In the past, youth and beauty were privileged over old age, but now the ideal of a healthy and active later life is also being promoted in part because so many people are living longer.

Activity 6.10c

1. open-ended answer, but the main point is that our likes and dislikes are traps for us that keep us locked in one way of looking at the world
2. Deconstructionism is also concerned about "pairs of opposites" that keep people from understanding the world.
3. Krishna says that those who focus on him can overcome the confusion caused by opposites.

Activity 6.10d

A deconstructionist critic would look at the way the use of language is associated with power. For example, Richard Wright must refer to white men as "sir" or "Mr." whereas he is called "boy." Similarly, Mellix had to use "proper" English if she wanted to fit into white, middle-class society. Her father also experienced language and its link to power when he insisted on being called "Mr."

Activity 6.10e

Sisyphus challenges the codes set down by the gods. He has a disregard for death that was shown when he put Death in chains. He also struggles to make a meaningless activity meaningful. He tries to change the order of *meaningless:meaningful* and *gods:human beings*.

Chapter 7
Activity 7.1

1. From these numbers, it's clear that the Nazis attempted to exterminate the Jewish population in Europe. World War II involved the genocide of the Jewish people. Also, more civilians than soldiers died in the war.
2. Open-ended. Activities 7.2 and 7.3 discuss the Holocaust in more detail.
3. Genocide occurs for a number of reasons. Among them are the following: (1) ideological reasons—A government uses a campaign against an ethnic group to consolidate political power. (2) Economic reasons—A government pursues a policy of repression against an ethnic group to obtain its land or wealth, as has been the case with Native Americans in both North and South America.

4. open-ended answer
   5. The story shows what can happen when a person projects his or her own evil onto someone else. The narrator's attention to strange details could be compared to the careful planning that is behind most genocides. However, unlike the narrator, few people who commit genocide actually confess to the crime.

Activity 7.2

1. anti-Semitism: racism against the Semitic or Jewish people.
2. Gestapo: The Nazis' secret state police *(Geheime Staatspolizei)* established in 1933 to suppress opposition. The Gestapo was known for having especially brutal tactics.
3. blitzkrieg: A German word that is also used in English to describe a surprise attack by air and/or land. In a blitzkrieg entire cities were often destroyed. Both the Germans and the Allied forces used a blitzkrieg strategy. *Blitz* means *lightning* in German; *Krieg* means *war*.
4. Aryan: A descendant of the earliest Europeans; characterized by having light-colored skin and hair. The Nazis believed the Aryan "race" was superior to all others.
5. concentration camp: A place where groups of people are kept as prisoners in inhumane conditions, usually for political reasons. The camps in World War II were also known as *death camps* because more than four million people died in the camps. Many of the death camps were disguised as work camps that used prison labor.
6. liquidation: The process of getting rid of something. The Nazis used this term as a code word for murder and genocide.
7. bath: The gas chambers were disguised as baths. Those who entered such baths expected water to come out of the faucets, but poisonous gas came out instead, killing all. Such "baths" were also called *disinfecting chambers.*
8. Zyklon-B: A poison gas used to kill insects. In World War II, it was used to kill people.

Activity 7.3a

1. By "delusion of reprieve" he means that he held onto the belief that somehow he would be rescued from the terrible situation he was in. Frankl believed this until he asked a guard to hide his manuscript and the guard swore at him.
2. He says it was a "real" bath because those who were gassed to death were killed in "disinfecting chambers." They expected water to come out of the shower faucets but Zyklon-B came out instead.
3. open-ended answer
4. Frankl had a hard time reading the situation because it was so inhuman, so unlike anything he had ever experienced. He did not know the rules of a death camp, and it took some time to understand exactly what was happening. According to reader response criticism, we can best read a text when we have strategies for interpreting it. However, the situation in the camps was so strange and unfamiliar to Frankl that he had no way to interpret what was happening there when he first arrived.
5. open-ended answer
6. Frankl humanizes and brings to life an experience that is usually presented as a mass statistic.

Activity 7.3b

1. Sample answer: Frankl says that even though people were prisoners in the camp, they still had the freedom to choose how they would behave.
2. He argues that people can give life meaning even in a seemingly hopeless and absurd situation. He sees this as a kind of personal freedom that not even the camps could take away.

3. Freud holds that a person's past will always influence how he or she behaves. In contrast, Frankl argues that people in the camps behaved in ways that could not be explained by their past experiences. They made a free choice to act as they did.

Activity 7.4

Open-ended answer. This question may not have a definitive answer, but it's worth exploring. Some may wonder why anyone would want to switch the binary opposites of *"normal" life: life in a death camp*. Others may feel that deconstructionism can not account for goodness and evil.

Activity 7.5

1. Feyerabend uses the phrase *benefactors of mankind* sarcastically because he feels these people do not really help others. The quotation marks around the word *primitive* show that he doesn't agree with calling such cultures "primitive."
2. He refers to the following binary oppositions: *majority:minority, "civilized" cultures:"primitive" cultures, doctors:patients.*
3–5. open-ended answers

Activity 7.6

1. chutzpah: self-confidence; boldness
   kibitzer: a person who looks on a situation and offers unasked for (and unwanted) advice
   ganef: a thief

Activity 7.7a

a. 7 i. 13
b. 5 j. 3
c. 6 k. 14
d. 12 l. 15
e. 9 m. 2
f. 10 n. 8
g. 11 o. 4
h. 1

Activity 7.7b

A. open-ended answer
B. 2. No day is like another.
   3. A woman can't get pregnant just by praying.
   4. All women are descendants of Eve.
   5. Even things that are hard to deal with come from God.
   6. You can't live without making mistakes.
   7. If you can't trust your own family, you can't even trust God.
   8. Everyone knows the truth and can "see" it, just like a person can see oil floating on water because water does not absorb oil.

Activity 7.9

1. open-ended answer
2. As the rabbi says, Gimpel has his own kind of wisdom.
3. He characterizes himself as being a fool, but his descriptions of himself unconsciously show he has a unique kind of wisdom.

4. The townspeople seem foolish for being so cruel to Gimpel.
5. Even though he is supposed to be a fool, he is wise.

Activity 7.10a

Some of the possible answers are as follows.
1. Everyone in the town knows everyone else, whereas in large cities people often don't know their neighbors.
2. The townspeople raised money for the wedding. In urban settings, couples and their families generally bear the wedding costs.
3. The rabbi or the religious leader plays an important role in the decisions people make. This is not always the case in urban environments.
4. The people follow religious ceremonies and rituals. Their social lives revolve around such events. Urban social life often does not have a religious basis or focus.

Activity 7.10b

a. Gimpel lives in a small Jewish community.
b. The people follow the teachings of the Jewish tradition. Traditions and rituals are very important.
c. Gimpel feels bound by the traditions of his community. Although he does what he is told, he does leave the "universe" of Frampol for the larger world.

Activity 7.10c

Sample answer: A feminist critic might note the fact that Elka does not conform to the stereotypical role of women in village life. She is apparently a strong woman with a "fierce tongue" and, as Gimpel says, people are afraid of her. As Gimpel also points out, she is not a typical homemaker; in fact, her house smells strongly from the filth. Elka is also unusual in that she is the one who threatened to divorce her husband—not a usual act for the time in which the story takes place. Finally, Elka is unfaithful to Gimpel and has a number of children by different men. Even if Gimpel dreams that Elka is eventually punished for her infidelity, Elka herself comes across as a fiercely independent character.

Activity 7.11

Sample answer: A Freudian critic might characterize Elka as representing the id while the townspeople would represent the superego that imposes its will on Gimpel. Gimpel, on the other hand, would be seen as characteristic of the ego: he tries to deal with both Elka (the id) and the townspeople (the superego). Like the ego, he has moments of clarity and insight, but at other times he does not realize or accept the truth of his situation. At the end of the story, he appears to have achieved a balance between the three parts of his psyche.

Activity 7.12

A deconstructionist critic would be interested in the ways that Gimpel is shown to be wise although he is always referred to as a fool, those who think themselves wise, such as the townspeople, appear foolish. Also, his final "devaluation" of traditional societal roles would be of interest.

Activity 7.13

Gimpel is an existentialist hero because he remains true to himself. He finds his own way to make life meaningful.

Activity 7.14

1. As Harrison points out, when Westernization takes place, traditions are lost and people become alienated from one another. There are many areas where native cultures are struggling to maintain their traditions, as are the tribal peoples of the Amazon region.
2 and 3. open-ended answers
4. He or she might say that urban life is privileged over village life. The balance could be restored by rethinking the way we plan urban communities and by developing activities that help to build relationships in urban settings.

Activity 7.15

1–2 open-ended answers
3. A sociological critic would be interested in the story as a social document that preserves the traditions of a destroyed community.

Chapter 8

Questions for "The Heart Tells All"
1. There are about one to two citations per paragraph. Only one citation is made up of at least one complete sentence. Four are phrases. Only one citation is over four lines long.
2. The author includes the following details: the narrator's emphatic way of speaking; his claim that he "heard all things in heaven and in the earth"; his excited speech; his confusion about his motive for the crime.
3. The author includes the following details: the long time it took the narrator to put his head into the old man's room; his waiting for the old man's eye to open before he can kill him; the dismemberment of the old man's body; the narrator's lack of concern about the smell of the old man's decomposing body.
4. The author includes the scene in which the policemen are in the old man's room with the narrator.

Questions for "The Eye of the Id"
1. There are six citations in the entire essay and one to two citations per paragraph. Two of the citations contain complete sentences. Four are short phrases. There is one citation over four lines.
2. The author gives the following examples:

   The narrator flatters his audience's cleverness.
   He claims to be calm and reasonable, but his speech is excited and emotional.
   The narrator's actions are irrational.
   He reveals his deed because he feels the police are mocking him.

3. The author provides the following details:

   It is the old man's eye and not the old man that distrubs the narrator.
   The narrator links the old man's eye to a vulture.
   The narraotr cannot explain why he is obsessed with the old man's eye.

4. The author uses the scene as evidence of the narrator's repressed sexuality.
5. Both essays analyze the narrator's madness, but the main difference is that the first does so from a formalistic point of view, while the latter does so from a Freudian point of view.